AF470822

THE PAST GLORY OF MILTON CREEK

DEDICATION

To a Milton Creek which is
clean and glorious again.

A fine painting in Milton Court Hall showing the Creek in 1866. It is not easy to identify the spot for certain, but the guess is Crown Quay. (Photo by Alan Cordell, courtesy of Swale Archaeological Research Group)

The Past Glory of Milton Creek

Tales of Slipways, Sails and Setting Booms

Compiled by:

Alan Cordell and Leslie Williams

Meresborough Books

1985

Published by Meresborough Books, 7 Station Road, Rainham, Gillingham, Kent.
ME8 7RS.

ISBN 0948193042

Front Cover: Prentis' Quay, near the Creek Head, about 1885. *Owner's Delight* (left) and *Water Lily* have set their sails for the portrait photographer. Both barges were owned by Cole of Milton, but later went to Burley.   (Courtesy of Bowaters and Tony Ellis)

Printed by Mackays of Chatham Ltd.

CONTENTS

FOREWORD

This book reveals to the reader a glimpse of a Milton Creek unknown to the present day inhabitants of the area, who now, sadly, see only a dead, malodorous expanse of muddy water, surrounded by a wasteland or by ugly industrial premises — a far cry from the busy waterway it once was. Mr Cordell and Mr Williams have performed a great service to future generations with their meticulous recording of the lives of past bargemen, their own personal anecdotes and a wealth of information not only on the barge industry itself but also on its associated industries and their effect on the life of the towns of Sittingbourne and Milton Regis. This collection brings vividly to life the world of the 19th and early 20th century bargeman and makes a most valuable contribution to our knowledge of local history.

Esmé Grisdale
Sittingbourne Archaeology Group

Alan Cordell was born at Sittingbourne in 1935. His grandfather, Jim Fenteman, had been a local barge skipper and at a later period was Harbourmaster of Milton Creek. The salt water seemed to get into Alan's veins as well and, as a boy, he spent many happy hours exploring the local creeks and rivers, making notes of the numerous barges (both active and derelict) which he saw. After attending Ufton Lane Primary School and Borden Grammar School, Alan qualified for a scientific career and he now works as a Technology Officer in the Research Group of Trinity House Lighthouse Service, based in London. As hobbies, Alan combines sailing, photography and writing. He was on the committee of the Society for Spritsail Barge Research for nearly ten years and also served for a similar period on the committee of the Thames Barge Sailing Club, during which time he won all four Club trophies for photography and literature. Alan enjoys both cruising and racing in the Club barges and was mate of the racing crew which won a trophy with the *Pudge* in the 1973 Greenwich Festival Match. However, he recently stood down from the committee (and the chance of a flag officer post) to concentrate on yachting in the Swale, Thames Estuary and Solent, to do some work for Sittingbourne's Court Hall and Dolphin Museums and to complete this book.

Alan's earlier employment caused him to move from Sittingbourne to Twickenham some twenty years ago. He would like to move back to the Swale area one day — after his daughter's schooling is complete — and he intends to continue writing for journals and books on subjects related to both the Swale and Twickenham areas.

Captain Leslie Williams was born at Sittingbourne in 1908. When he was very young, his parents emigrated to Canada, leaving Leslie and his sister in the care of relatives. The idea was that the children would eventually follow their parents — but they never did and Leslie was brought up by his grandfather and an aunt. Grandfather was in fact the well-known Harry 'Timson' Williams, who was skipper of the splendid local barge *Unique*. So during his time at St Michael's school (since demolished to make room for the road of the same name), Leslie spent most of his holidays away with the *Unique* and became her 3rd hand when he left school in 1922. He next obtained a mate's berth in the *Buckland* and was mate of several more barges (including a long spell in the powerful *Georgiana*). Promotion to skipper followed when he took the *Emma* (owned at Leigh) and then the *Bessie* (owned at Queenborough). But this was during the 'slump' time of the mid-1930s and Leslie soon had to give up barging or starve; so he worked at various other jobs, including a lengthy spell as a lighterman.

However, no less than 40 years after moving out of barges, Leslie made a come-back as one of the skippers of the Thames Barge Sailing Club craft *Pudge* and *Centaur*. Leslie held the post for the 1976-79 seasons and this means that he was Sittingbourne's very last active sailing barge skipper — a distinction which he is unlikely to lose!

Now living in retirement at Sittingbourne, Leslie (a widower with three grown-up children) spends much of his spare time writing for various nautical publications about his fascinating years afloat.

ACKNOWLEDGEMENTS

We should like to thank the following for their help and co-operation in the production of this book:—

All our contributors as named in the text. One of these, Ron Dickenson, has written both under his true name and also as 'Marlin Spike'.

All people who kindly lent photographs for copying and reproduction (each photograph has an acknowledgement where possible underneath). In particular we should like to mention the late George Goldsack (a clerk at Smeed Dean's works) and the late Bill Kennett (a bargeman), who were busy as amateur photographers with their glass ¼-plate cameras before the First World War, and also those eminent Sittingbourne professional photographers of a past era — Ferris, Ramell and Wrigglesworth. But for them the heyday of the Creek would have gone largely unrecorded.

Daphne Pipe of the National Maritime Museum, who spent many lunch-breaks getting information for us from the old mercantile registers.

Patricia O'Driscoll, of 'Coast & Country' magazine (previously called 'East Coast Digest' and 'Greenwich Times'), Graham Parrett of the 'East Kent Gazette', The Thames Barge Sailing Club and the Society for Spritsail Barge Research, for allowing selected articles and extracts from their respective publications to be reprinted in this book.

Tom Redshaw, who extracted from the 1912 Mercantile Register details of all the Milton Creek spritsail barges in commission at that time.

The respective staffs of the 'East Kent Gazette' and Sittingbourne Library, for making their files and reference works easily accessible.

The late Colin Cordell who, during the years of the Second World War when his health was by no means good, accompanied his eager son on cycle and foot all over the Medway and Swale area so that the nautical scene could be recorded.

Harold 'Jack' Butcher, Ron Dickenson, Peter Reeves, John Wills and 'Chippy' Wood, who checked the draft for accuracy.

Our admirable young typists, Louise Harris, Shirley Seymour and Louise Wallen, who coped well with manuscripts which were, at times, somewhat muddled!

Valerie Hayman, for tidying up the maps into a presentable state.

Rodney Spratling and Danny Steer, for assisting with the photographic printing.

Dennis Tanner, who drew the outline diagram showing the 'anatomy' of the Thames spritsail barge.

And last but by no means least, our respective late grandfathers, Jim Fenteman and Harry 'Timson' Williams, who put the salt water in our veins in the first place!

Alan Cordell
Leslie Williams
March 1984

PREFACE

Since the main text of this book was completed in June 1979, a number of changes to geography and architecture have already occurred, particularly in Milton Regis. Now, in March 1984, the photography, maps, diagrams and layout are almost complete, and it is time to up-date the earlier writing.

Some of the above-mentioned changes are unfortunately for the worse. One example is the incredible demolition of a considerable number of the historic memorial stones in the former Milton Congregational Church yard. Parts of Milton Creek have been infilled, which is surprising when one views the vast acres of seemingly derelict and unused land surrounding it. The Creek has seen two more barges fall derelict, *Nellie Parker* (at McKenzie's Wharf) and *Ardeer* (partially broken-up in a small tidal lagoon near Dolphin Yard). Both were brought to Dolphin Yard for maintenance, but they were eventually abandoned by their owners. The motor barge trade to the Ready Mixed Concrete South East Ltd depot at Station Brickworks Dock has ceased. And, sadly, 'Pip' Box, 'Jock' Kennett, 'Bony' Rossiter and 'Taffy' Taylor (former bargemen), John Wills (formerly a director of Wills and Packham) and Harold Coward — all of whom made useful contributions towards this book — have passed on.

However, there are also good things to record. Milton Creek is still a commercial waterway — just — because deliveries of aggregates (sand) to Eastwoods Wharf by motor barge continue. A new industrial estate has been built on the former Smeed Dean brickfields at the back of Shortlands Road, and has been appropriately named the 'Smeed Dean Centre'. The opening is commemorated by a brick-built plinth; this bears a beautiful metal plaque showing a fine spritsail barge (of the type owned by Smeed Dean for their coasting trade) under full sail. Col. Donald Dean, V.C., a former official at Smeed Deans, performed the unveiling ceremony. This was most fitting, because a Smeed Dean barge was named *Donald* after him, and was later renamed *V.C.* when he won this honour in the First World War. Murston Old Church and its grounds have been tidied-up by the local Boy Scouts. The activities of Milton Court Hall Museum have expanded, and the Dolphin Yard Museum (which re-opened shortly before the completion of the main text of this book) has survived despite some irksome problems. Barges lying afloat at the Yard, in varying states of usage and maintenance, are *Anglia*, *Celtic*, *Oak* and *Saxon*, plus the Dutch motor barge *Amicitia*. None of these were originally local craft, but they have come to the Yard for the convenient and economic facilities. The Milton Regis Society has started a campaign for cleaning and tidying the Creek — a pressing need in a waterway which has long been infamous for its polluted and neglected state.

Now, at last, we terminate this record with a piece of scintillating news. The famous Milton Creek barge *Olive May* (built by Wills and Packham in 1920) is fitting-out at Burnham-on-Crouch for a passage across the Atlantic. Her original spritsail rig has been replaced with that of a 'brailing boomie'*, which is more suitable for ocean voyaging. Miss Olive May Wenban (later Mrs O.M. Howton), after whom the barge was named, died recently; so if *Olive May* can successfully complete this task, it will represent a most fitting memorial to her late namesake. Let us wish her fair winds and a trouble-free passage, so that she may add a crowning contribution to the many great achievements of the Milton Creek barges and men.

* Brailing Boomie — authors' term for a boomie barge (otherwise known as a ketch barge) in which the mainsail brails up to a standing gaff when stowed, instead of being lowered.

INTRODUCTION

by Leslie Strevens

Milton Creek was originally the estuary of a small stream which arose in the vicinity of Bredgar and followed the valley that passes south-east of Borden and thence through Ufton Lane and Cockleshell Walk to Milton Regis. Between Bredgar and Borden (in the vicinity of Wren's Farm) is Hart's Delight (now wrongly spelt Heart's Delight), which in the middle ages was undoubtedly a watering place for wild animals, hence the name. I can remember, in my early days, seeing water flowing down the bed of the original stream through Cockleshell Walk after heavy rain and also through some allotments that were situated alongside Church Street, Milton, very near to the present head of the Creek (this part was known as the Periwinkle Stream). Another stream, the Bourne, ran down Crown Quay Lane and entered the Creek further to the east. I have heard that Sittingbourne derived its name from the Canterbury Pilgrims who sat by the Bourne Stream to refresh themselves before making the final 'leg' to Canterbury. The more 'classy' ones stayed at Milton which was later honoured by the addition of the suffix 'Regis'.

The Creek later became an important centre for the oyster and cockle fleets that worked in the Swale. Cockleshell Walk no doubt derived its name from this connection and the bed of the old stream in Cockleshell Walk was only filled in a few years ago, when the road was widened and the new one-way traffic system introduced. But by then the stream was nothing more than a rubbish dump. After widening, Cockleshell Walk became the west end of St Michael's Road.

The death knell of this stream was really sounded much earlier by the coming of the paper mills in the mid-19th century, as the demand for water for paper making is intense. The natural flow of water soon became inadequate and the paper mills (then Edward Lloyd Ltd, now Bowater) began sinking wells to supply their demands. This robbed Milton Creek of its natural flow of pure water and the descent into the polluted and mud-silted waterway it later became had begun.

However, the Creek derived a new commercial importance as a centre of the thriving stock brick manufacturing trade and also of the cement industry. The banks of the Creek, virtually from its head to the Swale, were lined on both sides by brick manufacturers. Among the better-known names were Smeed Dean Ltd, Chas. Burley Ltd and Wills and Packham Ltd. Of these, Smeed Dean were by far the largest, ranking second only in the country to the London Brick Co. in size. The reason for the proliferation of brick and cement manufacturers was that there was an almost inexhaustible supply of the chief raw materials in and around the Sittingbourne area, namely clay and chalk. Whilst the district provided the raw materials, the Creek provided the means of transporting the finished goods, and the 'work horse' was the Thames spritsail sailing barge.

All the main brick manufacturers had their own fleets of these vessels and many their own yards for construction, repair and maintenance. Again Smeed Dean Ltd were the biggest, owning or operating at their peak something in the region of 80 craft.

There were also independent barge yards which built and serviced vessels for those who did not have their own facilities. These were situated mainly near the head of the Creek.

With the coming of rail and road transport, the Thames barge lost its importance as the main means of conveyance and from the zenith of its popularity around the late 1800s and early 1900s it declined until it virtually ceased to exist with the coming of the Second World War. With the demise of the barge went also the importance of Milton Creek and although an occasional vessel can still be seen plying her way up, it is a rare occasion and confined almost solely to the carrying of aggregates to the ready-mixed concrete plant, now situated where one independent barge yard (White's) formerly operated, and also to the old Eastwoods wharf for concrete pipe manufacture.

Following the General Strike and the depression of the latter 1920s, the brick trade declined and the smaller manufacturers soon disappeared. A.P.C.M., Wills and Packham, and Chas. Burley remained, and indeed continued to make bricks throughout the 1939/45 war. In 1927 Smeed Dean had changed hands and was later acquired by A.P.C.M., now Blue Circle, who recently shut the cement works but remain as the only brick manufacturer in the town. As a result of the sale of Smeed Dean Ltd, two former directors, namely George Andrews and his son Harold, were left with a small fleet of barges (about six) with no home base, and accordingly sought suitable alternative premises with the idea (in spite of the parlous state of the Thames Barge trade) of building up a fleet of some 20-25 vessels and engaging in the trade of general freightage contractors. They found what they were looking for in the then virtually bankrupt independent boat and barge yard near the head of Milton Creek, at that time known as the Sittingbourne Shipbuilding Co. Ltd (occupying the former White's yard), and Harold Andrews acquired the business in 1930. Another former S.D. official, Sid Ellis, also brought in some barges and (whilst there was no legal partnership) all barges wore the same bob* and became known as belonging to Ellis and Andrews.

On acquiring the S.S. Co. Ltd Mr Andrews retained the services of the founder of the Company, Mr H.W. Harvey, (an independent marine surveyor) as technical adviser. He also brought in from Smeed Dean Ltd Vic Horsford, then foreman shipwright, together with several members of his gang. It was at this time that my connection with Milton Creek began for on leaving school I joined the S.S. Co. Ltd as a trainee. During the 1930s, 40s and early 50s, many well known barges were rebuilt, converted and motorised, including *Hydrogen, Phoenician, Vicunia, Edith May* and *Trilby*. We also built versions of the East Coast barge-yacht, this being a scaled-down model of the real thing with the hold fitted out as accommodation. From the inception of the company it had been engaged in the construction of auxiliary Naval craft and with the expansion of this programme due to the war, the adjacent and larger building premises of Wills and Packham Ltd were acquired. Following the cessation of hostilities, however, and the virtual demise of the Thames barge, such extensive premises were no longer required and the main buildings were turned over to other uses, so that around 1952/53 the former S.S. Co. Ltd became a warehousing business of which I am still a director.

Having spent approximately 50 years working alongside Milton Creek, including some ten years or more as Chairman of the Conservators, I am pleased to be associated with a book about it. Whilst unimpressive today, the Creek has a very distinguished past. In order to marvel at the tales of thriving commerce, wreck and rescue, record-breaking feats, witty characters, and brave deeds, I urge the reader to — read on!

*bob — a barge's flag, flown at the topmast truck.

The Milton Creek trade was linked with the work of the local mills. This was the last of several windmills in the area — it was on 'The Meads' near the Quinton Road railway bridge. Working until c.1914, it then stood disused until demolished in 1955. The site is now a housing estate.

(Photo by Alan Cordell, 1954)

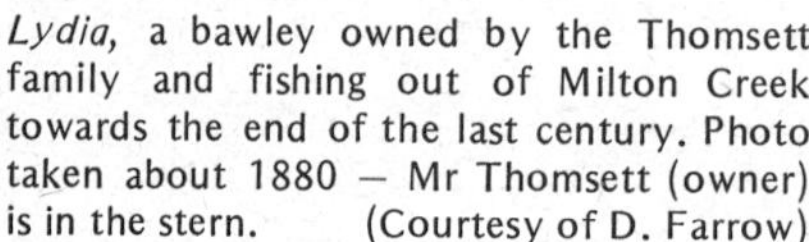

Lydia, a bawley owned by the Thomsett family and fishing out of Milton Creek towards the end of the last century. Photo taken about 1880 — Mr Thomsett (owner) is in the stern.   (Courtesy of D. Farrow)

CHAPTER 1

A GENERAL SURVEY

by Leslie Williams

History

Milton Regis is a very ancient town and must have had an important position in the past. The old town stood where the church is now — until it was burnt by Earl Godwin's men in 1052. Before that, it had been plundered by the Danes (in 893), although all they gained was probably fish and corn. There are some Danish Earthworks beside the Creek at Kemsley — called Castle Rough. I have always thought myself that the Danes probably beached their ships on the point at Kemsley Down, where they could have run them into the water at any state of tide. I believe that longships have been dug out of the saltings around that area and I think that when the sea wall was broken at Grovehurst Dock (before my time) one was washed out into the Swale, but this is only what I have heard. In Queen Elizabeth I's time Sittingbourne had only 88 houses and two quays — Crown and Holdredges. Milton Regis had 130 houses and four quays: Fluddmill, Whitlock's, Reynolds' and Hamond's; also Milton had 26 ships and vessels (20 under 10 tons, the rest 12-20 tons). 24 people were engaged in trade and fishing (according to the historian Hasted) so presumably these people were the owners of the above vessels. When Hasted did his survey of Kent in 1778-99, he recorded that Milton then had 5 mills, 5 quays, 32 fisheries, 230 houses and 1200 inhabitants. The Company of Fishermen and Dredgers paid the Lord of the Manor £100 and four bushels of oysters annually and there were 140 Freemen of the river, so fish and oysters were a valuable industry. There was a large duck decoy to the north of the town which I believe was later called Cornford's Lake (there are still Cornfords in Milton today). Hasted did not give the size of Sittingbourne in his time, but he mentioned the two best-known inns — the Red Lion, where King Henry V, on his triumphant return from the Battle of Agincourt in 1415, was entertained by Northwood; and the Rose, which Hasted described as the "most superb of any throughout the kingdom".[1]

In the French Wars many Milton men served in the Navy but probably not from choice. My own great-great-grandfather served on the *Victory* at Trafalgar — he was a quartermaster and was at the wheel. Milton was one of the ports which sent grain to London and it must have been a busy place — some of the mills were windmills; the others were watermills, for even in my time there were many streams running into the Creek. Milton and Sittingbourne are sitting on vast deposits of brickearth and there are Roman bricks built into Milton old church which stands out on the edge of the marshes; but the large expansion of brick making did not take place until about 1850 when almost all the land around the Creek became brick-fields. Most of the bricks were sent to London and the spritsail barge[2] was perfect for the job. With its light draught and the help of the tidal stream a barge could be loaded one day and in London the next. A barge would carry enough bricks to build one average house.

THE RIVER SWALE 97

Cods Reach.—N. & S. Good anchorage is available here, with 8 feet at low water.

Horse Reach.—E.S.E. & W.N.W. There is a "horse" here, which is covered at quarter flood. Craft must keep well to the West, as the water is shallow. At the top of this Reach to the Eastward the water at low tide is 4 feet 6 inches.

Bridge Reach (King's Ferry).—N. & S. Care must be taken in navigating King's Ferry Bridge. The centre arch is 58 feet in width, and the small arches 38 feet. There are six working arches at high water, but only three can be navigated at low water, viz. the centre arch and two to the eastward. The centre arch span is raised for vessels with fixed masts. There is a white light on the centre of the middle arch. The depth of water under the centre arch at low tide is 20 feet. The other two arches have 9 feet 5 inches of water. There is not sufficient water to navigate the arch to the westward of the centre at low tide.

Clay Reach.—S.S.E. & N.N.W. Half-a-mile above King's Ferry Bridge on the West is Ridham Dock (Edward Lloyd, Ltd.), 750 feet long and 250 feet wide at entrance, with 29 feet at H.W. on spring tide and 13 feet at L.W. on spring tide.

Elmley Reach.—N. & S. This Reach is narrow and shallow in places at low tide. At the top of the Reach is the entrance to Milton Creek.

Milton Creek.—This Creek has several Reaches. A south-west wind is a contrary wind for navigating the Creek on a flood tide, but if a vessel cannot get to her destination she can anchor in any part of the Creek. The rise and fall of tide at Murston is 11 feet. The following are the wharves on the way up:

Kemsley	Edward Lloyd, Ltd.
Churchfield No. 1	C. Burley, Ltd.
Murston	Smeed, Dean & Co.
Adelaide	Smeed, Dean & Co.

G

98 HANDBOOK FOR BARGEMEN AND LIGHTERMEN

Wood's	Wm. Wood, Ltd.
Dolphin Cement Works	C. Burley, Ltd.
Crown Quay	H. Filmer, Ltd.
Crown Quay	Wills & Packham, Ltd.
Gransden's	Gransden & Son
Churchfield No. 2	C. Burley, Ltd.
Murrell's	Milton U.D.C.
Station Brickworks	C. Burley, Ltd.
Lloyd's Wharf	Edward Lloyd, Ltd.
Prestis Quay	Edward Lloyd, Ltd.

At the entrance of the Creek on the East of the Swale there is a good anchorage with a depth of 15 feet at low water. A deep-water jetty for working large vessels is in contemplation and may shortly be erected.

The Eastern Swale

The Eastern Swale extends from Milton Creek Beacon to Columbine Spit Buoy, and has a depth in the fairway of about 3 feet at low water. It is buoyed for the use of vessels bound eastward to the open sea.

Milton Creek to Elmley Ferry is the 1st Reach. —N.W. & S.E.

Elmley Ferry to Conyer Creek.—N.W. & S.E. The stretch of water between Elmley Ferry and the eastern end of Fowley Island is known locally as "The Grounds," and extends for a distance of about two nautical miles. This channel is marked for the use of shipping by four buoys which are placed on the low-water line on the south side. They are marked " E. L., Ltd.," are painted red, and numbered 1 to 4, counting from the Elmley end of the channel.

Here is **Conyer Creek.** At the entrance is Eastwood's Conyer Works; at the top of the Creek is their Teynham Works; and at Conyer Quay, Teynham, is W. E. White's Bargeyard.

Conyer Creek to Windmill Creek.—N.W. & S.E.

Description of Milton Creek taken from 'A Handbook for Bargemen, Lightermen and Tug-men' by Charles T. Perfect (1930).

A 'staysail' barge, which was the common type in Milton Creek. This is the *Yieldsted*, pictured at Lloyd's Wharf in 1899 with part-owner and skipper Jim Fenteman at the wheel. (Photo by Ramell, a man who came from Deal and ran a photographic business in West Street for over 40 years; when he died in 1936 he was taken back to Deal for burial in his family grave.)

The 'stumpy' rig was favoured in small barges which worked to the non-tidal reaches of the Thames and the London canal system. Here is the well-known local 'stumpy' *Garfield*, about 1930, when she was wearing the 'Red Triangle' emblem which signified Smeed Dean's amalgamation with the Red Triangle Group. Her skipper around the turn of the century, Tommy Shrubsall, named his house in Tonge Road after the barge (which in turn was named after an American President). The barge ahead is the *Lady Mary*, owned by Everards of Greenhithe, Kent. *Garfield* was broken up in Northfleet Creek about 1965 after lying derelict there for several years; *Lady Mary* is derelict at Erith today.

(Courtesy of Thames Barge Sailing Club)

I have read somewhere that Milton Regis got some privileges from the Crown for carrying food to London in the Plague years. Knowing Kentish Men and Men of Kent, I bet they were paid well over the odds!

The coming of Lloyds Paper Mills (about 1870) transformed old Milton — I believe 17 streets were pulled down to make way for it. At one time all the materials for paper-making were brought in by spritsail barges, but after the Bargemen's Strike of 1912, which was very bitter, Lloyds turned to tugs and lighters. The Mills, which brought prosperity for some, were the ruin of many more, for the effluent killed most of the fish in the local waters. Hence the fishing fleet — about 90 smacks — had nothing to do. I doubt if the crews got any compensation and so they had either to emigrate or go into the Mill for 7 pence an hour, old money. I have been told that two smacks are buried under the shoal bank[3] in the middle of the Creek opposite Prentis' Wharf and another is under the saltings opposite Murston Quay. The Redshaw brothers were the very last Milton fishermen and got a living of sorts until the 1950s, although towards the end they kept their boat in the cleaner Medway. I do not think there are any boys left in the family. They were the last Freemen of Milton Creek. At one time two men had got a living fishing between Crown Quay and the top of the Creek, but this was before the Paper Mill started. There are two pieces of public land where the fishermen of Milton dried and repaired their nets. One has been 'stolen' but you can use the other if you know where it is (the barge

For coasting work, a bigger barge, rigged with a bowsprit, was commonly used. This is the superb 'mule-rigged' coaster *Hydrogen*. The photograph was taken about 1920 at a time when she was giving Smeed Dean's office staff their annual day-trip — as seen by the numerous people on deck. Two houses in Sittingbourne were named after her: *Gen-Hydro* (Arthur Coward, skipper, Woodstock Road) and *Hydrogen* (Harold 'Jack' Butcher, mate, Canterbury Road).   (Courtesy of Harold Butcher)

Ketch, or 'boomie', barges were not very popular for the Milton Creek work because their rig was less versatile than that of the spritsail barges. However, for coasting work they came into their own more. This is the ketch-barge *Ethel Edith*, which was skipper-owned for a few years around 1920 by local man Arthur Wenban. She and the ketch-barge *Edith Wood* regularly brought coal from the north to Milton for Dives' coal merchant's business in Hawthorn Road. *Ethel Edith* is today derelict and very much broken down at Pin Mill, Suffolk. (Courtesy of Peter Wenband — note the different spelling in some branches of the family.)

A ketch running up Milton Creek with a fair wind under flying jib alone, about 1908.
(Photo by Bill Kennett)

Saxon has lain there in recent times). The head of the Creek was a pleasant enough place 40 years ago, with the 'Periwinkle' stream running into it under a bridge to the floodgates. Periwinkle was a strong stream that has dried up now, but at one time the horses could stand in it and drink. The Portreeve's house stood on Prentis' Quay — a big house in red brick. It was still occupied before the Second War, but the office of Portreeve (which at one time was elected) was no longer in being — a pity for it sounds as if it went back to Saxon times.

If you unloaded on Prentis' Quay, you had to work with a gin[4] on the sprit (or on the topsail halyard and sheet) for there were no cranes. However, Lloyd's Wharf had cranes and there was also one on the Council Wharf for ballast and coal. At one time Eastwoods had an office at the top of the Creek but that was before my time. I do not remember many barges using Prentis' Quay although I believe wool was loaded — but only two or three freights a year, carried either by their own barge *Pomona* or Burley's barges. Bricks were sometimes loaded at the Parish Wharf at the bottom of Flushing Street. They were brought down by horse and cart and carried by Wood's barges. Lloyds had a bargeyard at the end of Prentis' Quay which was previously owned by Eastwoods, and before that by Shrubsall. They repaired their own wooden lighters and afterwards took over Sittingbourne Shipbuilding Company's Yard[5] (formerly owned by White — who built some famous racing barges in his time).

Wills and Packham had a dock (Station Brickworks Dock) by Whites yard where they loaded bricks. This dock was also used by Burley to unload rough-stuff but, compared to Smeed Deans, these brick fields were small. Gransden had a field on the Milton side of the Creek with a wharf which held three barges. Filmer's Dock on Crown Quay has a grain warehouse and Wills and Packham had at one time done all their work for them; there were nearly always three barges waiting to unload. It is now Parrett's Printing Works. Crown Quay was the public

Thomas Scholey discharging coal at Prentis' Quay about 1912. The building behind her still stands today.   (Courtesy of Bowaters and Tony Ellis)

Head of the Creek, with Prentis' Quay on the left, about 1928.   (From an old postcard)

Barges forcing a passage past Crown Quay during the icy winter of 1895. In the background is Burley's cement works. (Courtesy of Clifford Dolding)

wharf where the smacks unloaded their catch. Grandad used to say that the sprats were worth 6d. a bushel. I have seen timber unloaded there too. It was also a lay-by for Wills and Packham's barges for it was a large wharf and had a public weighbridge.

Further down the Creek, Burleys had a barge yard and a cement works but only a small one. I believe they turned out a very good grade of cement and had a Government contract for a time. Next was the Smeed-Dean complex which was the largest on the Creek. I think they had 90 hand berths turning out over 1,000,000 bricks a year each. Also there were three machine berths working all the year round. The cement works at Murston Quay would load about 500 tons a day into barges mostly for the London River but also to go down Channel and to the northern ports. The nearby brick works would also load about six barges a day with bricks and brick rubbish. There was once a brisk trade in flints (mostly exported for road-making) but the deposits had begun to run out by the time I started work. The stand-by return freight for all the local barge firms was London refuse, otherwise called 'rough-stuff' or 'dust'. Huge stacks were on each side of the Creek. It was sifted and the 'firing', which was the half-burnt coal (for London was coal fired at that time), was used for burning the bricks (in kilns). The fire dust was mixed with brick earth to make bricks. As they were paid to bring it away from London, our firms were in pocket both ways. However, we bargemen were not so deliriously happy — it could be an obnoxious freight, especially in the summer!

Paper was sent to a few places by sailing barge, mostly to Norwich. China clay was transferred from ketches and topsail schooners into barges and lighters at Ridham Dock and then brought up the Creek. Wood pulp had at one time been unloaded out of ships at Queenborough into barges, but this ceased with the building of Ridham Dock just before World War I. Large freights of esparto grass were once brought up the Creek for paper making, but I have never seen any.

The Masters family were barge-builders at Milton Creek for a century or more. In addition to operating a barge yard for some years, they were also well-known for building barges in the open on the seawall at almost any convenient place. A site just upstream of Adelaide Dock was often used. For the last barge they built in this fashion (the *J.D. Drake*), they selected part of the seawall at Drake's Dock (which later became known as Kemsley Wharf, and is by the Kemsley terminus of the Light Railway). This was done, of course, because the brickmaker Drake owned the dock and the barge was built for him. This photo shows a Masters' barge under construction on the seawall. It is interesting that three consecutive Elmley Cattle Ferry boats were built by successive generations of Masters: 1. By John Masters, c.1835; 2. By his son C.T. Masters, c.1880; 3. By his grandson F.G. Masters (a barge-builder with Wills & Packham), 1925.   (Courtesy of Dolphin Sailing Barge Museum)

Small steamboats used to lie at Elmley Ferry and be loaded by barge with cement. This was a Smeed Dean job — quick but poorly paid, about 1/- (5p) a ton. There was talk at one time of building a jetty at Elmley and having a ropeway across the marshes, but it never came off.

Slop was a cargo carried at times by Burleys barges. This came from the London drains and was semi-liquid when loaded, but the plugs were pulled out of the barge when she grounded and the excess water ran out. It would take a week to load at times, but as the crew and owners were paid wet-weight, everybody was happy.

Leigh sand was brought in by the brick firms. It was used to prevent clay from sticking to the moulds and it was left to be washed by the rain and snow before drying for use. Clay for cement making was loaded off the saltings but only by Smeed-Deans and Burleys. Oranges and sugar were at one time brought by barge for the jam factory at Bell Road.

The 'anatomy' of the Thames spritsail barge. This drawing shows a 'staysail' barge, with the modest sheer which was typical of many Milton Creek barges because they had to do so much bridge work and everything had to be kept low.

Types of craft and their builders

The sailing or spritsail barge was the main vessel to be built at and to use Milton Creek. Although I expect that small sailing ships were built before the sailing barge era (1840-1940) I have never heard much about brigs or schooners. Smeed (later Smeed-Dean) built some large flat-bottomed craft with leeboards but they were more usually barquentine-rigged. In my time there were some big mulies[6] using the Creek, particularly the *Olive May* and the *Hydrogen*. Some small motor craft would at times come up to load cement at Murston, also an occasional West Country ketch or schooner.

The smacks that I have seen locally were small, two-man crewed. They had almost all gone by the turn of the century. Burleys had a motor barge — the *Queen Philippa*. This vessel and Lloyd's tug were the only powered vessels to use the Creek before the A.P.C.M. took over Smeed-Dean's cement and brick works and began to use a tug and lighters (about 1932).

At one time all the barges were small, about 60 tons, and were swim-headed[7] and steered by a tiller. My Grandad could remember the round-headed barges coming into fashion. His own father always had a coasting barge with three hands, but apart from saying his father took him to sea because he would not go to school, Grandad never said what the barges were like. I wish he had, but from what I picked up from the older men, many had their wives as mate.

During the First War Wills and Packham built flying boat hulls for the Navy. After it was over they built two motor barges, the *Harparees* and the *Heather Pet* (both of which left the Creek for distant owners). Also from this yard came four big spritsail barges. The *Olive May* (1920) was in fact the biggest spritsail barge of all time and the only barge ever launched with an auxiliary motor already installed. She was followed by *Raybel*, *Olive Mary* (later renamed *Arcades*) and finally, *Phoenician* in 1922, which was the last barge launched in Milton Creek and proved to be a consistent racing champion. These were strongly-built barges, because Wills and Packham had been well-equipped by the Government for their

The *Unique*, a fine barge built by Wills and Packham in 1903; this picture shows her on completion, with restraining ropes holding her steady for the photographer! *Unique* was of composite construction (wooden planking on iron frames), as were several other Wills and Packham built barges; she was later fitted out with a bowsprit for coasting work. On the right can be seen Burley's sail loft, which today is the main building of the Dolphin Sailing Barge Museum. *Unique* was wrecked off the Essex coast about 1940.   (Courtesy of Mrs Nash)

Launch of the *Olive May*, 1920. Note the large crowd of spectators — there were just as many on the opposite bank. Certainly Sittingbourne folk seemed very interested in their Creek in those days.   (Photo by Ferris, courtesy of Tom Redshaw)

The *Esther Smeed*

war-work; three are in commission today (although *Olive May* is now rigged as a half-sprit mulie), but *Arcades* was lost by fire in 1947.

I believe Wills & Packham rebuilt some of their own barges, *H.T. Wills* and *Llandudno* in particular.

Many years earlier (in 1868) the biggest barge of all time, the barque-rigged *Esther Smeed*, had been launched into the Creek by Smeed. She was an enormous 494 registered tons and could carry 800 tons of cargo (ie 8 times as much as an average Milton Creek spritsail barge). Around the same time several slightly smaller sisters were built — *Emily Smeed, Eliza Smeed, Sarah Smeed, Ellen Smeed*, etc — and their rigs varied between barquentine, brigantine, brig and schooner. These craft were designed primarily for the coal run from the Tyne and at this they were very successful, mainly because their shallow draft enabled them to sail over sandbanks which other craft had to go round.

But after this Smeed and Smeed-Dean confined their building and rebuilding activities almost entirely to spritsail barges. In fact, Smeed Dean were rebuilding during my time (1922 onwards) and the barges were to all purposes brand new when rebuilt. I have read somewhere that the old gear was put back in them; this is nonsense. The masts, sails and ironwork were new as were even the anchor and chain.

Burley built several barges around the turn of the century — all named after members of the family — *W.B., May, Charles Burley* etc. As mentioned elsewhere in this book, Burley also bought barges into the firm from elsewhere. One of these had been a German schooner and was a First World War prize. I remember going aboard her when she first came up the Creek. Burley named her *Fulson* (after Fulson Manor[8], one of the family houses) and re-rigged her as a spritsail barge. She was painfully slow and a cow to handle — we used to get out of her way in the Creek. Being steel she would have done us a bit of no good.

Raybel just after her launch in 1920. On the left is *Olive May*, which was partially fitted out by this time — note her large mule-type mizzen. (Photo by Ferris)

Launch of the *Harparees*, 1920. (Photo by Ferris)

Nelson, built in 1905 by Alfred White Snr, was (as seen here) a good racing competitor between the wars. She was the Medway Bowsprit Class Champion in 1931. *Nelson* was burnt on the saltings of the Swale near Queenborough about 1965. (Courtesy of Tom Redshaw)

Construction of the motor barge *Harparees* at Wills and Packham's Yard.   (Photo by Ferris)

Two local yards were well-known for producing fast barges which put up good performances in the annual barge races on the Thames and Medway. Robert Mark Shrubsall was building regularly during the last thirty years of the 19th century and produced about 70 fast craft, of which at least 9 — *Anglo-Norman, Laura, Early Bird, Whimbrel, Godwit, Britannia, Gazelle, Pastime* and *Dunstable* (ex R.G.H.) — were racing champions. After Robert Mark died in 1901 his yard was taken over by Eastwoods, a brickmaking firm. Their foreman shipwright, Alex Styles, launched 10 barges (mostly named after counties) between 1902 and 1908. Eastwoods retained the yard for maintenance work until 1912 and then moved to Otterham Quay, Rainham.

The Shrubsall/Eastwoods yard was near Prentis' Quay. Almost opposite, on the other side of the Creek, was the yard where Alfred White (Senior — his son built barges at Conyer) launched many speedy craft during the period from about 1895 to 1910; his champion barges were *Vectis, Clara, Nelson, Queen* and *Dreadnought*.

Both Eastwood's and White's yards eventually went to Lloyd (later Bowater) for the maintenance of lighters.

Other well-remembered local builders were Mantle, Masters, Spencelaugh, Stephen and John Taylor and the Burham Brick, Cement and Lime Co.

Ironwork (ie winches, steering gear etc) for these builders came mainly from the firm of Littlewood, whose foundry was, and still is, on Milton Hill. The original building is still there today (June 1979), but it is in a very dilapidated state. R. Gardiner was another local firm which made barges' ironwork. Gardiner owned the East Kent Iron Works in Frederick Street.

An R. Gardiner 'chaff-cutter' type of barge steering wheel mounted in the 'White Hart' public house, Crown Quay Lane, Sittingbourne. (Photo by Alan Cordell)

Nancibelle as a houseboat at Falmouth, c.1978. (Courtesy of Ms M.E. Martin)

A rubbing from a brass plate picked up off the ground near Milton Creek. It is something of a mystery because nobody can remember a firm called Swale Launch Works Ltd. Possibly they were a subsidiary of Wills and Packham or Sittingbourne Shipbuilding Company.
(Courtesy of Henry Attwater Jnr)

The last few sailing craft built at Milton Creek were also amongst the most interesting. They were all East Coast barge-yachts[9] of the type developed by the yachtsman E.B. Tredwen in the 1890s. These craft (generally varying in length from about 22 feet to 35 feet) had flat bottoms and rectangular hull sections; leeboards were usually fitted to give them sufficient grip of the water for windward sailing. Hence they had most of the advantages of their larger sisters the spritsail barges — shallow draught, ability to sit upright on the bottom at low tide, stiffness (within reason) under sail, and generous interior room for their size.

Around 1930 several East Coast barge-yachts were launched from the Sittingbourne Shipbuilding Company's yard. Amongst them were the *Elizabeth Anne,*

The Essex barge *Portlight* at Crown Quay in 1956 with a cargo of canned tomato juice for the cold storage warehouse. This was the next-to-last freight ever brought to the Creek by a pure sailing barge. *Portlight* later became a motor barge and present rumour has it that she will soon be re-rigged as a sailing-barge-yacht. (Photo by Alan Cordell)

the *Hugodian* and (best-known of them all) the *Nancibelle*. A large example of her type, *Nancibelle* measured 43 feet long by 13 feet beam, and she was spritsail rigged. Launched in 1930, she used Conyer as her home port initially, but she later went to the West Country and in 1979 was still afloat as a houseboat at Falmouth. During the Second War *Nancibelle* had the distinction of being one of the Dunkirk 'Little Ships' — an honour shared with several full-size Sittingbourne-built barges, including the *Spurgeon*, *Ada Mary*, *Beatrice Maud*, *Burton* and *Monarch*.

In 1938, Mr Gash (a lighterman working at the A.P.C.M. Murston Cement Works) built the East Coast barge-yacht *Iduna* at the Murston Yard. She was smaller, about 22 feet long by 7 feet beam, and she was constructed mainly from waste timber — for example, from the hatches of laid-up and derelict barges. She was rigged as a gaff-ketch and looked very traditional until, later, her lee-boards were replaced with a centre-plate. *Iduna* (named after a goddess in Scandinavian mythology)[10] was still afloat at Conyer in 1979, although she had but rarely left her berth in 20 years.

As I have said, Milton Creek was geared to the barge — at the time I started work about 200 barges were based at Milton, Sittingbourne and Murston. But it was two 'foreigners' who brought the last sailing barge freights to the Creek — the Essexman *Portlight* in 1956, and Everard's *Cambria* about 1960.

Barge owners

The largest barge owners on Milton Creek were Smeed-Dean with over 80 barges. This was a Murston firm and they owned most of the land and all of the houses and farms. They were a pretty good firm to work for — you were never refused gear. Though they were not over-generous as regards pay, you did get Union rates and light-sailing[11] money. Their barges were some of the handiest

31

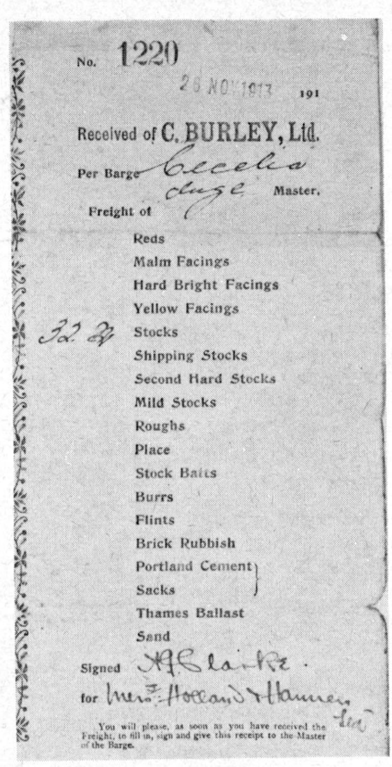

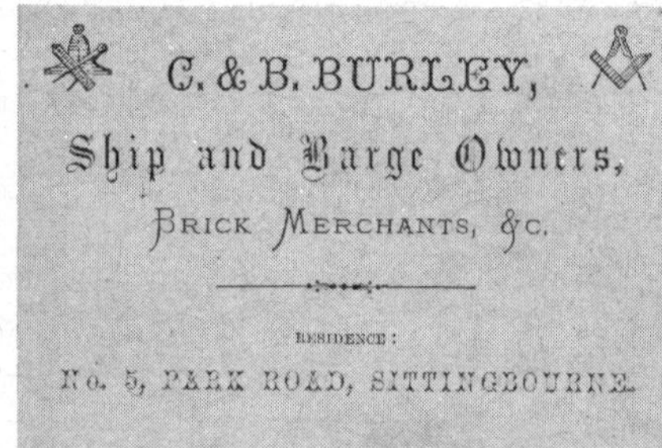

Papers from the firm of C. Burley Ltd. *Fanny Rapson* was a big ketch-barge which they owned towards the end of the last century. *Cecelia* was a spritsail barge; there is a slight anomaly in that the Mercantile Registers spell the latter's name *Cecilia*.

(Courtesy of Mrs Wright)

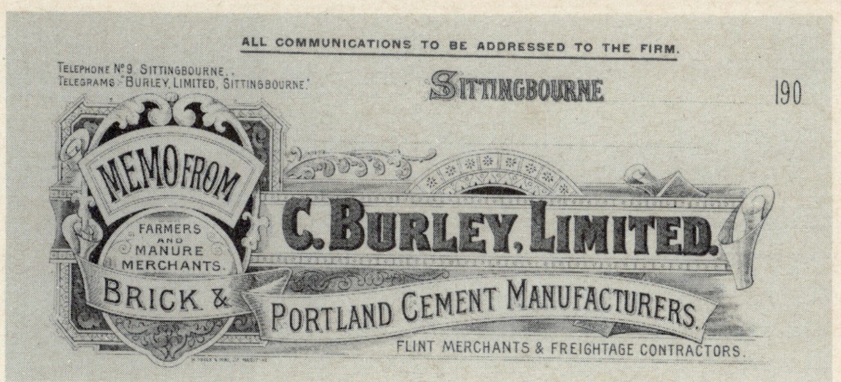

in the Creek — they would wend[12] in their own length. Their average tonnage was about 100[13].

Wills and Packham was a good firm with fine barges, but they did not have a lot of work of their own; so they often had to wait for a freight. About 20 barges, all well found, 90-ton average, comprised their fleet. Burley was a firm that bought up other people's old barges as long as they were big, and they also built 9 for themselves. As a matter of policy, maintenance was kept to a minimum in this fleet (rather like some haulage firms today). Hence most of their craft finished up derelict, rather than being sold. They had about 30 barges. Woods had a few small barges — the biggest was *Vera* (100 tons), and by hearsay you often had to wait for your money. They had mostly untidily rigged and oldish barges (about 8 barges, 80-ton average). Gransdens had only three barges but they were a good firm. When trade was slack they found work for the crews in the brickfield. Their barges were well found and of 100 tons average size. Lloyds had at one time some big sailing barges, but after the Bargemen's Strike the gear was taken out and they were towed. Pay was on a weekly basis instead of by the freight.

Filmers at one time had a barge of their own, the *Windward* — sold before I started work. When the A.P.C.M. took over Smeed-Deans, Ellis and Andrews took their barges out of the firm and with Bingham's *Shamrock*, worked china clay for Lloyd, corn for Payne and ballast where wanted. They did fairly well until after the Second War, but then they sold out and their barges were dispersed. However, their *Maria*, *Pimlico* and *Victoria* were the last locally-owned barges and regularly worked the Creek until about 1950.

I have never seen an Eastwood barge up the Creek although one of the wharves was called by their name. They also had a barge-building yard in the Creek during the period 1902-1908, an office about the same time near Prentis' Quay, and a brickfield (c.1890-1907) where Eastwood Road is now.

Lavers, Drake, Prentis and Watson were before my time and I know little of them myself.

Kent Barge Owners' Mutual Insurance Association

(LIMITED).

Offices: 90, High Street, Sittingbourne,

30 August 188_1_

Sir,

A Meeting of the Directors will be held at the Bull Hotel, on Friday next, the 2nd Sept. at Six o'clock precisely.

Business:

To read & confirm minutes of last meeting
The Case of the "Garibaldi"
    Ditto   "Water Lily"
    Ditto   "George & Frances"
    Ditto   "Sophia"
    Ditto   "Energy"

Damage to the "W. B."
The "Bethell" & "Prince Consort"
The "Cæsar" & "Conqueror"
The "Alert" & "Trinity"
The "Columbus" & "Samuel Abbott"
The "Sibyl" & "Rua"
The "Surprise" & "Sarah"

Yours faithfully,

F. USHERWOOD,

Secretary.

A paper from the local barge insurance association.　　　　(Courtesy of Mrs Wright)

Harold Andrews followed his father into the administrative side of Smeed Dean, later becoming a barge-owner and proprietor of the Sittingbourne Shipbuilding Company. In private life he was active as a sportsman, playing cricket, football and hockey for Gore Court. This photo, dated 1917, shows him in another spare-time activity — as Choirmaster of the Sittingbourne Congregational Church Young Worshippers League Choir. The barge families of Bones and Fenteman are also represented. (Courtesy of Leslie Strevens)

This is part of the Smeed Dean brick-making 'empire', as seen from Murston New Church about 1920. It well illustrates the vast areas occupied by these activities. (Photo by Ferris)

July 14th 1921 was a 'Red Letter' day for Sittingbourne — H.R.H. The Duke of York came to tour the local brick industries. Here he is seen in one of the Burley fields, accompanied by members of the Burley family. (Courtesy of Mrs Wright)

The Duke of York (later King George VI) meets Sittingbourne brick industry workers. (Courtesy of Mrs Wright)

Loading Smeed Dean bricks into the *Histed* at Adelaide Dock about 1930.

(Courtesy of E. Pearce)

Barge trades

The main cargoes from Milton Creek were bricks, cement, brick rubbish for roads or foundations and some flints; also the odd freight of wool. Ingoing freights were at one time coke for the old kilns; coal for the rotary kilns; mud for cement making; corn for Filmers Dock and Paynes; Leigh sand which was used by all the brick firms; some work for Lloyds (china clay, wood pulp and ballast); and of course London refuse ('rough-stuff') for firing the brick kilns.

It is interesting to reflect at this point that a scheme which was dreamed up 60 years ago would have greatly improved cargo handling. The idea was to put a lock at the mouth of the Creek. Then the barges would have remained afloat and could reach their berths, or change berths at any time. Equally, they could have locked in or out at any state of tide. But the idea never materialised.

Smeed Dean's and Eastwood's bricks in a partially demolished cemetery wall at Twickenham. The Smeed Dean ones were obviously made at Murston. The Eastwood ones could have come from the Milton field, but might equally have been made in one of Eastwood's other centres in the Thames Estuary area. Probably both types were conveyed by barge to Twickenham Draw Dock.

(Photo by Alan Cordell)

A complete view of Adelaide Dock taken about 1930. Three of the barges have been identified — nearest is *Histed*, with *Argosy* alongside, and second from right (with short topmast) is *Leslie*. Milton Old Church is visible in the background. Today, *Histed* has disappeared, *Argosy* is derelict in the River Crouch and *Leslie* is a housebarge at Allington, nr Maidstone.

(Courtesy of E. Pearce)

The above view as seen today, showing the silted, polluted and deserted wilderness which most of the Creek has become. Former Smeed Dean bargeman Ron Dickenson looks on — speechless!

(Photo by Alan Cordell)

Reels of newsprint paper being loaded into the spritsail barge *Pioneer* and a lighter at Lloyd's Wharf about 1910. *Pioneer's* sails are missing and her spars are on deck, so presumably this trip to London will be done under tow by Lloyd's tug. In actual fact Lloyd gave up sailing barges about 1920 and the *Pioneer* and her sister *Protector* were converted to lighters. They finished up as derelict hulks in the Creek, but have now disappeared. The multitude of chimneys in the background illustrates the vast extent of the Sittingbourne brickfields at that time.   (From an old postcard, by courtesy of Clifford Dolding)

Barge life

The life afloat was neither better nor worse than has often been described. It was hard at times but with many compensations. You always had a change of scenery and life was never boring. A boy was often a bit stupid when he first started at 14, but by the time he was 17 he was of use to himself and his skipper. Once you had found out the hard way that food comes first you were alright. It was tiresome to be windbound in the Swale or Lower Hope but this was not very often. People nowadays think we did not get a lot of sleep, but you had to get it when you could and you knew that if you had to keep up and about for a long time you were earning money. It was not work but the lack of it that got bargemen down. Normal work was never too hard — it is no trouble to get the anchor up and set the sails if you know what you are doing, for you always do things in the same order, viz: topsail sheet out, shorten chain, give skipper the mainsail and set foresail (held to windward on the bowline), heave up anchor, let go foresail bowline and set topsail. I do not suppose my skipper Jim Brooks said any more than 'Let go' (meaning the bowline) when we got under way. If we were in company with any of our other barges, when we brought up we would go aboard the one with the biggest cabin for a yarn. There was so much to see on the River Thames 50 years ago, for every wharf had a ship on it. I have counted 150 ships pass me at Gravesend on a Saturday or Wednesday which were the busiest nights. At other times the only thing moving would be yourself. There were no such things as hours or conditions — you made them yourself. If you were busy you might only get one good night in a week. And you never laid at a

Smeed Dean bargemen at the Camberwell 'vestry' (ie refuse depot). Four have been identified: back row — left, George Faint — middle, George Aspin; front row — left, Bert Kennett — middle, 'Justice' Hawkins. The building in the background was a gramophone record factory.
(Courtesy of George Faint)

One branch of the large Farrington family. This photo, taken about 1907, shows Frank (at the back) and Hedley with their four sisters. Two other brothers are missing. Frank (later known as 'Pilot') became a skipper with Smeed Dean and a member of several racing crews between the wars; Hedley did likewise and in the 1960s and 70s was a very successful racing skipper in the barge-yacht matches.   (Photo by Bill Kennett)

wharf after you were unloaded for we always had an order waiting, if only for London refuse. The best times were when we got to a wharf on a Saturday, which meant two nights in. Jim would usually go home and I did as I liked. At Blackfriars we always seemed to drop up to take the berth at night and come off in the afternoon; I cannot remember that we ever dropped up in the day. I am not saying that we never worked hard, we have all had sore shoulders after working a barge up a Creek against a head wind — no good saying 'start the motor' then! I think my best years were when I was 19-21; we were busy and I had a comfortable barge and knew what I was doing. After this times got worse (1931-2) and I wanted to take charge myself and began to have friction with Jim, for by that time I was as good as he was. He did try to get me three barges and recommended me, but the firm was getting rid of their barges, so that was that. As regards pay and prices, they were pretty low by today's standards. Food was pretty cheap: salt beef 3½-4d/lb, bread 4d/loaf, potatoes 6d/7lb, a hand of pork 5/- and other things in proportion. But pay was low — if we took 100 tons of cement to London, and loaded coal home, the mate's money would be £5. Bricks would yield something less. Mate's money for a freight of London refuse was about 30/-, ballast gave 25/- to the mate if we took it to London, less if to Leigh or Southend. I doubt if I averaged £2 a week all the time I was mate, taking good times with bad, and I was little better off when I took charge. Even when I went on the *Burton* as mate and shared the money[14] it did not come to £3 a week. Corn freights paid a bit more but you could lie a month waiting for orders. There was very little money to be earned in barging after about 1926. I have known barge skippers loading London refuse at Duke's Shore (where the market rubbish came in) to look in the boxes for bacon and fruit; they said it did not taste bad, but it would have done to me! I was never so badly off as that — when I thought I was getting nowhere, I moved on.

Bargemen

Many fine seamen sailed out of Milton Creek. What is seldom realised, even by their own family, is that a barge captain is a master mariner. When you were recommended as fit to take charge you were given a test by the ship's husband (the man in charge of stores, a senior skipper). One of the things asked was 'How far can you take a barge?' The right answer is 'As far as the tide ebbs or flows'. Another: 'Which is the best light in Sea Reach?' Some would say 'Chapman Head' but the right answer is 'Daylight'.

When you think of it, a barge skipper must be able to take his barge anywhere within reason, without any advice or orders, in a vessel that is really the size of a ship and with one hand or at the most two. Until recently bargemen were looked down on slightly due to the fact that to most people a barge is a box towed by a tug, or a narrow boat pulled by a horse. If I were called a 'Bargee', of which there is no such animal, I would disappear in a blue haze!

I remember my own grandfather, short tempered but kind, who always did his best for me — Harry Williams ('Timson') of the *Unique*. Also I recall Capt. Sandy of the *H.T. Wills*, Capt. Inge of the *Samuel Bowly*, Capt. England of the *C.I.V.* and *Five Sisters*, Dick Scattergood, 'Guggy' Wise, Harry Kitney of the *Carisbrooke Castle*, Capt. Port of the *Premier* and *Bexhill*, Arthur Coward of the *Hydrogen*, 'Dibby' Coward of the *Levitt* and *Gannet*, 'Scranny' Hambrook of the *Yieldsted*, Bill Gorf of the *Persevere* and *George Smeed*. Bill once blew all

A photo taken aboard the ketch-barge *Ethel Edith* about 1917. Skipper-owner Arthur Wenban (seated, centre) has his wife and daughters aboard for a few days' holiday. On his left is Madge, next is Olive May, then Mrs Wenban. Standing behind at the wheel is mate Ted 'Talking Tommy' Wraight and standing on the left is the young third hand. A few years later Arthur Wenban was the controlling shareholder of Kent Coasters when they had the biggest spritsail barge of all time built; she was named after Olive May.   (Courtesy of Peter Wenband)

his sails away down Channel but drifted ashore on the only nearby piece of beach; the barge was recovered.

I recall Sam Gorf of the *Harry*. When previously skipper of the *Favorite*, coming down from the Humber, his mate went mad; so he shut him down the cabin for four days until he made the Creek!

Tom Pearce of the *Youngarth* had her from new and was never in serious trouble. He trained Ernie Hearne of the *Jane Mead* and *Hambrook*, also 'Pilot' Farrington of the *Sam* and *Leslie*. I remember also Capt. Mitchell of the *Harold*, Capt. H. Farrington of the *Alan Dean*, Capt. D. Dorrington of the 'Big' *Maria*, Capt. Ellis ('Donkey') of the *Victoria*, Capt. B. Aspin Snr. of the *Gordon*, Capt. B. Aspin Jnr. of the *Maid of Munster*, Capt. H. Aspin of the 'Small' *Maria*, Capt. G. Aspin of the *Fred*, Capt. E. Aspin of the *New Hope*, Capt. J. Brooks of the *Martin Luther* and *Georgiana*, Capt. E. Brooks of the *Myrtle* and *Martin Luther*, 'Dadger' Goldfinch of the *Levitt*, Capt. W. Allen of the *Burton* and *Hambrook*, 'Happy Days' Irons of the *Russell*, Capt. Bill Allen of the *Ada Mary*, and Capt. S. Stevens of the *Esther*.

There were many more whose names I cannot recall, all competent bargemen, which you had to be to get a living.

The barging families were Farringtons, Wises, Shrubsalls, Cowards, Aspins, Brooks and Spices.

In the barge heyday, when you were outward bound from Milton Creek, it was quite common to give friends and relatives a sail as far as Queenborough. It was easy to put them ashore on the causeway and they then had a frequent and quick train service back to Sittingbourne. Here Tom Cockell (at the wheel) and Albert 'Bony' Rossiter, skipper and mate respectively of the *George Smeed* about 1925, have two smart young ladies aboard for such a trip. Alice Sharp, in the foreground, later became Mrs Rossiter. *George Smeed* is today a housebarge at Maldon, Essex. (Courtesy of Albert 'Bony' Rossiter)

The hufflers[15] at Kingsferry Bridge, all ex-bargemen, were Patsy Austin, Erne Spice, Jim Spice, 'Dolly' Higgins, 'Bonny' Stowers, Harry Jeffery, Fred Box, George Hambrook, 'Doggy' Fletcher, the Stone brothers, Dan'l Wescott and Fred Hadlow. They were later joined by Dick Evenden who stayed on until the early 1950s and by that time was the last huffler at the Bridge.

George Winn was probably one of the first well-known Sittingbourne coasting skippers. I do not think he ever lay windbound — he would put all loose gear down below, double-lash the spars and then let her run. It was a joke that he went under water at Dover and came up at the Isle of Wight. He always had his gear made stronger than normal. His son 'Spider' got his name when he was taking a spider iron for the sprit end aboard. You could normally sling them over your shoulder, no trouble, but 'Spider' had to push his down in a wheelbarrow it was so heavy. As he was a lanky fellow, he got the name 'Spider', which stuck all his life.

Another good tale about George Winn concerns the time when he lay in company with a large fleet of anchored barges in Dover Harbour. All were bound down-Channel. George got under way in half-a-gale from the south-west whilst the others preferred to remain at anchor. He spent several hair-raising days and nights beating down-Channel, delivered his cargo to the West Country, then ran back light before the same heavy blow, bound for Murston. When he reached Dover, the same barges were still at anchor, so (to rub it in) George triumphantly sailed into the south-west end of the harbour, through the fleet, and out of the north-east end!

Watch-chain emblem of the Bargemen's Brotherhood; pity about the missing fluke. (Photo by Alan Cordell)

A group of bargemen at the opening of the 'Bargemen's Hut' about 1921. This was the clubhouse of the Bargemen's Brotherhood, a social and spiritual organisation for bargemen; it stood in Crown Quay Lane on the triangle of grass opposite the 'White Hart' public house.

The sailors at each end were local men serving in the Royal Navy at Chatham. Left to right:

Back row (standing): Jock Spencer (RN), Bill Chapman Snr ('Hair Oil'), Steve Wise Jnr, Sid Wood, Alf Eaglestone, Arthur Woodall, Ted Bingham, Bert Aspin Jnr, Bert Aspin Snr, Ernie Hearn Snr, George Faint or Bill Kitney, Henry Attwater Snr, Ernie Spice, Bill Pudney, A. Stone, George Aspin or Ern Humphrey (RN).

Middle row (kneeling): Bill Allen, Ernie Hearn Jnr, Albert Rossiter ('Bony'), Wilf Box ('Pip'), Bill Chapman Jnr, Sid Court Jnr, A. Court Jnr or Archie Glandfield, Sid Court Snr.

Front row (sitting): Fred Wills ('Wilkie'), Ebbie Earl, C. Bishop or Jim Kitney, Tommy Schmidt, Frank Farrington ('Pilot'), A. Eaglestone or Bert Stone, E. Coleman ('Pudden').

The hut was demolished around 1942.   (Courtesy of Henry Attwater Jnr)

George used to come and go so quickly he was known as the 'Channel Ghost'. He left Sittingbourne around the time of World War I and went to live at Leigh-on-Sea.

Like others such as Chris Dickenson, George ran out of luck when he bought a boomie[16] for its reputed sea keeping qualities. He was wrecked in his *Diana* near the Old Harry Cliffs at Swanage, whilst Chris lost the *Rosebud* on Brighton beach. These incidents happened in the early 1920s and both men survived to sail again.

The Bargemen's Brotherhood

I believe that most members of the Bargemen's Brotherhood are now dead. Even in my barging days it was mainly the older skippers who belonged to it. From my own impression it was a thing that ran from about 1900 to 1927 and had been formed by the Rev. Parry-Evans who edited a magazine called 'The Bargeman'. I last saw a copy about 1915 and I could read it although I was only seven. I remember going to two garden parties with Grandad and also to a church parade with the banner; about 80 bargemen were there. The banner depicted a barge on one side and Milton Church on the other.

The Brotherhood had a clubhouse in Crown Quay Lane (opened c.1921) which was running when I was a young mate, but it closed when the Depression hit us. The Rev. Parry-Evans was a good friend to bargemen and his wife was a real lady. I have heard that she had a title. They both used to come round to see Grandad when he had the gout, which was nearly every year. I believe that they left Sittingbourne about 1922 and died about 1950. Members of the Brotherhood were entitled to wear a watch-chain emblem, in the shape of an anchor, and to fly a pennant with the letters 'B B' on it at their sprit-end.

Tugs and lighters

By 1946 sailing barge traffic to Milton Creek had almost ceased; there was still quite a lot of cargo carried, but it was almost all by tug and lighter.

At one time the only lighters in the Creek were owned by Bowater-Lloyd, who had turned over to powered craft about 1912, after the Bargemen's strike. The tug when I started work was the *Sirdar*, an old steam tug. Lloyd's lighters were all 'resident' which meant that the men lived aboard their own lighters all the time. These lighters could carry about 200 tons; some were wood, some steel. They carried wood pulp to the Mills and loaded paper away, mostly to the wharf below Cannon Street Station. China clay was loaded out of ships in Ridham Dock and lightered up to the Sittingbourne Mills. Lloyd's tug used to work Milton Creek every tide except Sunday and we would often try to get in her way, so that the skipper had to give us a 'snatch' (tow) to get us out of his path! When as lads we saw the tug, we would all sing 'There's a barge across the Creek, Jimmy Dean' — you can guess to what tune! Jimmy Dean was of course the skipper's name.

The *Sirdar* was blown up during the Second World War by a magnetic mine (in Cods Reach of the Swale, above Queenborough); all the crew were killed, but I believe Jimmy Dean was off duty ashore, or possibly he had retired by then. Bowaters then bought the tug *Elizabeth Murre*, which they ran until they finished with lighters in the 1960s. She was a diesel tug.

Burleys ran a motor ship, the *Queen Philippa*, which loaded rubbish herself and towed two lighters (also loaded) behind her. I think the drill was as follows:

A view of Murston Quay looking downstream in 1957. An A.P.C.M. lighter is on the repair blocks on the left and more are at the Quay beyond the sunken sailing barge *Thomas and Frances*. Bowater's tug *Elizabeth Murre* is leaving the Creek with one of their lighters. The area in the foreground is the site of the earlier Smeed Dean barge building and repair shed.

(Photo by Alan Cordell)

Big lighters, towed by tugs, ousted the sailing barges from the Milton Creek trade. This view, taken in 1956 and looking upstream, shows several A.P.C.M. lighters at Murston Quay.

(Photo by Alan Cordell)

Today there are no locally owned commercial craft using the Creek. However a few steel motor craft owned elsewhere still bring in occasional sand and ballast. Here is the *Ferrocrete* discharging sand at Eastwoods Wharf (mainly for Milton Pipes) in 1977.

(Photo by Alan Cordell)

she would bring two lighters home, take the berth herself and unload; then she would go away, taking two empty lighters behind her, leaving the other lighters to unload while she was away. When she got to the 'dust' wharf in London, she would load first again, pick up two loaded lighters and come down the River, leaving the 'empties' to load. You can see that the job would be carried on with 6 lighters. The *Queen Philippa* and the lighters were on a weekly wage, but not overpaid (if I know Burleys!). Burleys lost the 'dust' contract about twenty years ago and the fleet was sold, mostly for scrap I believe. I was recently told that the *Queen Philippa* is down in Ramsgate.

When the A.P.C.M. took over Smeed-Dean and Co., about 1932, their own tugs and lighters were brought into Milton Creek right away. The tugs were the *Leopard* and *Panther* (both steam). The sailing barges were sold off as quickly as possible — you could say 'given away', for a barge in sea-going condition was typically sold for about £50. At the same time the firm ordered some new lighters to work the Creek; these could carry 250 tons in about 6 feet of water. A.P.C.M. also had some lighters built to work the Surrey Canal. A motor boat, the *Cemarco*, was based in Milton Creek. 'Pilot' Farrington took her new, at the time when he gave up barging (ie. when A.P.C.M. moved in).

I do not believe that any sailing barges loaded away after 1939 from the quays at Murston. Even from about 1932 both bricks and cement were taken away mostly by lighter. The ingoing cargoes were coal, refuse and some coke. Cargoes away were mainly cement, with some clinker. No bricks were exported by water after the Second World War, when I rejoined the firm. At that time the towing was done by the *Cromford*, a small motor vessel; she was ballasted with stones to give her some weight. She was not very powerful, but she seldom

A FORMER anti-submarine frigate has come to its last resting place, near Sittingbourne

The 1,200 ton H.M.S Kepple, which was launched in August, 1954, has been brought to the Linguria Maritime ship breakers' at Milton Regis to be scrapped.

She was the largest ship ever to be brought into Milton Creek and caused quite a headache for the breakers, who had to manoeuvre her 310 feet length and 33 feet width into the berth.

H.M.S. Kepple, which sailed from Portsmouth dockyard on her last journey, has been scrapped because she is outdated and in poor condition.

Her metal will be taken off and used for scrap.

Extract from the 'East Kent Gazette', 10th May 1979.

had more than two or three lighters to tow although she would bring four up if needed, for she had the tide from Queenborough. Leaving Murston with two loaded lighters gave her just about as much as she could drag over the west tide[17]. There was a barge repair yard at Murston on the site of Smeed-Deans yard. Here, one or two lighters were always to be found being chipped and painted; this was to keep the lightermen busy in their spare time, for all the lightermen were not wanted every day. Before the War, if you did not have a job on a particular day, you signed on the 'dole'. It was rare to get a full week's work then; but after the War you either had to have a full week's pay every week or be stood off, not half-and-half. People cry out about being exploited now; we were then, and knew it, but could do nothing about it. The A.P.C.M. lighters ranged in size from 80 to 320 tons and were busy enough up to about 20 years ago. Then the policy of the firm changed — as much was put on road and rail transport as possible and most of the tugs and lighters were sold. As a waterman, I think this is a mistake; water transport will come back in time, in some form or other.

The largest vessel I ever saw go up the Creek with a cargo was a motor ship just after the Second World War. I believe she took 800 tons of pulp to Lloyd's Wharf on a 'hot' (high) spring tide — of course the Creek was not swabbed up so much then.

Today the Creek is almost dead — some ship breaking at Churchfield Wharf (which sometimes brings in larger craft than ever seen before in the Creek) and a little sand and ballast (for concrete) work to Milton are the only activities left. There is a nice wharf at Wills and Packham's old yard where foodstuff has been unloaded, but not for many years. A reflection on the state of the creek:— with its miles of water and wharves, there is not one yacht berth in Milton Creek although they are at a premium everywhere else!

The Creek today

The Creek is a disgrace to the Town and the Water Authorities. There is hardly a berth where you could put a barge — most of the wharves have swabbed up level and only two berths are worked, (Eastwood's Wharf and Packham's Dock[18], sand and ballast). Lloyd's wharf has water but the piles are falling. Crown Quay is now built on and Filmer's Dock is infilled. Prentis's is reasonable but private. All the sluices in the Creek are broken and useless. It seems to be the policy now that if you pull a house down, put the rubbish on the edge of the Creek, and if it falls in, so much the better! Bottle hunters have been allowed to dig the banks away, and the whole Creek area looks as if an Atom Bomb has hit it!

1 The Rose Inn building has been converted into shops, one of which is Woolworth's.
2 The definition of a barge is: a flat-bottomed freight-boat. A spritsail barge is a vessel of this type fitted with a spritsail rig.
3 Called the Duckle.
4 Gin (sometimes called a gin wheel) — a type of pulley wheel which could be suspended from the sprit, or between the topsail halyard and topsail sheet (after these had been unshackled). Cargo could then be handled with it.
5 This was about 1938, when S.S. Co. moved out to take over Wills and Packham's yard.
6 Mulie — a hybrid rig used in some big barges; it consists of spritsail main rigging combined with a ketch-barge's gaff-and-boom mizzen. A half-sprit mulie has this type of mizzen, but the loose footed mainsail has a gaff instead of a sprit; the gaff is left standing, so that the mainsail is brailed up when stowed, instead of being lowered.
7 Swim-headed — having a wedge-shaped bow, like a traditional lighter.
8 Sometimes spelt 'Fulston'.
9 East Coast barge-yacht — a pleasure yacht built on the lines of a trading barge, ie. with a flat bottom.
10 The name is also said to signify 'I done her'!
11 Light-sailing — sailing without cargo.
12 Wend — go about on to the opposite tack.
13 Tonnages in this book are given as 'Burden Tons' which is an indication of the weight of cargo a vessel could carry. This is the term usually quoted by bargemen. Another measure is 'Registered Tons', which is an indication of the volume of the cargo space and is carved on the vessel's main beam. This is the figure quoted in Mercantile Registers.
14 In the hard times of the 1930s it was not uncommon for two recognised skippers to form the crew of a barge and share the earnings equally.
15 Huffler — a waterman who earned his living by assisting barges through a bridge. (As this exercise often involved lowering and raising the barge's gear, ie. mast, sails and rigging, extra manpower was needed). The term was also applied to local pilots who assisted barges up the narrow creeks and rivers.
16 Boomie — a barge rigged as a ketch, with a gaff and a boom instead of a sprit on both main and mizzen masts; otherwise known as a ketch-barge.
17 West tide — in the Swale between Milton Creek and Queenborough, the tide runs from west to east for the first two hours of the ebb. This is called the west tide. After that it reverses and runs from east to west. Between Milton Creek and Shellness, the ebb tide runs from west to east all the time. The term 'west tide' is really a misnomer, because tides are usually described in terms of the direction towards which they are going, rather than from which they are coming.
18 Packham's Dock — often called Station Brickworks Dock.

CHAPTER 2

BIOGRAPHIES OF THE SAILORMEN

In Chapter 1, a large number of the better-known Milton Creek skippers are listed. Fortunately, we are able to present here short biographies of some of them to give an overall picture of the lives of the local bargemen.

TED BINGHAM
Extracted from an 'East Kent Gazette' of February 1951

Everything is trim and ship-shape in the eight-roomed house at 43 Staplehurst Road, Sittingbourne, the home of bearded 88-year-old ex-barge captain, Edward John Bingham.

He has been living there alone since his wife's death, but housework is nothing new to him, for his wife was an invalid for a number of years before she died. The living room stove is black and brilliant. "I always liked a clean stove, whether ashore or afloat", he told an East Kent Gazette reporter, "and people have given me credit for it then and now".

This fine old man is remarkably fit (if a little deafness is not taken into account) for his 88 years. But he is fighting the battle of the old — the fight against loneliness. Housework, a love of cribbage and whist and a long memory (even longer when he sits pulling at his pipe) are his only weapons against it.

Milton bred and born, he is the son of the late Mr John Page Bingham, a smack captain, who lived in Crown Road, Milton; and he was born in Charlotte Street in 1863.

"I think 1896 was the best time I knew in England," he said. "Things were cheap, there was plenty of work and you earned a decent screw. Everything was flourishing. You could go and buy meat for 5d. a lb., suet included. I used to buy it — a hundredweight at a time. Butchers used to chase me all over the town for my order".

"I had two men besides myself to keep and feed on the ship, and it only cost me about £1 a week to keep the three of us. We had four meals a day — breakfast, dinner and tea, and a meal at midnight. You could do it for 6s. 8d. a week a man and live well — far better than you can today. My ration this week was a little bit of steak. It's supposed to last me a week. I could eat it for breakfast".

Ask him what he thinks of the youngsters today, and Mr Bingham, who patronises 'neither pictures nor pub', will say: "They're a funny lot. They're too gay, too frivolous. All they think about is being up and down the street and at whist drives and dances — that is all they seem to live for. It is a different world altogether we are living in now. People are far too fickle minded".

"Sittingbourne and Milton have changed a lot, too. At one time, if a party of three of us were out in the town, one of us would be sure to know the people we met in the street. That is how small Sittingbourne and Milton were. My! Haven't things changed! Staplehurst Road was a blind lane when I first came here, with wheel ruts up to your knees. The beginning of Chalkwell Road used to be a pond, and now there is a row of houses there."

Mr Bingham can remember the two oyster fishing firms in Milton 75 years ago, Austin's and Hills. In the '80s he was the captain of a barge which ran coal here for Charlie Wood, a grocer who had a store on Prentis's wharf.

He can remember the times when, during neap[1] tides, it was possible to walk on craft from Prentis's Quay to Crown Quay, a distance of over half-a-mile. "Smeed Dean had over 80 barges, let alone ships. Wills and Packham had about 25, Burley as many — and in addition to those there were the casual vessels visiting here".

Mr Bingham was with Wills and Packham for 35 years and worked for Robert Mark Shrubsall, the barge builder, for another ten. "I left Shrubsall and took a ketch named the *Lord Beaconsfield*. We used to run down Channel; and across to the Continent, touching Yarmouth and all the intermediate places between."

After a lifetime of working for other people, Mr Bingham decided to go into business on his own and bought the 120 ton barge *Shamrock* which he had captained for Mr Wills. "I stopped sailing her when I was 68", he said, "and by then had another barge besides. The man who was in partnership with me took her".

"When the flint work fell off, the barges were no use to me and my barge became a barge yacht. They called her the *Black Swan* and when I last heard of her, two years ago, she was lying alongside the Thames Embankment, fitted out to cruise the Dutch rivers".

Milton has changed, and not for the better, thinks Mr Bingham. "When I was a boy there was no wharf where the sailors' home used to be. There was a sloping hard and the bawleys used to lie there for cleaning. There was quite a fleet of them out of Milton then, and they caught mussels, sprats and 'five-fingers' to sell to the farmers as manure at about 6d. a bushel when times were bad".

"Milton Creek was a lot different then to what it is now. The craft working up and down it kept it open. I was down there last summer near the cement works. Now the channel will only carry one barge. There used to be room for two. It is all silting up." He recalls with pleasure the times he has seen 300 barges meeting in the Jenkin Swatch[2] as they came out of the Swale and the Medway.

He knew that barging was dying, however. One of the main causes, he thinks, was the journey overland from the waterways where the barges were unloaded, which made cartage an expensive item. "I have had 23 horses and carts unload my bricks in a day. It was very expensive."

When he first knew Bowater-Lloyd, it was just a little tide mill at Brunswick Wharf[3]. From there, down to Wills and Packham, was a sea wall. "Flushing Street was the finest street in Milton when I was a boy — all cobble paved and with fine, white painted, red brick houses. In it were the Jolly Sailors public house and Scott's baker's shop. A little further up a pipe maker had his business and used to put the initial 'W' on his pipes."

Lloyd's three barges, the *Annie Lloyd, Frank Lloyd* and *Harris Lloyd,* carried the paper from Milton to Bow.

Back of the tide mill was a big reed pond, said Mr Bingham, extending from Scott's corner down to where Wills and Packham's offices are now. Somewhere between the pond and Scott's corner was a piece of ground, left by a Mr Huggens, for the fishermen of Milton to dry their nets and leave their gear. Mr Bingham wonders what has happened to it.

Mr Bingham is a little shy of people. "I used to be a hail-fellow-well-met, but I never associated with anybody", he said. "I discovered that if you were familiar with two or three people, you would find that they would be pulling somebody to pieces who was not there. Invariably you would be drawn into the conversation and would have to give some sort of answer. That answer, misrepresented, would soon find its way to the person discussed."

"When I was barging, I never made a chum, but I was always ready to give a hand when somebody needed help. The only chum I ever had was my wife. When I was home, I was Home!"

He had two sons and would have been married 68 years this May. Both sons are in Canada. The older is aged 66 and the younger 64. There is one grandchild and three great grandchildren one aged 18. He has visited them on several occasions and saw his younger son in 1939 when he was here on holiday.

Mr Bingham's grandmother lived in a row of houses where Milton's overhead railway now is. "She had a pig which got its living from the creek. When it was killed they couldn't eat it — it was too fishy. You could go and pick up half a bushel of flounders when the tide was out. Now you do not see any fish in the creek. The water kills them. It polluted all the oyster beds."

There was a lot to learn from an oyster, he said. "The man who knows them can keep them alive for days. The oyster has a reservoir of water. If you pack them flat side downwards they soon die because they gape, and every time they do a little water escapes. Pack them the other way up and they live long."

There is a way to eat oysters, too. Mr Bingham likes them fried with a bit of steak. "I can remember, when a boy, going round the farms with a bucket of oysters and exchanging it for a bucket of eggs. We used to call it 'dressing the hat'. It was a change for the farmers and a change for us."

There were coast guard ships in the creek when Mr Bingham was a lad, one lying off Craft Marsh[4] and the other in the second reach. Smuggling was their main concern.

We have heard a lot about the flooding of the creek just lately. Mr Bingham remembers people rowing up as far as the King's Arms in Milton High Street to get a pint of beer.

His grandfather was Milton's policeman. "I can remember him chasing me and other boys up and down the alleys and passages in Milton. If he didn't catch me I would find him waiting at the bottom of the stairs as I came down to breakfast . . ."

Drunks were usually imprisoned in the old Court Hall, and there must have been many of them, for public houses kept open as long as they had customers. There were some 'notorious chaps' who went barging in those days.

Mr Bingham likes to tell the story of one who fooled a policeman. He stole the policeman's chickens and was taking them aboard his barge in a sack late one night. The policeman's torch suddenly pierced the gloom, illuminating the bargeman and his loot. He complained fiercely, saying that the sudden light might have made him fall. The policeman apologised and handed down the sack, containing his chickens, to the irate bargeman.

"However, these bargemen were no trouble at sea," Mr Bingham concluded.

Arthur Coward, with son Harold on his left, at the wheel of *Hydrogen* about 1930. *Hydrogen* later became a motor barge and is today re-rigging for work as an advertising barge for Bell's Scotch Whisky.

(Courtesy of Harold Coward)

ARTHUR COWARD
By his son, Harold Coward

Arthur William Thomas Coward, the eldest of three children of Eastman Gill and Lydia Elizabeth Coward, was born on the 19th May 1865 in a house in a street of Milton that has long since disappeared due to the growth of the paper mills — Dean Street.

He commenced his long career on the water at the early age of 12 in 1877. He joined his father, who at that time was master of the Milton built and owned barge *Paragon* of 120 tons burden, as third hand. In the following year Eastman Coward took command of the *Marie Stuart*, another Milton built and owned barge and Arthur went with his father as third hand, taking the mate's berth in 1879 when he was 14 years old.

For seven years he sailed as mate with his father and, in 1886 (at the age of 21) secured his first command, that of the *Swiftsure*, built by R. Shrubsall at Milton and owned by Mr Edwin Neal Clark of Milton.

Work was scarce and freights were difficult to obtain in those days and two years later Mr Clark hired his barge to Messrs E.J. Goldsmith & Sons, the well known barge masters and freighters of Grays, Essex. Arthur Coward's skill, hard work and enthusiasm for his job soon attracted the notice of Messrs Goldsmith and in the same year, 1888, they offered him the command of their barge *Cambridge* of 90 tons burden.

Eastman Coward was very much against his son going to Messrs Goldsmith but in spite of his objection, Arthur decided to accept their offer and so began an association which lasted for 24 years and during the course of which he came to be one of the leading and most respected racing captains of the day. He commanded the *Cambridge* for three years and in 1891 took charge of a Sittingbourne built barge, the *Surprise* of 110 tons.

In the following year he moved into the *Gazelle*, 120 tons, and in 1895 he took command of that famous racing barge, the *James Piper* of 150 tons. It was about this time that he commenced his racing career, sailing as mate with the famous Captain Harry Munns. In 1896 he sailed his first race as skipper in the *James Piper* gaining third place in the Thames race and fourth in the Medway.

Arthur was well satisfied with his command of the *James Piper* she being in many respects a very fine barge. He was not at all pleased when in 1897 Mr Walter Goldsmith told him that he had been selected to take charge of their new barge, the *Giralda*, then building at Mr James Piper's yard at Greenwich. Arthur was to race her in the Diamond Jubilee races of that year.

Captain Munns had previously been asked to race this barge, but he flatly refused, declaring that in his opinion she would never win a race, and he preferred to put his faith in the graceful *Haughty Belle*.

Arthur protested strongly that he was quite satisfied with the *James Piper* and did not want to take the *Giralda*.

On Mr Goldsmith's orders he visited Mr Piper's yard and inspected the *Giralda* which was then on the stocks and he returned disgusted with her build and appearance and refused to take command of her. Messrs Walter and Edward Goldsmith however were convinced that they had a champion barge in the making and were confident that Arthur Coward was the man to prove so, and they insisted that he should sail her in the races. Reluctantly Arthur agreed to do so on the condition that he should return to the *James Piper* after the races were over.

The first trials of the *Giralda* proved very disappointing and as she was then she seemed to be anything but a champion. In the Medway race, however, she finished second to the *Satanita*, being beaten by 65 seconds.

Arthur was convinced that she needed trimming by the stern and in the two days before the Thames race he and his crew worked hard to do this. Racing barges were not allowed to carry ballast for trimming and the only way to get her stern down was to move everything that was movable, even the kitchener in the forecastle, from forward to aft. This proved to be her secret and in the Thames race she easily secured the first place, the gold cup and the honour to fly the Diamond Jubilee champion barge's burgee from her sprit end.

Captain Harry Munns was beaten into third place and this event prompted some lay poet to compose the following lines:— 'and when *Giralda* passed Gravesend, they fired off the gun and someone cried aloud, Oh where! Oh where! is that *Haughty Belle*, and that artful Harry Munns?' Although he did not race in her again, the secret of her trim was passed on by Arthur to subsequent skippers and enabled this most famous of barges to maintain her place as champion for many years to follow.

Arthur Coward did not return to the *James Piper* after the races but took command of the *Thetis* of 180 tons burden, a coasting barge. In the summer of 1898 he was commissioned by Messrs Goldsmith to supervise the building of a number of steel barges which they were having built at Woolston, Southampton, and later in the same year he took charge of the first of the barges, the *Gloria* of 130 tons.

He raced this barge in the races of 1899, securing third place in the Thames and fourth in the Medway. In 1901 he took command of the *Marconi* of 130 tons built by Messrs White of Conyer and took part in both the Thames and Medway races of that year, securing third and second places respectively.

How many can recall the Thames race of '01 which was sailed in a strong westerly breeze? Arthur Coward sailed the *Marconi* with all the skill he possessed and in beating back against the strong wind, the gallant little barge was lying over so far that her lee rail was awash. Lady spectators on the Committee Boat were fainting and averting their gaze, whilst bets were being laid amongst some of the men that she would go over in the next heavy puff! Arthur Coward, however, knew nothing of this at the time, so concentrated was he on his job, and he succeeded in bringing the *Marconi* home in third place.

In the following year he took command of the fine coasting barge *Perseus* and he remained in this vessel for the next ten years until the conclusion of his association with Messrs Goldsmith.

His racing days were not yet over, however, for in the same year, 1902, he secured third place in the Thames and second in the Medway in that famous racer *Sara*, built at Mr White's yard at Conyer. In 1903 Arthur sailed Mr White's latest barge, the *Torment*, gaining third place in the Thames and after finishing first in the Medway, was disqualified on a technical point which occurred at the start.

He sailed his last race in 1904 in yet another of Mr White's barges, the *Resurga*, securing fourth place in the Thames race.

Over the eight years 1896-1904, Arthur Coward secured a place in every race in which he took part and rose to be one of the leading and most respected racing skippers of the day. His tussles with his famous contemporary Capt. Harry Munns will long be remembered by those who were fortunate enough to have witnessed these races. They were contested in a keen spirit of friendly rivalry, every member of the crews of the contestants doing their utmost to bring their vessel home first. Arthur Coward was fortunate in having some very fine bargemen among his crews and, win or lose, he was always generous in his praise for their support. He continued his coasting career in the *Perseus*, working mainly to the East Coast ports (Harwich, Lowestoft, Yarmouth) and to the Humber ports (Grimsby, Hull, Goole, Keadby).

In 1912 came a transport strike and Arthur Coward, although not directly involved, had a disagreement with his employers as a result of which he and Messrs Goldsmith parted company.

The old saying 'It's an ill wind that blows nobody any good' was proved to be very true in this case, for as Arthur Coward was returning home from London with his kit, he travelled on the same train as the late Mr George Andrews, the well known managing director of Messrs Smeed Dean & Co. and himself a barge owner.

Leaving the station at Sittingbourne, he overtook Arthur and noticing his kit bag and gear said, "Well, Captain, does this mean you are without a barge?" Arthur replied that this was the case. Mr Andrews, a shrewd businessman, knew of Arthur Coward's great reputation as a barge captain and at once offered to find him a command, stipulating as a condition that he was to have a share in the vessel. Arthur Coward did not altogether view this proposition with favour, but Mr Andrews was determined to obtain a vessel worthy of his command. During the following days, several barges which were at that time on the market were inspected, but none met with Arthur's approval until, however, he and Mr Andrews viewed that fine mule-rigged coasting barge, the *Hydrogen*. Arthur had of course seen this fine vessel and had heard of her renown and after discussing her sailing qualities with her captain, his old friend George Dines of Grays, he told Mr Andrews that if he was still determined to make him a working partner, then this was the barge for him. Her purchase was concluded in the face of keen competition, the keenest of which came from Messrs Goldsmith, who as Arthur was afterwards to be told by Mr Pearson, their General Manager, intended to buy the vessel and offer the command of her to himself. Thus began a partnership between Arthur Coward and George Andrews which lasted until Mr Andrews' death twenty years later.

It gave Arthur Coward the command of one of the largest and finest wooden-built sailing barges ever built. At that time she was six years old, having been built by Messrs Gill & Sons of Rochester in 1906 and was capable of carrying a deadweight cargo of 220 tons to sea and nearly 250 tons in the sheltered waters of the Thames and Medway.

She was owned by Messrs Burt, Boulton and Haywood, Chemical Manufacturers of Silvertown, and was fitted with tanks for the carriage of tar, oils etc. These were removed and some alterations made in her deck and hatchways and in August 1912 Arthur Coward made his first trip in her, carrying a cargo of 1,000 quarters of barley from London to Yarmouth.

For twenty years until his retirement in 1932, Arthur Coward commanded this fine vessel, carrying cargoes of cement, coal, grain, paper and many other commodities to and from the East Coast ports from Dover to the Humber. He made many fast passages in her and the writer of these notes was privileged to take part in one which must surely rank among the best made in a Thames barge. On 28th June 1919, the *Hydrogen*, loaded with 210 tons of coal from the port of Goole on the Yorkshire Ouse, sailed past Spurn Point at the mouth of the Humber at 7.00 a.m., homeward bound to Sittingbourne. Dusk fell that evening as she was abreast of Yarmouth, where the firework display commemorating the celebration of peace after the 1914-18 war could be seen. The fine nor'westerly breeze which had prevailed all day fell light as darkness came on, and with the tide against her, progress was slowed down. Dawn on Sunday, 29th June found her abreast of Southwold and as the sun rose higher there came a gentle breeze from the westward, which tended to souther as the day progressed. At 2.00 p.m. however, the anchor was dropped just above Elmley Ferry, in spite of some delay being caused by the breaking of the topsail headstick as she was turning up the East Grounds of the River Swale.

The time of 31 hours for a journey of over 200 miles by a fully laden barge is pretty good going! Subsequently, this fine run was beaten by one from the Humber to Queenborough made in 24 hours! Another shorter trip made when she was light was one of 5 hours from Harwich to Queenborough and yet another fine trip was one from Yarmouth to Queenborough in 10 hours. On this occasion the *Hydrogen* left Yarmouth pier heads at 7.00 a.m. and the clock on the Town Hall at Queenborough was chiming five o'clock in the afternoon as the crew were making fast to one of the buoys in the Swale.

Yet another notable occasion was a voyage from Queenborough to Yarmouth loaded with cement. Getting under way just before 9.00 a.m. at Queenborough the *Hydrogen* sailed in between the pier heads of Yarmouth Harbour as the clock at Gorleston Church was chiming 8.00 p.m. in the same evening.

Although perhaps not so fast to windward as some craft, with the sailing breeze abaft her beam *Hydrogen* could show her name and port of registry on her stern to almost any barge afloat.

Over the twenty years that Arthur Coward commanded the *Hydrogen* she must have brought many thousands of tons of Yorkshire coal from the Humber ports to Sittingbourne.

Countless dinners have been cooked and many streets and homes lit by gas made from the coal brought by this vessel to the Sittingbourne Gas Co.'s Wharf at Murston.

For a number of years the *Hydrogen* carried cargoes of reels of news-print from Messrs Lloyd's Kemsley mill to Norwich for the East Anglian press.

During his twenty years in the *Hydrogen*, Arthur Coward was well served by some excellent and loyal crews. The vessel was manned by a crew of three: skipper, mate and third hand (who also acted as cook). His first mate, Frank Downs of Sittingbourne, was mate with him in the *Perseus*, but he did not stay long in the *Hydrogen*, leaving in the spring of 1913. His place was taken by Albert Tuff of Sittingbourne, who sailed with him throughout the war years of 1914-18. Soon after the conclusion of hostilities Albert Tuff left to take command of a barge of his own.

Arthur Coward was then joined by Harold Butcher, an Essexman from Brightlingsea (that home of many a fine bargeman). Harold Butcher settled in Sittingbourne and he remained in the *Hydrogen* until the conclusion of Arthur's captaincy in 1932.

In that year, at the age of 67 and after having spent some fifty-five years of his life afloat, Arthur Coward decided to retire. Relinquishing his command of the *Hydrogen*, he also sold his share of 16/64ths in her, but he did not altogether sever his connection with the salt water on which he had spent so much of his life. In 1929 he had purchased a motor launch, the *Queen Mary*, which he had converted to a cabin cruiser. In the later years of his life he spent many hours cruising under power over the waters of the Thames, Medway and Swale, where before he had so often battled with wind and tide in sailing barges.

In 1891 Arthur Coward married Miss Esther Phipps, daughter of Mr and Mrs Richard Phipps, formerly of Murston Road, Sittingbourne, and together they enjoyed a long and happy married life.

Their Golden Wedding Anniversary in March 1941 in the dark days of the 1939-45 war was quietly celebrated in their home 'Genhydro' in Woodstock Road, Sittingbourne, to which they had moved (to pass the remaining years of retirement) in 1932.

Arthur suffered a grievous blow on the loss of his wife in 1946, a blow from which he never recovered. A partial seizure gradually deprived him of the use of his legs, and for the last year or so of his life, he was confined to his bed. Notwithstanding his physical enfeeblement, he remained mentally alert and in full command of his faculties. He could recall and discuss incidents which happened in his career more than half a century earlier with wonderful clarity and accuracy. He enjoyed very fine eyesight and up to a day or so before his death, he took great pleasure in reading books and newsprint without the aid of glasses.

Following a second seizure he sank into a coma and passed peacefully away on 9th November 1948, at the age of 83.

His death severed a notable link with the past as he was one of the last of the men whose skill and industry had brought the graceful Thames sailing barges to such perfection during the latter years of the last century and the early decades of this.

It is to be regretted that with the passing of these fine vessels before the march of progress, also passes a splendid class of British seaman.

Frank 'Pilot' Farrington (holding his 'Kentish barge-hound') aboard the *Sam* about 1925. On his right is his cousin Harold Farrington-House, who was mate of the barge at that time. The photo was taken at the Camberwell 'vestry' or refuse depot.

(Courtesy of Harold Farrington-House)

FRANK 'PILOT' FARRINGTON
By Ron Dickenson

Among the thousands of 'Sailormen' who manned the red-sailed Thames barges, there were many who, for one reason or another, had an outstanding personality; some good, some bad, happy, miserable; some for downright 'cussedness' and others for being thoroughly likeable men. Many through their unusual character gained 'nicknames' like 'Frenchy' Reed and 'Doggy' Fletcher, 'The Admiral' etc. Such a man was 'Pilot' Frank Farrington, though how he came to be so called I never knew. He was known by that 'handle' to every man who sailed out of Milton Creek. Twinkling blue eyes, impish grin, more than a bit 'wild' in his younger days I believe, till (like many other 'wild' men) he married and settled down a bit; as much as his liveliness would let him, anyhow. It was said that, for a dare, he dived overboard from the crosstrees; though I did not see this myself.

Around 1926 I joined 'Pilot' in the *Sam*, a very nippy little barge which, however, leaked like an old boot; no good for anything but bricks away and 'rough-stuff' home from Camberwell (and go easy with the bricks!). 'Pilot' belonged to a family of Sailormen — Harold and Perce House were his cousins. All the family were able to play some musical instrument or other and 'Pilot's' was the twelve-stringed mandolin, and maybe that drew us together, because I too had a twelve-stringed mandolin. We would 'have a go' while lying wind-bound, or waiting turn somewhere. In contrast we had a set of boxing gloves hanging in the cabin and would frequently knock 'seven bells' out of each other, and we carried the marks to prove it! He was immensely popular with all the other young bargemen; indeed with most of the older ones, too. Our cabin was always an attraction wherever we moored up or lay at anchor and discussion would vary from sailing to whether man would ever walk on the moon. Yet one must not think by all this that 'Pilot' was a playboy; if one did, one would wake up and find him half way down the next reach!

We finally took *Sam* home in a sinking condition and were told to take over the *Murston*, then having a refit on the hard. The *McKinley* was there too and, as she had no mate, I had to help her skipper fit a new tops'l. He asked me if I would like the mate's berth. Well, *McKinley* was a good berth but I turned it down because few mates could sail with that skipper for very long. When I told 'Pilot' what had happened he completely lost his 'marbles'. Breathing sulphur, he went for the master of the *McKinley* and said, 'If my mate wants to better him-self, that's O.K., but don't try to take him behind my back' — and more to that effect. Soon after this we were bound home 'rough'[5] loaded and brought up in Lower Hope to make our passage home next ebb. When I turned out to 'shove the kettle on', 'Pilot' looked out from his bunk and said he felt too queer to turn to — did I think I could get her under way? I sailed *Murston* home with only the huffler's help at Kingsferry Bridge and moored at Marsh Berth, Milton Creek. When I went below, just about all in, 'Pilot' was waiting, bag packed ready for home.

"Sorry to do this to you Rufus," he said, "I knew you could do it, now they all know."

That did more for my ego than a row of medals!

Such a man was 'Pilot' Frank Farrington, Sailorman Extraordinary. Is my name 'Rufus'? No, but I had ginger hair in those days and 'Pilot' called me everything, except: Ron . . .

Compiler's note:
Some years ago we heard the following explanation of how 'Pilot' Farrington got his name. His father was a Milton Creek barge skipper and as a boy before the First World War, Frank was of course always hanging around the Creek. One day a 'foreign' barge arrived off the Creek mouth and her crew were unsure of the navigation in the Creek. Frank offered to be their Pilot — and the name stuck.

The 1905 painting of the *Yieldsted*. (Courtesy of Mrs E. Fenteman)

Jim Fenteman and second wife Julia with seven of the family at the Shortlands Road house about 1898. Left to right are: Lizzie, Dick, Nell, Jim Jnr, Kit, Julia (holding Bert) and Jim Snr (holding Bill). Rose and Sarah were probably away 'in service' at this time and Elsie and Mary were still a twinkle in Jim's eye. (Courtesy of Mrs Colman)

JIM FENTEMAN
By Alan Cordell

I often wonder what thoughts cross the minds of my many correspondents when they address their envelopes to my house called *Yieldsted* in Twickenham; probably something like this: '*Yieldsted*? what the devil does that mean?' Well if they knew me better, they would realise that a house or boat owned by me can be named after only one thing; a spritsail barge. Such is my enthusiasm; and *Yieldsted* was the barge skippered and part-owned by my grandfather for many years. As I can only just remember Grandad (he died when I was four), it is difficult to see why his love for barges and the sea rubbed off on me, but nevertheless it did!

My grandfather, Jim Fenteman, was born at Sittingbourne in 1855 and as a boy he worked on a farm at Murston. Later, around 1872, he took a fancy to the water and shipped on the *John Ward*, a smart ketch barge which had been built at Murston for the Burham Cement Company. Most of Jim's time on the *John Ward* was spent trading to Rotterdam, but his last voyage in her was to Queenstown, Ireland. Very bad weather was encountered and the crossing took a month. From Queenstown, they went to Cork to load oats for London, and in contrast, the return passage was made in about five days.

Jim then moved into the spritsail barges, becoming mate of the *Georgiana*. Sometimes this barge was engaged in coasting, but generally she worked in the Thames. Whilst Jim was in her a freight of 3,000 bushels of sprats was loaded from the smacks at Brightlingsea and taken to Milton Creek. Mr George Smeed, who owned the *Georgiana*, used the cargo (which was worth about £100) for fertilizer on his farms.

When he was twenty years old Jim was appointed skipper of the spritsail barge *Wave*, which also belonged to Mr Smeed. She was a minute thing, only about 60 burden tons, and had been built at Chiswick in 1851. She was known as the 'Little' *Wave* to distinguish her from another of Mr Smeed's barges the 'Big' *Wave*! When the subsequently well-known firm of Smeed Dean and Co. Ltd. was formed around 1877, it took over the brickfields and cement works of Smeed and the Burham Cement Co. at Murston; and Jim Fenteman with his little *Wave* took away the very first freight of bricks for the new company.

Around 1887 came the day which was to shape the future of my address! Jim moved from the *Wave* to take charge of the bigger spritsail barge *Yieldsted*. She was a 39 registered-ton barge which had been built at Rochester in 1870 and had been owned initially by Joseph Alexander of Hollingbourne, Kent. She was named after a small downland hamlet roughly halfway between Sittingbourne and Maidstone; maps and signposts spell the name 'Yelsted' nowadays. I think that Alexander probably owned some land there.

A new owner, George Goodhew of Newington, Kent, bought the *Yieldsted* in 1884. I believe that he was distantly related to Grandad and I expect that is why Jim became skipper of the barge shortly afterwards. Then in 1895 came another change of ownership, when the barge was bought by a syndicate consisting of Gransden, Matson and Fenteman, with the last-named as managing owner. Gransden owned a few barges, a brickfield, a wharf near the head of Milton Creek and the well-known local rope-walk. In those days, when Milton

Jim Fenteman pictured about 1923 when he was Milton Creek Harbourmaster. The damaged barge on the right is probably the *Vincent*. Around that time her stern was knocked off in collision with a steamer in the Thames. The bulkhead which was built to refloat her can be clearly seen and she was brought back to Murston, repaired and put back in trade.

(Courtesy of Mrs Daniels)

Creek was the home port for some 200 barges, the rope-walk must have been very busy. *Yieldsted* entered into the brick, rough-stuff, coal and ashes trade to Gransden's wharf.

In 1899 the syndicate decided to have the *Yieldsted* rebuilt. To raise the necessary capital, Jim sold his house in Shortlands Road, Sittingbourne; after paying his share he had enough money left over to put down the initial payment on a new house in Ufton Lane.

It is interesting to digress here for a moment and comment on the beautiful maritime names these bargemen used to give to their houses. Many chose the names of their barges, of course, but grandfather's new house was called 'The Haven'. His brother-in-law 'Bushy' Rossiter (master of the *Empress*) bought an identical new house further down the lane and called it 'The Anchorage'. Both these houses retain the same names today and I had the pleasure of visiting Miss Rossiter at 'The Anchorage' recently to talk about her father and photograph her fine painting of the *Empress*.

So the *Yieldsted* was rebuilt by the well-known Robert Shrubsall at Milton, who had previously built several crack racing barges like the *Pastime* and the *Gazelle*. It must have been one of his last jobs, because shortly afterwards his yard passed to Eastwoods Ltd. There is some evidence to suggest that, before being rebuilt, the *Yieldsted* was a stumpy, but the accompanying photographs show that when she left Shrubsall's yard she was a compact little topsail barge.

Contemporary registers show that she lost a registered ton in the rebuild, being reduced to 38. Most unusual! She had a 'full' stern and (for a Kentish brick barge) a pretty sheer. Instead of the conventional 'bob', a vane (the rampant horse of Kent) flew at her topmast truck, and a sling[6] of black, brown and green bands was worn in her sprit and mizzen sprit. For handling the leeboards, tackles were used in place of the usual winches; I bet that Grandad and his mate kept pretty fit looking after those leeboards!

During the period roughly 1899-1901, Grandad's eldest son, also named Jim, was mate with him. Jim junior left the barge to join the London Fire Brigade and there met one Charles Montague Clarke, who was a good artist and had been in barges. Clarke was persuaded in 1905 to produce an oil-painting of the barge; it is an accurate and strikingly beautiful work, reproduced here. It seems that Jim senior was a bit jealous of his son's fine picture, for in 1906 Clarke did a smaller painting for grandfather, and this is now one of my treasured possessions.

In 1903 health considerations forced Jim to come ashore, although he retained his controlling shares in the *Yieldsted*. He became wharf manager at Milton for Murrell, the London contracting firm, and was appointed a director of the Kent Barge Owners' Association. One of his tasks in this capacity was to examine barge mates to assess their suitability for promotion to master. Then in 1912 he added yet another occupation to those described above, that of Harbour Master to the Milton Creek Conservancy. I am the proud owner of the 1912 Mercantile Register which he obtained when he took the job. It seems that neither he nor the Conservancy Board ever felt that the expense of a later one was justified and the original had to serve until the old chap retired in 1930. A pity — a complete set would have been very useful for barge research purposes and would have saved Miss Pipe (of the National Maritime Museum) and me a lot of trouble!

While all this was going on, the *Yieldsted* was still plying her steady trade between Milton Creek and London. Soon after Jim came ashore, a regular skipper called 'Scranny' (or sometimes 'Scranny Jack') Hambrook settled in and was to sail the barge for over twenty years. 'Scranny' was a tough, amusing and popular character who was renowned for the way he chewed vast quantities of tobacco and spat the exhausted wads with unerring accuracy over the lee quarter from his seat at the wheel!

Around 1910 part-owner Matson died and the syndicate broke up. Shares in the *Yieldsted* were redistributed between J. Fenteman (managing owner) and H. Andrews, an official in Smeed Dean Ltd. So the barge transferred to the Murston brick and cement trade and exchanged her vane for the blue-white-blue striped 'bob' which was worn by all the privately-owned barges working for Smeed Dean. The company's own barges wore these stripes with 'S D' superimposed in red over them. The 'S D' was later replaced with a red triangle.

Then came 1914 and the disastrous December gale, tales of which are still recounted with horror to this day. *Yieldsted* was amongst the fleet of barges which were caught loaded in Sea Reach. Many sank and drowned their crews, but the *Yieldsted* managed to ride it out at anchor off Canvey Island. Unfortunately the iron bar for securing her foc's'le hatch was lost, but 'Scranny Jack' prevented the hatch from washing away and the barge from sinking by standing on it for the whole night of the gale! He chewed his way through ¼lb of tobacco during that spell! The barge sustained some damage to her gear and had to go back to Queenborough for repairs.

Remains of the *Yieldsted* at Kingsferry Bridge, 1957.   (Photo by Alan Cordell)

'Scranny' Hambrook was still master of the *Yieldsted* when her sailing days came to a rather unexpected end in 1930. Whilst lying unattended at Cremer's Berth, Murston, an unexplained fire burned out her cabin, cabintop and part of her deck. This was at the time of the 'slump' and repairs were not worth while.

But even now the gallant old *Yieldsted* was determined to make herself useful for a few years more. She was sold to Dick Evenden, the well-known (and later the last) Kingsferry Bridge huffler. He removed her gear and cut out a section of her stern above the waterline. Then the old girl was able to serve as a floating dock to help Dick with his part-time occupation of small-boat maintenance. When Dick wanted to work on the bottom of a small cruiser or fishing boat, his first move was to pull out the *Yieldsted*'s plug. Then at high tide, with the barge sunk in a fathom of water, he could float the craft into the barge's main hold via the gap in her stern. At low tide, when all the water had gone, Dick would put the plug back and thereafter the craft would nestle in the *Yieldsted*'s dry hold until the work was done and it was time to float her out again. Dick had another barge, the *Livingstone*, which he also used as a floating dock; and I have come across one or two other barges with their sterns cut out in a similar manner. But nevertheless, it was a pretty unusual end for a spritsail barge.

Within a few months of parting with the *Yieldsted* and at the ripe old age of 75, grandfather retired from his Harbour Master's job. Nine years later, in 1939, he died and he now rests with his second wife (he had three wives and eleven children!) in Sittingbourne cemetery. I know that in his days as Harbour Master he was disturbed by the growing pollution of Milton Creek. If he can see the silted, polluted, smelly mess that it is now, he must be turning in his grave. It is time that the authorities took action.

The *Yieldsted* must have sensed that her old master had gone, because around 1939 she fell derelict and was thereafter used only to supply Dick Evenden with wood for his stoves. An accompanying picture shows the remains as they looked in late 1957. How I wish that I had pinched one of those deadeyes while I had the chance! In 1958 the new Kingsferry Bridge was built, and as the remains were lying in the way, they were broken up completely.

I would like to finish with a little story about grandfather which is still recounted with some amusement in the family. Friends, relatives and the people of Sittingbourne generally held Jim in fairly high regard, but a criticism which is sometimes heard concerns the rather tight hold he used to keep on his money! Once, when he had the *Yieldsted*, he was enduring a frustrating spell lying becalmed. Grandad was a firm believer, so he would never resort to bad language or blasphemy. Better, he thought, to raise a breeze by the mariner's time-proven method of throwing a penny over the side. Jim knew full well that the Lord would always take notice of this and instruct his line-managers (the gods of Wind) to improve matters in the vicinity of the barge. In an uncharacteristic fit of sheer reckless generosity Jim spurred the astounded gods into action by throwing TWO pennies over the *Yieldsted*'s side. He brought her home dismasted!

Bill Kennett (in dark suit) aboard the committee boat at the 1960 Thames Barge Match. On his right is Alf Mills, who was Bill's mate in the *Mercy* about 1915 and who went on to become a barge skipper himself. (Photo by Alan Cordell)

BILL KENNETT
By Alan Cordell

Captain W.H. (Bill) Kennett was a very well-known and respected Sittingbourne barge skipper. His career in barges lasted from 1895, when he was 16, to 1946. During that time he was mate of the *Derby, Levitt, Esther, Jessie, Harry* and *Mercy*; and skipper of the *Garfield, Monitor, Mercy, Spurgeon, Sam, Harriet, Burton* and *Sidweli*. His stay in the *Sidwell* was very long, from 1918 until both he and the barge retired in 1946.

Much of Bill's work took him up through the London bridges and it has been said that his skill in handling a barge in that area was unsurpassed by his contemporaries. Also, when in a hurry, Bill would shoot Kingsferry Bridge (which connects the Isle of Sheppey to the North-East Kent mainland) at night without a huffler. And that was something which only the most skilful and confident of skippers would attempt.

Lindum Villa,
Sittingbourne.

June 25. 94

I have great pleasure in testifying to the character and abilities of William Kennett, whom I have known from infancy.

When at school he was quick, attentive to his duties, and his work executed with care and neatness.

Wm H. Roper

A glowing reference for Bill Kennett from his headmaster.

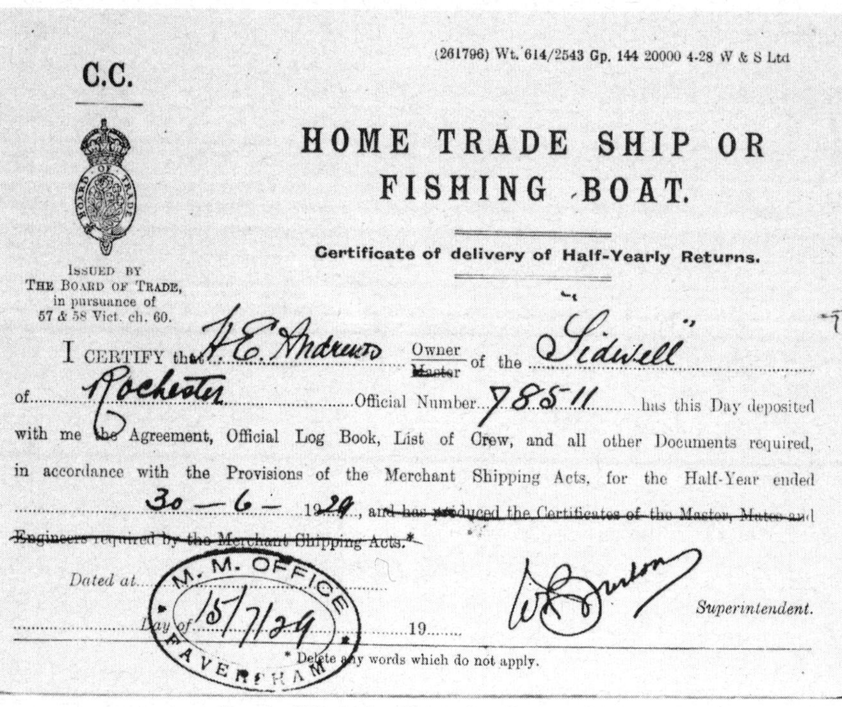

Board of Trade Certificate for the *Sidwell*.

Bill was also highly respected for his kind and good-tempered nature. The late Harold Farrington-House, a recent Thames Barge Sailing Club skipper, was mate with Bill for a while in *Sidwell*, and used to say 'He was a nice old boy to sail with'. When working in London so much of the time, the barge was bound to get into an awkward predicament now and again. Harold recalls such an occasion when the fast-running spring tide caused the *Sidwell* to drag her anchor in the Pool. Despite frantic efforts by Bill and Harold, she only stopped when her gear fouled Tower Bridge! But, Harold said, Bill never lost his temper and he would never blame his mate.

A further tribute to Bill's kindliness was paid by the late Frank Farrington, Harold's cousin. On one occasion, when Frank was skipper of the *Sam* (in about 1925), she and the *Sidwell* were among a group of loaded barges bound for London. The wind was fresh from the north and, off the Nore, *Sam* started to leak badly. Frank suspected that she had 'dropped a lap', i.e. that a joint in her bottom was leaking. He was forced to shorten sail to ease the barge, and then he and the mate had to work a pump each. Frank began to make plans to put *Sam* ashore on the Yantlet Sand. However Bill Kennett, with *Sidwell* under full sail, soon overhauled him and asked what the trouble was. When told, Bill first got his own mate to shorten sail, then rig the navigation lights as it was already dusk, and he then put his mate aboard *Sam* to help with the pumping. So, together, the two barges jogged along up the Thames, *Sam* with two pumps going and Bill keeping the *Sidwell* within easy reach, but unable to leave the helm. At high tide they anchored together off Dartford Creek and by this time *Sam*'s bad leak had stopped. So, in order to help another barge's crew, Bill had gone without food for eight hours and had only got as far as Dartford when he could easily have reached Greenwich. When Frank thanked him Bill merely said 'You would have done the same for me. Anyway you are off my mind now. I thought it was better to keep my mate on your barge, just in case'.

There was one further feature which made Bill very popular with his fellow bargemen — his enthusiastic and clever playing of the concertina. This was something which he had taught himself in those odd hours when both he and the barge were idle — windbound; beneaped; waiting for the dockers; and all those other times when a barge is held up. Fortunately when he was 84 (in 1963) Bill became a recording star and made a tape — his own spoken introduction followed by a selection of tunes on his concertina. There are several copies of it in existence among the barge folk of Sittingbourne and my copy is one of my most treasured possessions.

After Bill retired from the water I got to know him very well. We lived near each other in Sittingbourne and as a young schoolboy I used to go and listen wide-eyed to his fascinating and often thrilling tales of the sea. The 'fee' for this favour was to have to play him at draughts. This was another skill which he had acquired in the barge's cabin and he used to wipe the floor with me! I wonder whether any of his mates fared better.

Memorial Service

IN THE

SALVATION ARMY HALL,

—SHORTLANDS ROAD,—

SITTINGBOURNE,

On SUNDAY, NOVEMBER 5th, 1916,

At Three o'clock,

FOR THE

Bargemen and Soldiers of Sittingbourne.

Parade will leave Station Yard at 2.30.

ALL BARGEMEN AND SOLDIERS

In Town are heartily invited to take part
in the Parade.

A souvenir from Bill Kennett's collection.

Harry — brand new barge — at Murston, 1898. Although she is lying at Smeed Dean's barge yard, she was actually built by White, near the Creek Head.
(Photo by a professional Sittingbourne photographer, probably Ramell)

One of his best yarns was about an occasion around 1914 when he was skipper of the stumpy-rigged barge *Garfield*. The owners of the oyster beds in Stangate Creek[7] chartered him to fetch a freight of imported oysters from the London docks. Then, to satisfy the final clause in his contract, Bill had to sail the barge up and down the creek, while the consignees threw the cargo overboard!

Later on, when I had my own cruising yacht, Bill used to come sailing sometimes. He often came to the barge races and I also recall an occasion in 1965 when he helped me out of a spot of bother. It was August Sunday and I was lying at anchor in Queenborough. I had to take the yacht back to her home berth at Conyer the next day, but unfortunately my crew told me they could not come and my engine had decided to have one of its frequent strikes. I was faced with the prospect of taking the yacht through Kingsferry Bridge under sail, on my own — not difficult, we know, if conditions are good — but very difficult if they turn out to be bad. It only needs a strong tide setting you on to the buttresses, and no wind, and you might get faced with the job of trying to steer, drop your anchor and fend off all at the same time! However Bill saved the situation when, at very short notice, he decided to forsake watching his August Monday cricket[8] in favour of a trip with me. We had a wonderful sail that day. Bill, in spite of his 86 years, was as pleased as punch to be under sail again and enlivened the proceedings with a fascinating string of yarns about how they used to do it in the barges!

Harry derelict at Wallasea Island, River Crouch (Essex), 1964.   (Photo by Alan Cordell)

Bill made his last passage (to the Better Land) in the autumn of 1969 at the age of 90. His funeral service was beautifully conducted by the Revd H. Williams at the Wesleyan Church, Sittingbourne, where Bill had been an organ-blower when he was a boy. The service included the very appropriate hymn 'Eternal Father', and the equally fitting Tennyson poem 'Crossing the Bar'.[9] He was then laid to rest in Sittingbourne cemetery, in his family grave. He had never married.

During his long career afloat Bill collected together many fine photographs and documents connected with barges. Due to the kindness of Mrs Irene Rhodes, his niece, and Captain Harold Farrington-House, his friend to the last, these were passed on to me after Bill died. His best document, I think, is his thrilling account of the loss of the *Mercy* when he was wrecked in her down Swin in 1918, which appears elsewhere in this book. For this chapter I have chosen Bill's interesting description of an incident at Kingsferry Bridge, around 1938, when *Charles Burley* got athwart the bridge just as Bill in *Sidwell* was following in her wake:

"This morning at about 8.45 a.m. we got under way in Bridge Reach to proceed up through Kingsferry Bridge. The bridge was already lifted and there was a strong S.S.W. wind. The *Charles Burley* started first. We let her get a good lead over us and then followed. We had half-mains'l, tops'l, fores'l and mizzen set, and we hauled over to the S.W. shore, winded, and stood up for the bridge on the starboard tack. The *Charles Burley* had only half-mains'l, fores'l and mizzen, with the tops'l lowered, and as we approached the bridge we were rapidly overhauling her so I had to lower my tops'l. The *Charles Burley* was not making a good wind and fell to leeward and stopped across the N.E. buttress. I had to luff my barge up to avoid colliding with her and unfortunately could not get her to bear away again in time. We hit the S.W. buttress stem-on and stopped athwart the bridge, head across the S.W. buttress and stern alongside the *Charles Burley*.

We were pinned by the tide, and stopped the bridge traffic for some time until one of Gazeley's tugs came down from Ridham and cleared us. We were deep loaded with ballast and it was half-flood tide, i.e. there was a fair tide running through the bridge. We are badly damaged, with a broken stem and waterways, and the deck planking is open."

I have also selected from Bill's collection a very fine picture of the *Harry* taken at Murston in 1898 when she was brand-new. The picture used to hang in Bill's lounge. Bill, then mate, is seen in the bows, and the skipper, George Bourne, is at the wheel. George Bourne later fell out with the Smeed Dean management. He emigrated to Australia, founded a brickmaking firm and died a wealthy man.

The *Harry* was a fine, fast barge, built by Alfred White Sen. at Sittingbourne. Compare this picture with the one which shows *Harry* as she is today, derelict at Wallasea Island, River Crouch.

In conclusion, I must say that I have derived a lot of pleasure from writing this account and I hope it has done justice to a very fine character and seaman.

Taffy Taylor surveys the deserted Murston Quay of today.   (Photo by Alan Cordell)

HARRY 'TAFFY' TAYLOR
By Alan Cordell

There was little about young Harry Taylor's early life to indicate that he would take up a nautical career. Born at Sittingbourne in 1903 and nicknamed 'Taffy' by his school chums, Master Taylor was, for a start, rather fortunate to live long enough to take up a career at all. A bomb which was dropped during the first Zeppelin raid of World War One blew Taffy out of bed — and the chimney-pot of his parents' house came through the roof and landed on the bed which Taffy had just unknowingly vacated; a mercy indeed!

Vectis deep-loaded in the Thames; Taffy Taylor in the bows preparing to anchor her.
(Courtesy of Thames Barge Sailing Club)

After leaving school Taffy spent a few years in 'casual' jobs such as boot-shine boy, making wicks for candles (the wax for them came from butcher's fat) and collecting rate and gas money. Strangely, Taffy had a barrow for this latter job; he says that it could not be done like that today — crime has escalated so much that the risk would be too great. During this period Taffy was an amateur footballer with the local Milton Invicta Club.

In 1920 Taffy's mother thought he looked too frail and suggested that it would be good for him to join the North Sea fishing fleets so as to toughen him up a bit. Accordingly, Taffy left home and spent some months in a Hull trawler; then he shipped in a collier trading between Blyth and Oslo where he stayed for two years. The 'toughening up' process seems to have worked well, because today Taffy is as tough-looking an ex-sailorman as you could wish to meet!

Round about 1922, whilst enjoying a weekend at home, Taffy was strolling along Sittingbourne High Street when he was 'collared' by the well-known local barge skipper 'Ebbie' Shrubsall. Ebbie explained that he needed a mate for his barge *Aberdeen* (owned by Wills and Packham, brickmakers). This firm had a reputation for taking exceptionally good care of their barges and Taffy decided to take the berth, so he joined the barge at Filmer's Dock, Milton Creek. Ebbie was a bit surprised that his new mate had not brought any bedding along — but Taffy explained that he did not need it for one trip! No doubt, however, Taffy moved some bedding aboard later because he stayed for several months with Ebbie. He then moved to another Wills and Packham barge, *C.I.V.* (named after the City Imperial Volunteers — a Boer War regiment); her skipper was a well-known and somewhat eccentric fellow named Dick Scattergood. Dick was an addictive tobacco chewer and he did not waste the spent wads — he dried them on the cabin stove, mixed them with dried spent tea leaves and then smoked the mixture!

In the mid-1920s Taffy became one of Wills and Packham's relief skippers. He did a few freights with *Llandudno* when her regular skipper Teddy Simmons was ill (including a freight of ballast to Kemsley Dock for construction of the paper mill) and he also did a freight or two with *Rover*. However, to get a permanent skipper's berth, Taffy had to move to another Sittingbourne brick firm — William Wood and Co. He spent a few years as skipper of their *Mary*, *Violet*, *Excelsior* and *Vera*.

Taffy later moved again to the fleet of C. Burley Ltd., a Sittingbourne firm which had brickfields, a cement works and farms. His first command for this firm was *Surprise* and his second *Vectis*. This latter barge had once been a fine craft. She won the Thames Championship in 1895 when she was brand new from the Sittingbourne yard of the renowned Alfred White Senior. At that time she belonged to Keep (a London firm), but she passed to C. Burley well before the First World War. This firm's barges were rather modestly maintained, so by the time Burley entered *Vectis* for the 1930 races, she was not exactly the trim craft of 30 years before. Taffy has an amusing tale to tell about the preparations (at Burley's yard) for those races. For a start, *Vectis*'s wooden wheel disintegrated when an attempt was made to clean it up for varnishing; she had to have a chaff cutter[10] instead! Then, owing to lack of time, some leaky seams were repaired by covering them with canvas which was held on with battens and then tarred.

At length *Vectis* was 'ready', so Taffy sailed her round for the Thames Match and anchored amongst the elegant fleet of competitors (Everard's, Goldsmith's, L.R.B.C's, Horlock's etc.) at the 'Ship and Lobster', Gravesend. Presently, the Committee — led by the famous Mr Goldsmith of Grays — came alongside in their launch to carry out their inspection. "Thank you very much, Skipper", said Mr Goldsmith, viewing *Vectis*'s array of horizontal battens, "You're the only barge here with a ladder up the side!" However, *Vectis* was not too badly disgraced for Taffy brought her home in the middle of the field in both matches.

Life in *Vectis* was also somewhat troubled by the numerous rats which lived aboard. Taffy tackled them by igniting a sulphur compound below and then battening her down.

In 1932, whilst he was still in charge of *Vectis*, Taffy's wife died; they had been married 10 years and there were five small children. Fortunately, a friend moved in to look after the children and subsequently became Taffy's present wife, bearing him three girls and a boy who unfortunately died at the age of 9½ years.

Around 1934 Taffy moved into one of Burley's big barges, *Our Boys*. Whereas all his previous barge work had been in the Thames Estuary, he now did a fair amount of cross-Channel work. *Our Boys* was not very fast and not particularly sound, but Taffy always enthuses over her handiness and dryness at sea — even loaded in the Channel he could steer her in his carpet slippers without getting his feet wet.

Rats were again a problem — sometimes they ran over the crew as they lay in their bunks. Once, the 'four legged friends' (as Taffy calls them!) stole two sausages out of the frying pan! Again, Taffy gassed them and picked up thirty dead bodies afterwards.

One of Burley's barge mates used to energetically chase the rats on his barge and kill them with a coal shovel. One day, whilst engaged in this exciting sport when the barge was lying afloat at a London wharf, unfortunately he tripped over the side and disappeared. A day or two later, when the barge had gone, his flattened body was found at low tide in the hard berth she had just vacated. The poor fellow had become trapped underneath his barge, which had then sat on him as the tide fell.

Taffy says that Burley's barges were largely ruined by the hard, uneven berths they used in London. Stepney Electric Light Co. and Duke's Shore were the two wharves most commonly used; these berths were so hard and uneven that it was possible at low tide to see right under the barges' bottoms at some points. Frequently the barges used to lean heavily against each other when aground and straining was so severe that Taffy has at times seen stars through the opened-up deck seams above his bunk.

Due to this type of treatment and 'economic' maintenance, most of Burley's craft leaked so much that a few courses of bricks were always carried underneath cement cargoes to stop the cement from getting wet. In the mid-1930s most of these barges were condemned as unfit for further trading and this fate befell *Our Boys*. In 1936 she leaked badly on a return voyage from France and Taffy had to patch her port bow to nurse her home. When he eventually moored her at Burley's barge yard, next to their cement mill in Milton Creek, it was for the last time.

Burley's fleet was now diminishing rapidly and Taffy had to move to another company once again for his next command. He moved to the firm of Surridge, who had a regular contract to take London household refuse down to the disposal tips at Mucking in Essex. This firm's barges also did quite a lot of sand work. Together with its associated companies (Lower Hope Development Co. and Stuart Sand and Shingle Co.) the firm owned about twenty craft, many of them having been in the Associated Portland Cement Manufacturer's fleet before that firm went over to tugs and lighters. Taffy commanded three Surridge barges, *R.A. Gibbons*, *Caledonia* and *Minicoy*.

Edward Perry, a well-known authority on London barges, makes this nice comment on Surridge's fleet: 'A thing I liked about Surridge barges was the way in which, despite the facts that expenses were cut to the bone and the nature of their work was lowly, they tried to look as smart as possible. Although sails were patched and ill-fitting and the hulls showed evidence of many years' hard work, the bright blue paint and uniform insignia on bowboards and galley stacks gave them an almost jaunty air'.

By the late 1930s, work in Surridge's fleet was becoming slack so Taffy stepped ashore. But within a very short time the war came and Taffy was directed by His Majesty's Government to help the war effort — by becoming a bargeman! At this time the demand for barges grew; they were needed for ammunition work, barrage balloon flying and for keeping the nation's coastal trade going. Taffy found himself back in Burley's firm again, this time as skipper of their *Scud*.

Like her sisters *Serb* and *Scout*, *Scud* was a big barge built with small timbers and not very strong. She leaked badly when deep-loaded and eventually Taffy got into the habit of never loading her deep enough to put her wale[11] in the water. Although she was theoretically capable of carrying 80,000 bricks, Taffy used to settle for 60,000. Even so, on one occasion during the war, Taffy sailed *Scud* away from Stepney with 18 inches of freeboard. By the time she reached the mouth of Milton Creek her deck amidships was level with the water (despite the crew's energetic pumping); and when she got to her berth, she promptly sank! But a bit of quick repair work from Burley's barge yard got her going again.

Scud's wartime armament consisted of two rifles (with 600 rounds of ammunition) and a Lewis gun mounted on deck. The authorities gave no training for these, so Taffy and his mate had to train themselves by firing at bottles and flares. The trouble was that when the Lewis gun was fired the deck sprang up!

One day in 1945 Taffy arrived in Milton Creek with *Scud* and, as was quite common, the conditions required a lot of work with the boom.[12] This demanded quite a measure of skill, so Taffy put his mate at the wheel and took the boom himself. Unfortunately, the inexperienced mate turned the wheel the wrong way at one stage and the barge rode against the boom — putting Taffy's shoulder out of joint.

So Taffy Taylor's barging career was terminated at that point by doctor's orders. Fortunately his nautical career continued; he did twenty years in the A.P.C.M. lighters; enough to earn him the A.P.C.M. house in Sittingbourne where he now lives in retirement with his wife.

HARRY 'TIMSON' WILLIAMS
By Leslie Williams

Our grandfather could never be mistaken for anything but a seaman — short, like most of his generation; always with a blue jersey and flat cap; and a slight limp, for he was subject to gout for a long while. He had been on the water all of his life, starting as a boy of eight in the fishing boats which worked out of Harwich in the summer season, going down from the Medway and Swale. He received 2s.6d. a week and was the best-off member of the crew if the fishing was poor.

His older brothers were on the boat with him and on the last trip took most of his money off him to pay his own share of the beer and food. I think that finished Grandad with fishing.

He then went as a boy with his father on, I believe, the *Dover Castle* — running to France and Belgium. It was just after the Franco-Prussian War and there were plenty of freights if you were able to do them. He said that after one spell running across the Channel for three months without going home, they found themselves working down Sea Reach with a light northerly wind. The 'Old Man' said: 'I think we'll run into the Swale for the weekend and go home and have dinner with your mother', which just suited the boys. As they ran down the Swatch the wind freshened and when they reached Sheerness harbour they had no orders from their father to bear up. When at last the mate asked "Why?", the skipper said: "What! Lose this fair wind! We shall be over in Calais by the morning", so that was their weekend gone.

Grandfather stopped with his father for some years, working anywhere from the Isle of Wight to the Humber, until he took charge himself at the age of 19; incidentally he also married then.

Grandfather took the *Arthur Blake*, running out of Milton Creek with bricks mostly, and did well. Six freights a month at £4.10s. a load. Eventually, with the growth of the owners, Wills and Packham, he changed over to *Five Sisters* when new-built, keeping her until the *Unique* was built for him in 1903.

All my early memories of barges are of summer holidays on Grandad's barge for my grandmother always went with him, if she could, and I was always with her. They tell me I was carried aboard the *Unique* as a baby and in my early years was always aboard. After my grandmother's death in 1915 I spent all my school holidays afloat.

I remember one summer when I was about eight we were bound, I believe, to Woodbridge Haven. We had brought up at the top of the Swatch and after breakfast, which I still remember after more than 50 years for it was ham and eggs done to a turn, got under way with a fine southerly wind and were off Harwich by four o'clock. It was a fine sunny day and everything was about as right as you can expect in this imperfect world.

Grandad had no formal education, but wrote a good copper plate hand (strange, for his spelling and composition were pretty weird), but he told me that he had taught himself to read and write out of a copy book, so his letter formation was almost perfect.

There was nothing anybody could teach him on coastal seamanship. He taught me how to lay a course and fix a position before I was higher than the wheel; and he told me that once at Colchester, when I was about three, he tied me with a bit of line so that I could just reach both quarterboards, which I objected to rather strongly. When I was on deck by myself, I threw all the ropes I could reach overboard. I cannot remember this incident myself, but it always seemed to amuse him.

The *Unique* was a fine barge, 120 tons with fine lines, for she was built from plans by Harvey of Sittingbourne. When Grandad first had her she did a lot of coasting work, but after the First World War he preferred to work in the London River as he was getting older. Also work was slackening off.

I was considered weakly as a boy and when I was 13 got permission to leave school for my health's sake. I went third hand with Grandad for about a year until I got the chance of going mate in Smeed Dean's barges, which I took, and I remained with the firm until they came to an end.

Grandad was always known as 'Timson'. I do not know why, for his name was Harry Williams; he was almost the last of a line of seamen that went back as far as we are able to trace. His own grandfather was picked up for smuggling down in Essex and given the choice of prison or the Navy; not being stupid he joined the Navy, being put on board the *HMS Victory* and was made a P.O. He was at the wheel when she broke the French line at Trafalgar. I joke with my relations at times and say that had the shot which carried away the wheel taken great-great-grandfather as well, none of us would be here. I looked up the roll of the *Victory* when I was last in Portsmouth and found his name and prize money — £25.

Grandad worked until he was 75 and, when he retired after 50 years service, was given a certificate — but no pension as the firm could not see their way clear to pay him 5s. weekly.

I lived with Grandad when I was married and he was failing then; unfortunately I did not see him at the last. I was in Egypt in the 8th Army and did not know of his death for three months, but I believe he died very peacefully.

He was well thought of by all who knew him. Nobody could be kinder, and I never knew him to refuse help to anybody. Even now, 30 years after his death, people who knew him always say, "He was a good old man!"

1 At neap tides there was insufficient water at the head of the Creek for loaded barges to get away. Hence large numbers of them would be stuck there until the tides improved.
2 Jenkin Swatch — the channel providing a 'short cut' between the Medway and the Thames for shallow-draft vessels. Often just called 'the Swatch'.
3 Near the Creek head.
4 Craft Marsh — the area between Crown Quay Reach and Milton Old Church.
5 'Rough' loaded — carrying household refuse, usually known as 'rough-stuff' or 'dust'.
6 Sling — coloured bands painted on a barge's sprit. Many firms had their own particular design.
7 Near the mouth of the River Medway.
8 Considering that these old bargemen spent most of their working lives away from Sittingbourne, it is astonishing how interested they were in the local sport. In particular, I have often heard them reminisce about the great years of Sittingbourne F.C. during the 1920s and early '30s. During nine seasons under the captaincy of centre-half Bill Dickie, Sittingbourne were in the Kent Senior Cup Final five times — winning twice. In those days a home match at the Bull Ground would draw a crowd of 3,000 — as opposed to the 130 *or so who turn up now. See Chapter 24.*
9 This is a poem in which Tennyson likened death to crossing a harbour bar. See Appendix 5.
10 Chaff cutter — a cast iron type of steering wheel frequently fitted to barges.
11 Wale — the uppermost strake of a barge's side planking.
12 Boom — long pole which was pushed into the river or creek bed to propel the barge when it was impossible to sail. Often called a Setting Boom.

A painting of the *Dunstable* by Bill Martin, who was skipper of the *Ada Mary*. Bill (who was also known as Bill Allen) was an active barge artist and several of his paintings are still around amongst the barge folk of Sittingbourne. One (of the *Alan Dean*) is in the Dolphin Yard Museum. *Dunstable* was broken up in Northfleet Creek about 1965 after lying derelict there for several years. The picture was painted in 1930 when *Dunstable* wore the 'Red Triangle' emblem, so the 'Blue Circle' emblem and 'sling' in the sprit were superimposed later.

(Courtesy of Wilf 'Pip' Box)

'Pip' Box and Mrs Hewitt (Ernie Britton's daughter) holding the trophy presented to Ernie when *Dunstable* won the 1937 Thames Match (staysail class).

(Photo by Alan Cordell)

CHAPTER 3

AUTOBIOGRAPHIES OF THE SAILORMEN

Continuing in the vein of Chapter 2, we have fortunately persuaded some local bargemen to write about themselves. These autobiographies add further to Milton Creek's great maritime history.

MY LIFE AFLOAT
By Wilf 'Pip' Box, the very last APCM Barge Skipper

When I left school in 1914 I was 13 years of age and my one ambition in life was to go mate of a sailing barge and to follow in my father's footsteps. At that time my father was skipper of the *S/B Gordon*, owned by C. Burley, barge owners of Sittingbourne. Also his three brothers and their father were all sailing skippers. Coming from a barging family was the reason why I wanted to go on the water to keep the tradition of the family going.

I was very disappointed on leaving school, because my father would not let me go and my mother did not want me to go on the barges, so I had to be satisfied by working ashore; first at a bakery and then at a cement factory owned by Burleys. I remained at the cement factory until the end of the First World War. Then came the 'Slump' and I found myself out of work. I think I was on the dole about 16 months. Then I had the chance to go mate with Fred Inge (nicknamed 'Flicker', to bargemen). He was skipper of the *S/B Regent* a 70-ton stumpy owned by A.P.C.M. I was happy then because I was mate of a barge. I had about 6 months in the *Regent* taking freights of cement and lime to London and coke back from Beckton Gas Works. We also freighted cement to the Regent's Canal, where you had to get the leeboards aboard and lower the mast flat on the hatches because of the low bridges. Also there was a long tunnel up the canal where you had to get down on your back. It was called 'legging tunnel', because you had to use your legs on the roof above to help the barge through the tunnel. Most of the way up the canal we were towed by a horse.

After I had about 6 months in the *Regent* I got a mate's berth in the *S/B Spurgeon*, owned by Smeed Dean of Sittingbourne. I was sorry to leave Fred because I got on alright with him. He taught me to splice and whip ropes during the short time I had with him. When I joined *Spurgeon* as mate with Capt. W. Pudney it was much better for work and we were taking freights of cement, bricks and also flints to London, including going up through the London Bridges under oars as far as Mortlake Draw Dock. It needed a bit of skill to navigate a barge through the bridges down and up and I must say Capt. Pudney was pretty good at that. We also loaded back with refuse from the Council wharf, coke from the gas works or coal to Smeed Deans of Sittingbourne.

After about two years and a half in the *Spurgeon* with Capt. Pudney, she started leaking and getting a bit weak. The skipper had orders from the firm to put her on the shipyard to be rebuilt, so in the meantime my father got me a mate's berth in *S/B Jessie* with Capt. Britton, my third and last sailing skipper. The *Jessie* mainly did the sand work from Leigh-on-Sea to Smeed Dean's brickfields, Sittingbourne. The firm had 60 hand brick-making berths at that time and we used to do one freight of sand for each berth (this was mostly done in the winter months). During the summer months we used to do general cargo in the Thames and Medway, also going up through the bridges under oars. I must say Ernie Britton was a good man at navigating through the bridges. When I first went mate of the *Jessie* with him, some of the skippers and mates in the other barges said I would not last long with him — he would 'kill me' doing this sandwork! I already knew it was hard work, helping to sail a barge from Sittingbourne to Leigh-on-Sea and then back to Sittingbourne with a freight of sand which we helped to load, and I can assure you I felt pretty tired on arriving home. I did 16 winters at sand work altogether and it did not do me any harm (on an average about 3 freights a fortnight). Ernie Britton never seemed to get tired. He was always on the go, up through and down through Kingsferry Bridge all times of the night; just us two[1]. Ernie used to steer the barge and I lowered the gear down. I think in my time I hold the record for a mate of a barge lowering the gear at Kingsferry Bridge. I remember Capt. H. Farrington of Eastbourne Street saying to me once when Capt. Jimmy Spice took my place as mate (after I met with an accident aboard the barge), that they were coming up to Kingsferry in the early hours of the morning and Ernie said to Jimmy: "What do you want to do, have the wheel or the gear?" and Jimmy's reply was: "Feel more like lying down and going to sleep than lowering a barge's gear down. How young Pip sticks it I don't know. You'll kill him!" I thought they had been loading beer when I went back again (instead of sand). There were plenty of empty beer bottles down the cabin because old Jim used to like his pint. In 1926 Ernie Britton and myself went into the *S/B Mary Ann* (same firm as the *Jessie*) doing the same work on the sand hill. We only had about 9 months in *Mary Ann* (she was built at Sittingbourne by Whites, the well known barge builders). She was a very good barge, a little bigger and better than *Jessie*, for she carried 115 tons dead weight.

In March 1927 we both went into the *S/B Dunstable* which was formerly the *R.G.H.* She had been cut down[2], and was rebuilt for us to do the sand work.

I was quite proud of myself when I went into the *Dunstable* because my Uncle Bob, my father's brother, took her brand new in 1891 when built at Milton by Shrubsall, another well-known barge builder. During the latter part of 1927 they wanted a skipper for *S/B Providence* because the proper skipper had met with an accident, so my skipper put a word in for me to take her. I had to go up the office to see Mr Coward (who was the ships' husband at that time) to see if I would pass the examination he put me through. I got over that O.K. and then went skipper of the *Providence* for 9 months. When the skipper came back I went with Ernie in the *Dunstable* again, in the sand work during the winter and up through the bridges in the summer. There was also occasional dock work.

Around 1933, Smeed Dean was bought out by A.P.C.M. ('Blue Circle').

Over the years I had charge of the *Dunstable* several times when Ernie went racing in some of the other barges. In 1937 the *Dunstable* was fitted out by the Blue Circle Firm for the Coronation Race. We were entered in the staysail class and came first in the Thames and second in the Medway. After the barge race, Capt. Britton went into the lighterage as a lighterman for the Blue Circle Firm and I was made skipper of *Dunstable*. Henry Attwater came mate with me and we both carried on doing the sandwork to Sittingbourne and also to Greenhithe. Henry soon picked the job up (loading the sand) and was a pretty good worker, also a good barge mate. *Dunstable* remained in the sand work until 1940 and then the firm put us on the Northfleet bargeyard to have our limbers cleaned out to go in the cement trade in the Thames and Medway — that meant doing dock work and also going up through the bridges as far as Fulham. In the latter part of 1940 Henry was transferred to the lighterage dept. by the firm. I then had a young apprentice from Northfleet as mate with me until he got his 2-year river licence. Next I had another boy straight from school by the name of Bryan Hillyer from Gravesend — he also was an apprentice. Both of these mates went lightering for the Blue Circle. Bryan stayed as mate with me until March 1946, by which time work was far too slack. So after serving 19 years in *Dunstable*, mate and skipper, I gave one freight's notice, doing my last freight in her (which was a cargo of breeze from Southend to Greenhithe). Also it was the last freight *Dunstable* did under the Blue Circle Trade Mark, and I was the last sailing skipper for Blue Circle.

After leaving *Dunstable* I got a berth in the *M/B British King* owned by L.R.T.C. Ltd., Canal Road, Strood. I started as mate again to learn a bit about the engines. I had about a year in *M/B British King* and then went mate in the *Niagara*, same firm, with skipper Bill Filmer of Strood. She had a 66 diesel engine and it did not take me long to learn about that. I had charge of the *Niagara* quite a time because Bill was on the sick list. When he came back we went into the *M/B Atrato* and I also had charge of her when Bill was on holiday. After being with Bill about 2 years the owners asked me to take the *M/B Greta* which was doing freights of beer from Meux's Brewery, Nine Elms, to the depot at Chatham.

I took the *M/B Greta* about 1950 and remained skipper of her until 1959 when she went on the bargeyard for scrap, so that finished *Greta*. The firm gave me a job on the bargeyard, but the last 4 years I was ashore I spent in the sail loft (Canal Road) and then retired from the firm in 1966.

MATE WITH 'PIP' BOX
By Henry Attwater
(Sequel to the 'Pip' Box Autobiography)

It was April 1933 when I sailed out of Milton Creek, mate of the *S/B Diligent* (skipper Stan Horton); I was then 15 years of age. I had sailed out of Milton Creek many times before, as my father had been a barge skipper and I had spent many holidays away with him. If we were going up through the London bridges, I had to stand at the wheel and, while father and the mate rowed the barge, father would shout his instructions like this:— "Pull the wheel to you a bit" or "Push it away from you a bit". This saved father running from for'ard to aft, and they could keep good way on the barge.

But this mate's job was different — I now had to scrub the decks clean, scrub out the cabin, clean the stove with black lead, and polish the panelling in the

Henry Attwater in 1973
(Photo by Alan Cordell)

cabin. I shall always remember the skipper running his fingers along the top of the cabin door and round the panelling to see if I had missed any of the dust, but this was only a part of the duties of a bargemate. I think Stan was only making sure that I learned the right way to do things from the start, as Stan (who had been a barge mate under my own father before being made a skipper) must have been made to do the same.

I stopped with Stan for about two years and then I went mate in the *S/B Grace*, a much better barge (skipper Perce Farrington). Most of the freights were rough-stuff from Camberwell and we also had a few freights of bricks and timber, but by this time anybody could see that the sailing barges were going to be replaced by motor barges. After about 2 years in the *Grace* the firm started bringing in lighters and selling the sailing barges. Some went for as little as £100. A number (like the *Grace, Russell* and *Ada Mary*) were sold to the Leigh Building Supply, and kept working for a few more years.

Then in 1937 I joined the *S/B Dunstable* and started in a different kind of barge world — loading sand off Leigh sand hill for the brickfields at Murston. I do not think I have ever had to work harder in the whole of my life. Skipper 'Pip' Box was an old hand at the game and taught me how to use a fly tool. He could cut and carry a much bigger spit of sand than I could so, to make up the difference, I ran with my spit! When you think that we had to cut and throw into the barge about 15 tons each time the tide was away, it was no wonder that we were tired out. The sound of the flood tide running into the newly cut holes in the sand, signifying two or three hours' sleep, was like music to me! One of the jobs the mate had to do just before the tide left the barge dry on the sand hill was to make a big teapot of tea, sugar and milk all mixed in the teapot. This was placed in the barge boat and you just went to this for a drink. There was no stopping for anything else — you had to get in as much sand as you could while the tide was away. Even when the flood tide came and you did go back aboard, you still had to trim the loose sand off the decks, wash clean and dry the fly tools and then oil them ready for the next time.

There were still quite a few barges loading off the sand hill at that time:— the *Kappa* of Eastwoods, *Premier* of Gransdens, *Edinburgh* of Wills and Packham, *Mona* of Nash and Miller, *Good Templar* of London and Rochester Trading Co., *Lancaster* of Clarkes, *Charles Burley* of Burleys Ltd., and the *K.C.* and *Anthony* from Wakering. I know that as soon as we arrived in sight of the sand hill, a quick count of masts showing soon let you know how long you would have to wait for the regular sand-heaving gang to give you any help with the loading of your barge. The *Dunstable* was still carrying her racing gear and I remember that on one occasion after loading on the sandhill, we floated on the flood tide and, with a strong N. wind we sailed down Leigh Ray straight across to Sheerness and up through Kingsferry Bridge to reach our berth in Milton Creek on the very same tide. Also another time, we came off the sandhill on the flood tide and with the wind from the north sailed to Johnson Dock at Greenhithe and berthed ready to unload on the same tide.

After 30 years of working on the water in sailing barges, plus steam and diesel tugs, I feel there is nothing to equal the thrill of steering a sailing barge in a stiff breeze.

Compilers' note:
It was very kind of 'Pip' Box and Henry Attwater to set down their memories of the sand work for us; we are truly grateful. But after reading both articles we were left pondering one question:— how did they know how much sand to put in the barge, so that she would float at her correct loaded waterline when the tide came up? We have since talked to both 'Pip' and Henry and this is their answer, which they say will work for any barge:—
Fore Hold: Sand was thrown up against the for'ard bulkhead so that the top of the heap was level with the top of the hold and extended the full width of the hold. The top of the heap extended two carlings[3] aft from the bulkhead and then the 'skirt' ran down to a position vertically below the after coaming.
Main Hold: The top of the heap again went right across the top of the hold. It extended from 2 carlings before the middle tie beam to 4 carlings abaft the beam. The 'skirts' then ran down to positions below the for'ard and after coamings.
The wet sand was firm enough to remain in these positions whilst the barge was under sail — danger of the cargo shifting was negligible.

1908 TO 1960 — 52 YEARS OF HARD WORK NON-STOP
(Something which today's society does not understand)
By Harold 'Jack' Butcher

Leaving my Brightlingsea, Essex, School in March 1908 at thirteen, I went to work on a farm (62 hr. week for 2s.6d. — 12½p in today's money — rising to 5/- per week after 2 years). In 1910 I decided to go to sea — that's where this article begins. I got a job as fourth hand on the 300-ton barge *Britannic* (owners E.J. & W. Goldsmith of Grays), at that time trading with shingle from Brightlingsea beach to Immingham Docks, then building on the south bank of the Humber. We brought back coal to any port in the south of England. In most ports the crew had to heave it out, all 260 tons, in 1 cwt. baskets.

Harold 'Jack' Butcher at the wheel of *Hydrogen.*   (Courtesy of Harold Butcher)

This went on until 1914 when my service finished, bang! — just like that, in the *Britannic*. I was then mate of her — a 300-ton coaster — at 19 years of age. It happened as follows.

Whilst unloading coal from Keadby at Prentis's Quay, Milton, by ginny wheel[4] into horse and carts, one of the men on the winch said the ginny wheel wanted oiling. I said "I oiled it yesterday", he said "It is supposed to be oiled every day, that's what Mr Dives gives the 7s.6d. allowance to the crew for". This was news to me. I had been there before and I had never seen an allowance. I went to the mast head and oiled the wheel and when Mr Dives (the merchant) came down, I asked him if it was correct; he assured me it was, every trip for every barge, the skipper drew 7s.6d. for the crew to oil the gin daily. My skipper had drawn it, trip after trip and stuck to it. When he came down I asked him about it and he said "Yes", but he added it was nothing to do with me. I was paid by the month and to get up and oil the b . . . gin. I said if he wanted the gin oiled, then get up and do it himself. The sack followed (at a moment's notice!). So ended *Britannic* and me!

After getting the sack at Milton, I got a lodging and applied for a job at Smeed Dean's. I was given a mate's job right away, in an old barge called the *Edith*, a 'left handed' barge, skipper old Alf Mackee. Her sprit was on the port side of the mast; anchor snatch was on the starboard side of the stem; stay fall and anchor chain were both rove the opposite to the traditional way. Two trips and I was offered the mate's job in *Mary Ann*. She did a lot of beach work to Clacton, Walton and Frinton. As the War went on we worked a lot to the Guncotton Powder Works at Faversham. Then in 1917 I went into C. Burley's *Sportsman* in the cross-Channel work to Dunkirk, Calais, Boulogne, Tréport and Dieppe. 1918 brought the armistice. I stood at the foot of Calais lighthouse and saw it light up on 11th November 1918. From the *Sportsman* I went into the Merchant Navy, over a matter of money (not the skipper's fault). I sailed in a troopship called the *Marmari* (Shaw Saville and Albion) with troops home to New Zealand from the War Zone (one voyage took 6 months) then was transferred to *R.M.S. Athenic*

(Shaw Saville White Star) a big ship in the same trade to New Zealand. I did one trip as A.B., then was offered the job of Quartermaster, steering on the bridge; I took it as it appealed to me. On the last trip in 1920, on arrival at Panama, a letter came aboard for me from the manager of Smeed Dean's offering me the mate's job in the big coasting barge *Hydrogen*; when I got back to England would I come and see him? The outcome was that I took the job under Captain Arthur Coward, under 'special conditions'. These conditions gave me more than the mate's share of the freight. This lasted for 12 years until 1932 when the barge had been sold to Daniels of Whitstable. There was no more work from the Murston cement mills, which had also been sold, first to the Red Triangle then to Blue Circle; so I left and applied for a job at Lloyd's Ridham Dock. When interviewed by Mr Williams (the Manager) who knew me from the times we had loaded paper in Ridham for Norwich, he said "You don't really want a job ashore do you, Butcher?" I said "No Sir". He said "You want to get into our lighters don't you?" I said "Yes Sir", and he replied "OK, you start at the bottom in the log ships' hold, and when we call you to take a lighter away, at any time of the day or night Saturday or Sunday, we shall expect you to do it. The same applies when one of our skippers gets laid up or has his holiday". This was 1932. It soon happened that I was in bed after being at work all night when there was a knock at the door and a note to get to Ridham at once; one of the men had been taken ill, and away I went on my first trip to London with paper for Lloyds. This temporary system lasted until 1936 — in and out of the lighters. Then Mr Box (the ship's husband) offered me the *Calcutta* as my own lighter. After a short stay in the *Calcutta*, I was offered the *Bombay* — a better lighter, but still a wooden one. Next came the War in 1939; all sorts of regulations to comply with in and out of Sheerness and up and down the Thames. We were not allowed to use the Swatch after magnetic mines were dropped — had to go through the swept Channel below the Nore, before heading up the Thames. Four lighters were burnt out with fire bombs. Luck was in for the skippers as they were all home for the weekend. We normally lived on board as they were residential lighters — one man, one vessel, the skipper being responsible for the upkeep of the lighter and the cargo, ropes and tarpaulins. First casualty was the *Ballarat* on 7th September 1940 (Poplar Dock), then the *Hobart* and *Melbourne* (Waterloo) on 29th December 1940, then the *Ridham* in April 1941 (Blackfriars). These were all steel vessels, but they were repaired, after all woodwork was burnt out of them. The 12 wooden lighters trading to London in the Blitz did not get a scratch or a spark! In 1942 I was offered the steel lighter *Melbourne*, which I had for ten years; then in 1952 I was asked to take the *Adelaide*, which I had until 11th January 1960, when my foot got jammed at Northfleet Paper Mills between two lighters. I was then nearly 65. Five months in hospital followed, then attendance five times a week for another six months. Thus ended my working life.

A DABBLE IN SAIL
By Ron Dickenson

I was born on 14th December 1910 at No 13 Mill Street, Milton Regis, a stone's throw from the head of the Creek. My father was a sailing barge man and a good seaman. My mother was a God-fearing woman with a deep trust in everyone and a fixed intention that her sons should not follow their father. Both of them did.

Some of my earliest memories are of being away with my father, the smell of fish-oil, canvas and new rope. As a schoolboy I roamed the shores of the creek and learned to swim in it, so I grew up rather independent, somewhat aggressive, and with an urge always to see what was 'over the hill'.

I left school at 14 years and, out of loyalty to my mother, took a job in Wills and Packham's brickfield. Two months and three jobs later, I told my Dad I wanted to go to sea. So strong was the urge that I would have sailed on a tree stump, so my mother gave in. The *Gertrude May* of Smeed Deans, skippered by Walter King, was loading cement for Plymouth and needed a third hand. My dad had a pint with Walter and the job was mine. Up to Taylor and Streeter's, the outfitters in the High Street, where my father bought me an oilskin and sou'wester, back home where he gave me his second-best pair of sea-boots, and I was a Sailorman! I had plenty of room in my boots, but three pairs of socks helped a lot! I believe that the general comment was "That will cure him!", but I came home a month later with a 'North Atlantic roll' and an eagerness to get away again. This time it was cement to Truro, Cornwall — a good run for a sailing barge; the *Lady Jean* was there at the same time. We loaded alum back from Plymouth to Northfleet. Then *Gertrude May* went for a 'brush-up' on the yard, so as I was only on 10/- a week and 'grub', I was offered a berth as mate of the 'stumpy'⁵ *Garfield* with Jack Austin. I was a lively lad by then and, after 'Channel banging', being pulled up the Regent's Canal by a horse was not my idea of sailing. So a couple of freights later I heard that Jim Brooks wanted a mate in the *Martin Luther*. Jim was a nice man and we got along fine but my feet started 'itching' again and when I was 16, without telling anyone, I went to Chatham and joined the Navy as a boy. I came unstuck because I needed my parents' written consent. I was out-numbered, so I went back nursing an injured pride and joined 'Pilot' Farrington in the *Sam* and subsequently in the *Murston*. We had fun, but not much money, so I moved on to Andy Wood in the *Swift*.

She was a 'dry' barge and so carried cement and other better paying cargoes. Round about this time I met the girl who is now my wife; I was then about 17. During these years Smeed Dean had become the Red Triangle and we carried that insignia in our topsails. Soon they began to 'put the screws on' as things got worse for sail in the depression. Then the 'light sailing' money was stopped which meant that if we sailed home light (no cargo), or from home to London light, we did it for nothing. This was true of all trades except the 'rough-stuff' work; there the money was still paid because it was to the firm's advantage.

We discharged cement at Chelsea and received orders to sail light to Rochester buoys. I refused to sail for nothing and emptied my 'donkeys' breakfast' overboard and went home by train. I was lucky again because Lloyd's Paper Mill was then taking on hands for Ridham Dock on the log ships and I pestered the foreman till he took me on. This, I thought, is the end of my sailing days!

It was not to be, for at the end of the log season I was stood off with the rest. My father was skipper of the *Shamrock* (owned by Bingham and Ellis) and needed a mate just then, while I was out of work. So 'needs must when the Devil drives' and I joined her. Luckily *Shamrock* was in good work and we did better than most. Then, about 1930-31, my father's health failed and he went into hospital. I asked for command of the *Shamrock* and had things been normal I think I might have got her, but by then work was so bad that barges were being tied up and experienced skippers were taking mates' berths. I was refused and so decided that there was no future in sail and looked round for another job.

I found one with W.H. Howlett, a small lighterage firm having a contract with Bermondsey Council to take house refuse (or 'rough-stuff' as we called it) from London to Pitsea marshes. We had two motor barges towing a lighter alongside. I was lighterman-cum-mate and after sailing it was a piece of cake but, somehow, not as enjoyable. I was not paid a lot, but at least it was weekly, and I got married while in that job and moved to Gravesend. About 1937 (that made me 27) things were looking up on the river and I went back to A.P.C.M. at their Lighterage Depot at Northfleet. I was in good company there, because nearly all the gang were ex-Sailormen. Then, all too soon, came the war and I volunteered for the I.W.T. R.E.

My unit moved around the country doing patrol duties on lakes and other waterways until 1941, when we were posted to the Persian Gulf. We were there for three years, during which time I saw the river Tigris from Fao to Baghdad. Also I had nearly two of those years cruising the Gulf as acting Chief Mate of a small motor coaster on Charter to the British India Co. We carried a Royal Mail Pennant into Kuwait, Bushire, Bahrain, Dubai, etc. We heard about the Allied invasion of Europe over our radio, but it did not seem important just then because we were trying to find the estuary of the Tigris in a blinding sandstorm.

In 1944 I was sent home and saw a bit of Europe before being demobilised as W.O.II. I went back to lightering again and stayed with A.P.C.M. until they closed their Northfleet depot.

Men (a few) were kept on in order of service and sent to work at Greenwich Depot. I did not qualify, so I went ashore to a job with Vickers Armstrong at Dartford. I was then 51 and, after a life afloat, I did not settle down very easily; but the move was providential as things turned out with our family and I was able to help my wife through a bad time much more than if I had still been afloat. Soon after this my wife was persuaded to go into welfare work as Warden of Housing Centres for the Aged and, as I write, she is now Senior Warden of one of the biggest centres in Sevenoaks and Dartford. This has made retirement easy for me and I take some of the load as handyman about the place. Now, as I look back, I know that I have enjoyed my life (even the rough bits) but never with such freedom as in my 'rope and canvas' days.

1   Only rarely did the hufflers work at Kingsferry Bridge during the night.
2   *Dunstable*'s sides were reduced in height, so that it was easier to load her with sand.
3   Carling — a beam supporting the side-deck.
4   Ginny wheel — same thing as a gin wheel (described in Chapter 1)
5   Stumpy — a barge with no topmast, and therefore no topsail or staysail; this was a common rig on small barges in river and canal work.

Smeed Dean barges at Ashingdon's Wharf, February 1908. This is in Ballast Wall Reach which, around that time, was often the scene of rowing races between the local wherrymen. A bit of fishing, ferrying and odd-jobbing was the way these men scratched a living with their own small boats. 'Pickle' Coomber, 'Nutty' Spice and 'Chicken' (no other identity known!) are names which are still remembered. The last-mentioned actually lived on his boat on the mud-flat known as 'The Duckle' near the Creek Head.

(Photo by George Goldsack)

Smeed Dean barges in Adelaide Dock on a snowy day in January 1903.

(Photo by George Goldsack)

CHAPTER 4

UNDER THE SMEED DEAN BOB

By Leslie Williams

When I first started work for Smeed Dean & Co. (the barge owners at Murston) as mate aboard the S/B *Buckland* with Bill Barnard, I had already spent two years afloat as boy to my grandfather in Packham's *Unique*.

Then, in 1922, the Company's entire process (from manufacture to loading, unloading and carriage) was completed by hand. The only concession to mechanisation was the cranes which had been installed at the cement works and at Adelaide Dock. Incoming freights were thrown out by forks into barrows and bricks and bags of cement were always hand loaded. Apart from the brickworks, the cement-works and the barges, the Company was working 8 wharves below Murston Quay with 12 berths; the gas wharf; 8 berths at the cement works; a coke dock; the barge-yard which comprised sheds, a sawmill, two sail-lofts, various old hulks and the barge blocks; Adelaide Dock with 5 berths and a lay-by; a further 7 berths up to MacKenzie's Reach; 40 horses with carts and some Fodens. In those days there was horse-drawn rail traffic!

It was usual for a boy at Murston to start at around the age of 14 either with his father or with somebody who knew him. Then at the age of 20 he would be given charge himself. Many of the older skippers had formerly served in the brigs and schooners which enabled them to be able to take their barges almost anywhere. Some skippers, like Bill Gorf who had the *Persevere*, went coasting from the Humber as far round as Cornwall and even some of the smaller barges like the *Russell* (of which 'Happy' Irons was skipper) went in for short coasting passages. The firm had ten proper coasters, including the *George Smeed*, *Youngarth*, *Gertrude May* and *Victoria*, while there were a further 18 craft which worked in short coastal trades, *Hambrook*, *Silver Wedding*, *Burton*, *Harold* and *Grace* were some of these. The *Graham*, *Young Jack*, *Winnie*, *Livingstone* and *East Hall* were in the mudwork; *Favorite*, *Histed* and *Edith* were working coke; while the remainder of the fleet (52 barges at the time) were in general river work, including the small *Maria*, *Vincent*, *Derby*, *Whitehall*, *Garfield* and *Agnes*, all of which worked up into the Regent's Canal.

In the river work it was usual to sail for turn at most places. So if you had been lying windbound, say in the Swale, it was a race to get under-way afterwards before any other barge by any means you could. Once you arrived there was seldom any argument; you sailed for turn and that was it, except that if you overhauled a stumpy barge you always gave her the turn.

Working on the London River you were never very far from a shop, so unless you were on a coasting passage you never bothered to carry many vegetables aboard. Tinned food was not much in favour in those days, but the open fire-places were coming to be replaced by stoves with ovens, so that we could have a

A 'Mystery Pic'! Three barges dressed overall in Adelaide Dock during the Red Triangle era, around 1930. They are thought to be, left to right, *Favorite*, *Georgiana* and *Valdora*. However, as they have obviously 'scrounged' pennants from other barges as well, the names are not certain. Another problem is that nobody knows what they were celebrating!

(Courtesy of George Faint)

change from boiled foods, although not a lot of baking was done. The usual meat was salt beef which was then 3½d. a pound; most of the other food was fried. Bacon, cheese and jam were bought as standbys, with fresh bread when you could get it. Although bread never went off, it began to taste queer after a couple of days, probably due to the bilges! It was understandable then that sometimes you could run out of food when lying windbound, especially if it was too dangerous to go ashore.

If you had been stuck aboard, say for a fortnight, and then managed a quick turn around in London you naturally wanted to get ashore. But in a strange place there was nowhere to go except to the cinema or to a pub. We only drank mild beer and while I never saw anyone ever get vicious I did see them do some funny things!

I saw a mate once jump off Colchester bridge and then swim down to his barge at the Hythe! Of all things, the skipper of the *George Smeed* once threw a jar of peppermints all over a billiard table — ruined it — and had to pay up £5 damage. One night the skipper of the *Derby* and myself took our mates ashore for a drink in the Army & Navy at Southend. When we came out at closing time I found that my barge had blown off the shore about ten feet. I would never have been able to get the mate back aboard in his condition, so we put him to bed in a skip in the yard and left him there 'till the morning. He did not complain too much either!

My first freight aboard the *Buckland* was with bricks from Murston up the Surrey Canal to Peckham, which in those days was a pretty rough place. As soon as we came up on deck we were pelted with stones and rubbish by the local kids. I was not sorry when we dropped down to Camberwell Vestry[1] to load rubbish back for Murston. The *Buckland* was only an 80-ton barge and after the *Unique*

(which was a fine coaster) it was rather like being on a barge boat. At that time
Smeed Dean was running a number of loads of bricks and brick rubble over to
the Essex shore of the Estuary and we came to do a lot of this in the *Buckland*.
It was hard work, sailing to places like Pitsea, Vange and Benfleet, where at times
the channel was not much wider than the barge, and it was unusual if you did
not get up and out again at the cost of sore shoulders and aching limbs.

It always seemed that we got to the awkward places so, after a year, I left her
to join the 80-ton stumpy barge *Lowe*, first under Bill Spillett and then under
Sid York. After two years in her I served for a spell in the recently re-built
Fred, which was doing sand work from Leigh, with shorter spells in *V.C.*, *Alan
Dean*, *Providence* and *New Hope*, before going as mate with Jim Brooks in the
Martin Luther. Jim was a skipper who was happy for me to get on with carrying
out work on the running rigging, or painting, as well as the cooking and cleaning;
you learn faster that way. He was offered the *Georgiana* after a while, and I went
along with him. The circumstances were curious. Her skipper had lost his nerve
and lay at anchor for a month in the Swale laden with brick rubble. Finally he
went home sick, never to go back on the water again; so we took the barge.

The *Georgiana* was a nice barge. She was 110 tons and had just had her cabin
painted out in dark oak and light elm. It was a roomy cabin and I always looked
after it, polishing the brass and panelling every day.

The barge had worked out of Dover at one time, getting cargo out of ships
wrecked on the Goodwins. This was a well-paid job and had helped to build
Smeed Dean and Company up when they were only a young firm. On many
occasions the crew had to leave things as they were to run for shelter. But that
trade came to an end when the Great War finished and there were no longer big
sailing ships to get into distress.

The *Georgiana* worked anywhere between Harwich and Dover. At the time
we joined her she was mainly working to the Essex backwaters with brick rubbish
and flints. When that work fell off we returned to London River to carry bricks
and cement up and return with household refuse. However, if there was a chance
of other work coming up we took it, even ballast, so sometimes we were away
from Murston for up to a month at a time.

Our London work was to the big builders' merchants. We went to Horseshoe
Jetty, when the Dagenham Estate was being laid out, and to Young Wharf at
Blackfriars, where you could always find Smeed Dean barges lying on the buoy
below the bridge. However, other work was to any wharf, hard or landing where
you were wanted. Perhaps we would unload bricks over the side above bridges
one day, then on the next load a freight of corn to Ipswich, Colchester or
Dover. *Georgiana* was fitted with a removable tie beam to enable us to easily
load a freight of timber or machinery. Times were still good, at least for us then,
and I reckon that we often averaged 6 freights a month, including inward and
outward cargoes. We unloaded dust at Murston one day and the same night were
up in London loading coal; sailed all night back to Murston to start unloading
before breakfast and then were away back to London with cement. I enjoyed
working to Bell Wharf at Leigh, where you could sail right up to the Wharf, or
lie out on the sands. It always seemed to be summer, then. Perhaps we only
worked there in summer . . . I cannot remember.

Our inward cargoes to Murston were mostly household refuse from Camberwell or Battersea, which after sifting was used in the brick-making process. It was

50 years ago . . .

Ships being held up by the new German U boat were a common occurence. On Wednesday evening last week the largest coasting vessel belonging to this district, the S.D., owned by Messrs. Smeed, Dean and Co. Ltd., was stopped by a German boat.

Covered by a revolver, the Master was compelled to hand over the ship's certificate of registry, her bill of landing and other official papers to the officer-in-charge, who then gave the crew five minutes only in which to get clear of the vessel.

Four bombs were placed on board, two in the cabin and two in the forecastle, and the red ensign lowered and taken, together with the lifebuoy bearing the ship's name, and all the food on board. The bombs soon exploded and blew the vessel to pieces.

Extract from the 'East Kent Gazette', 6th April 1966, recalling the fate of the *S.D.* during the 1st World War. Fortunately Skipper Dorrell and his crew eventually reached land in the barge boat.

RULES.

Contributions to be sixpence per week. Payments over **eight weeks** in arrears to disqualify from benefit. Payments over four months in arrears to cancel Membership.

Sick Pay.—10/0 per week for the first 13 weeks, 5/0 per week for the next 13 weeks, and 2/6 per week for the succeeding 26 weeks.

Death.—In case of Death of a Member, £5, and in the case of Death of any Member's Wife Single Member's Mother who has been dependant upon him, £2/10/0.

Share-Out each Christmas.

Mates.—Messrs. SMEED, DEAN & CO., LTD., have again expressed their willingness to subsidise the payment of Mates who are Members and in their employ, by Twopence per week, leaving their Contributions at 4d. per week.

Contributions are due on the **1st of each Month**.

S. J. ELLIS, Secretary.

Smeed Dean & Co.'s Bargemen's Benefit Club

Name...H. Attwater... No. 67

192	1 wk.	2 wk.	3 wk.	4 wk.	5 wk.	TOTAL.
Jan...	0	6	6	6	6	
Feb...	6	6	6	6		4 6
Mar...	6	6	6			
Apr...			6	6		
May	6	6	6	6		
June	6	6	6	6		
July...	6	6	6	6		
Aug...	6	6	6	6		4 6
Sept...	6		6	6		
Oct...			6	6		
Nov...	6	6	6	6		
Dec...	6	6	6	6		4 0
				Total		

A souvenir of Smeed Dean's Benefit Club.

(Courtesy of Henry Attwater Jnr — the card belonged to his father)

Georgiana, deep-loaded, prepares to discharge her cargo at Clacton in Essex. Pity the poor horse — although perhaps it was a nice job in the summer! The bottom of the *Georgiana* today lies on the foreshore of the Swale at Queenborough.   (Courtesy of George Faint)

a light-loading freight which meant that we could usually be home the day after loading. We were so light-loaded (with a 2'6" side) that the weather had to be really bad to stop us coming down Sea Reach. As there were 8 unloading berths at Murston we never had to wait long to get unloaded; which was just as well because at times our cargoes were pretty ripe!

It was not too bad in winter but during the summer months when the refuse was just paper, tins and rotten fruit we had more flies than cargo. Luckily we could always run down if the wind was right: two tides from Battersea and one from the Surrey Docks. Smeed Dean barges were expected to work anywhere and Jim Brooks had once taken only 50 tons up to Marlow Lock in the *Providence*. We had to work the barges ourselves up as far as Kew, but if going above there we towed with Tough & Henderson, who picked up a full tow at Woolwich on most day tides bar Sundays. There was regular work to Barking Creek, Bow Creek including Old Ford, Bromley Lock, Hammersmith Creek, XYZ Wharf at Wandsworth, Wandsworth Creek, Mortlake and Nine Elms. We also had to go occasionally to Pebbley Brook. I had never heard of it before; when we found it, it was a little dock under a road, used by the Council for their Depot.

Before the cement mills changed over from hand kilns to rotary kilns we sometimes loaded coke in London; afterwards the kilns required coal which was loaded under the Albert Dock hoist. Having our own work, it was seldom that we ever sailed light-laden.

It was a good life, always with plenty of company. Most of our crews were Sittingbourne men and I had been to school with, or knew, many of the mates. We had to get on well together, and help each other, for with so much work being above bridges or through the canals our gear was always going up or down.

Georgiana in later years, after her bowsprit had been removed. This picture shows her leaving McKenzie's Wharf, deep-loaded, in 1923. A party of Wandsworth Sea Scouts is aboard, probably having a trip as far as Queenborough. Skipper of the barge at that time was Jimmy Toms, with his son Percy as mate.   (Photo by Ferris, courtesy of George Faint)

It was back-breaking work to rig a barge with only two hands, but the topmasts at least were easily handled as they were fitted with balanced fids[2], and all that you had to do was trip them with a length of spunyarn to save climbing aloft to house them.

I suppose that all this helped to make us pretty smart aboard. Certainly we could handle the gear quickly. Once when we were turning out of Sheerness in a breeze our tops'l halliard block shackle at the topmast head broke. I was able to trip the topmast, lower it, fit a new shackle and get the topmast up again, and set the tops'l without losing more than a board on the other barges who were sailing with us. Of course, mistakes were also made and I did not always do things right. The skipper of the *Harriet* who was sailing in company with us saw me lower the topmast and then called out to my skipper that "You've got a smart mate there!" The incident might have gone to my head . . . had I not proceeded to drop the staysail over the foc's'le funnel and it was burnt right out before I even noticed it!

All the gear aboard the Smeed barges was designed for easy working. There were patent sheaves in all the blocks except the stem head; we were given ash setting booms and hitchers and you were able to get any gear that you asked for. All river barges were fitted with a bridge sail and a short mast which was a great help up through in a fair breeze; for the Company's contracts were to keep the rubbish depots clear! I have seen smaller barges when light-laden actually turn up under bridge sail and mizzen. Coming back down we rigged as soon as we were in the Pool.

I remember that one night we locked out of the Surrey Dock gates when there was a flood at Westminster; the odd tidal set made us wait until half-ebb before we could get away. We were in company with the *Ada Mary* and our skippers took a boat ashore to row round the houses to see that the occupants were alright. I believe that on this occasion nobody was drowned. I have known a lot of freak tides. We were at Bow Creek once when the tide came up so fast that you could actually see it rising: and this was half tide. Eventually it stopped and was only a normal, good tide. It was not uncommon to see the tide ebb and then flow again after high water, usually on a neap tide. On another occasion we have berthed at Milton only two hours after low water, when we normally entered the creek two hours before high water. Sometimes we never got any water at all.

Milton Creek was not an easy place to work if there were 30 to 40 barges coming in and out and you had to rely on everybody keeping out of your way. If you got 'put by', as we used to say, and went on a lee shore then there was nothing else to do but push, or if there was not too much wind you could run a line ashore or use setting booms on the bow to keep way on. It was fortunate that most of our wharves were well down towards the mouth of the creek, for Wills & Packham's craft had twice as far to travel, but they usually took on a huffler. Below the cement works the channel narrowed and there was much more mud, but there was one deep hole, called 'Biddy's' after the landlord of the pub[3], where you could not even touch bottom with a setting boom. We usually managed to sail up the Creek as far as Adelaide Dock without much trouble.

Once alongside, the inward freights would be shovelled out, then the outward freight of bricks would be loaded by hand. A gang would load a full freight of 46,000 bricks in a day. Loaded, the mate was then expected to clear the barge ready for sea and in practice the mates turned round to help each other.

The Company was pretty circumspect in its dealings with its barges and its crews. The rule was that they employed their skippers who in turn employed their own mates. If the barge was on the yard the skipper would always be found a job somewhere but the mate had to look after himself. This happened while we were doing some work for Cremer to Oare Creek, taking ashes from Ebury Bridge Basin. It was bitterly cold when we left London and even the water tank was frozen solid. We ran round to the Medway mouth in a strong northerly wind, carrying the tide all the way down in snow showers. We shot Kingsferry Bridge, sailed through the 'grounds'[4] under half-sail and pushed through the ice to the mouth of Oare Creek, where the wind had shoved the ice floes on top of the flats at high water. Later the floes blocked the mouth of the Creek and in company with *Atlas* and *V.C.* we were iced in for three weeks. The Company found Jim Brooks a job in the yard — I did nothing.

On another occasion we lost time replacing our shrouds and were paid nothing for it. We were turning into Milton Creek in near gale force winds when we broke our starboard shrouds. We shot *Georgiana* into the Lower Berth, then got the topmast down in readiness to lower the gear the next day. We lowered down, unshipped and cleared the masthead and replaced the rigging. All on our own without any help — and we lost three days work. Those old shrouds still lie at Lower Berth after 50 years.

Soon work began to fall off with the increase in road traffic. When they had been in collision barges were no longer taken into the shed for repairs — they were written off. George Andrews, the Chairman then, did all he could to save the firm. He brought in an Economiser — who sacked a lot of men and if the Murston women could have got hold of him they would have strung him up — and one suggestion he made was to take topmasts out of the barges and sail them single-handed!

Smeed Dean sold out to the A.P.C.M.: 60 barges, 300 houses, farms, brick-fields, cement works etc. Barges came to be sold off, especially the larger barges which were too big for the Surrey Canal, and shipwrights came to be stood down. Somehow the *Georgiana* managed to shrink sufficiently to get under the Surrey Canal Bridges! But this was done by stripping the topmast, so that the mastcap just cleared the wheel, and by removing one leeboard. The only work left to us was to run light to Camberwell for household refuse. We did two months work then one month on the dole. To ease matters we used to help load the barge ourselves, which gave us 2/6d. — enough to grub us home again.

Then we lost the *Georgiana*. We had come away from the Lower Hope in a light westerly breeze into Sheerness Harbour and were heading into Queen-borough inside the line of warships which used to lie there. We were just abreast of the *Valiant* when a collier came round her head to drop off the pilot. They had not seen us although we had our lights up. It became obvious that she was going to hit us somewhere, so we pulled the boat up, got into it and hung over the quarter to wait.

At first it seemed that she was going right over us then at the last minute the helm was ported and the collier struck us on our stem — knocking us in the boat back 6 feet. Jim wanted to know what ship it was, but she would not answer; however the *Valiant* put a search light on and we saw that it was the *Colaris*.

We got back aboard *Georgiana* to find that the stem had been knocked back 4 feet and the deck had opened right out. We were not making much water, so we decided to sail her on up to Kingsferry, with the running shrouds set up for'ard to prevent the mast coming down. At Kingsferry we shipped the huffler, 'Doggy' Fletcher. Next day we towed up the creek and unrigged. *Georgiana* was declared a total loss. As the shipwrights had been discharged the skipper was paid 8/6d. and I received 5/6d. for un-rigging her: very generous!

Jim and I then took the old mud barge *Alliance* which should have been broken up 20 years before as she was only held together by force of habit! She was flush-decked[5] and had a minute cabin. She leaked terribly and we were caught out soon afterwards in a south-west gale in Sea Reach and dragged our anchor. The Southend life-boat came out to us but Jim refused to leave the barge, al-though I wanted to. Instead, we lowered the gear and rolled the gale out. I lay that night on the cabin floor so that when the water rose up and touched me I knew it was time to pump.

Lighters were being built now for the canal work and the old *Alliance* came to be tied up. Jim Brooks and I then parted company and he was taken on doing canal lightering. As for myself, I was given my first command. Theobald's over at Leigh offered me the stumpy *Emma*, having just bought her from the A.P.C.M.

So I left Murston and sailed up the Medway to load flints for Southend; it was supposed to be a regular run, but I only did two freights and then had to go into the ballast work, with timber work and sometimes ashes as they came along. The *Emma* was a most unsuitable barge for any of this work — she had been built for Peters of Wouldham as a lime barge and therefore designed always to be light loaded, as she had a 6ft 3in side and was a stumpy. I therefore found that I was always close to the ground on the sands and would lose my wind under the hills of Westcliff and Leigh. I often wished I had the old *Georgiana* in that work for it was the sort she had been built to do. If she had not been run down I would most probably have taken her over to Leigh instead.

I seemed to get on fairly well with the firm, who were still buying barges at that time even though they had a job to get crews. I tried to get a bigger barge but was not successful. I do not think it was anything personal, but if they had a job to get a crew for a 110-ton barge, it would have been more difficult to find one for the little *Emma*, so Theobald's kept me in her. I read in 'Down Tops'l' that the crew's share of the money was about fifty shillings a week. I recall however that at times I had been better off as mate of the *Georgiana*, when once my money had been six pounds a week for a year.

During the middle 1930s we were running a lot of ballast into Leigh, both into Bell Wharf and Theobald's. A lot of the crews were Kentish men whom I knew and we always helped each other, which made life easier. We also worked a lot up to Benfleet and to the wharf above the bridge there. It was not a very good place to take a barge, with the channel between shingle banks, and we had to be careful where we lay if we didn't get up on the tide. However, once I had learned where the water was I never had any real trouble in Benfleet Creek. I had only been up there once before and that was in the *Buckland* as a lad of fifteen. The *Emma* was a narrow barge and flat with it; coming down Sea Reach with the wind S.E. or N.E. (which meant a long and a short tack) I have seen her put solid water from the stem to the mastcase. I often thought she would keep going down, but she always came up. As a safety precaution I would keep the mate back aft with me, until we got down in the Ray. By this time we often had two feet of water to pump out. We must have looked a terrible sight, but I was there to try and get a living and I cannot remember ever lying windbound.

Finding suitable mates was a continual problem to most skippers by this time; I do not know where half of them came from, but they would arrive in just what they stood up in, without even blankets or mattress. If it rained they relied on being allowed to stop down in the cabin! Their worst fault was their reluctance to prepare any food. I think they used to try and eat enough stuff at Leigh to last them until they got back again, which did not work, of course — but they never learned! I always had a good cook-up at weekends, which helped to keep them going. If I had stopped all they owed me from their pay they would have drawn nothing.

I remember once, when a new boat lay off Bell Wharf, the police came round and asked if I knew anything about an anchor which had been stolen. As I did not, I said so, and they went away. Later on that day, as we were running up Sea Reach, my mate told me he had hidden the anchor down our fo'c'sle under the floor. I was very angry for I did not know anything about it and his dishonesty could have got me into trouble.

I sailed the *Emma* for about eighteen months, even after she stranded across Leigh Creek and sank, until it became so difficult to find good mates that I went half shares in the *Burton*. A new skipper came to take the *Emma*, who said he had been barging; though I have my doubts as he had orders for London and sailed off from Leigh going straight up Benfleet Creek! He obviously did not know the way to London so Billy Theobald promptly sent the motor boat off to tow him back to the sands, where he sacked him. Unfortunately the gear that I had left aboard the *Emma* went with him as I was ill with jaundice at the time and had not been able to collect it. I made a reasonable living whilst I had the *Burton* but things became very slack and eventually we got our cards. So after a very short spell as skipper of Allsworth's *Bessie*, I saw that there was little or no future on the barges. I felt that the time had come to look for different work so I came ashore, buried the anchor and had several jobs in factories including a number of years with Bowaters Paper Mills at Sittingbourne.

After the war I joined the APCM company as a lighterman thus returning to the water again and I remained with the firm until I retired in 1973. Recently I returned to barging again under the TBSC flag having been persuaded by Alan Cordell to join his charter party in 1975 and again in 1976 when I was delighted to be approached by the TBSC to go skipper of *Centaur* on a number of charters and some weekend sailing. It takes me back a few years . . .

1 Vestry — a term surprisingly used to describe the refuse-loading depot.
2 Fid — a metal pin which locks the topmast in place aloft.
3 The 'Brickmakers' Arms'. The pub, as well as the hole, was known as 'Biddy's'.
4 Grounds — area of the Swale between Elmley Ferry and Fowley Island.
5 Flush-decked — having no raised cabin top.

Murston Gas Works Wharf, with the 'Brickmakers Arms' on the left, in January 1903. Sailing past is Wills and Packham's *C.I.V.* She was launched in 1901 and named after the City Imperial Volunteers, a regiment which was raised at that time to fight in the Boer War. *C.I.V.* is still afloat today as a sailing-barge-yacht, although she sails very little.

(Photo by George Goldsack)

The top end of Murston Quay about 1920; *Joe* in the foreground with, astern of her, *Gladstone*. The hulk of the latter is still in the Creek today. (Courtesy of W. Marsh)

CHAPTER 5

THE HEYDAY OF MURSTON QUAY

By Leslie Williams

Murston Quay during the Smeed Dean era was never empty of craft; ten or more were always there. As you came up the Creek you would find barges at the brick berth two or three abreast. The outside barge would top his cross-tree and sling the anchor on the inside bow, to help other barges who might fall foul of him. At that time, before they built the rotary kilns, the only coal was for the gas works — all carried by Smeed's barges. At times (about twice a year) a barge called the *Tartaric* — a tank barge belonging to Rainham, Essex — would load away from the gas works a liquid of some sort. This was perhaps a tar; he would always give you a gallon — we called it black varnish. At that time a lot of ballast from Brightlingsea was being unloaded at the wharf below the cement-loading berth, for Smeeds were modernising the cement works. Such barges as the *Alan Dean, Youngarth, Victoria, Maria* and *George Smeed* would do this work.

At the cement berth there would always be at least two barges loading by courtesy of a gang with barrows, one bag at a time; this process was quicker than you might think, for they would often load both barges in a day. The clay berth above this had a crane, which used to drop the clay over a wall. I do not know how it was moved further, but probably by manual means at that time.

Then came (I believe) a lay-by, for I remember coke barges there, four deep at times. Next came another cement-loading wharf; the same system operated — barrows, plus a gang of men. Right at the top (below the painters' shop) was the coke dock, with another crane. These were all deep-water berths. In the coke

A barquentine at Murston, about 1920.   (Courtesy of W. Marsh)

Loading cement into a motor vessel via a chute, Murston, about 1930.   (Courtesy of E. Pearce)

The lower end of Murston Quay about 1926. A lighter, which would eventually sound the death-knell of the barges, is ominously present. The 'Brickmakers Arms', at this time known as 'Biddy's' (after the landlord), can be seen in the background.   (Courtesy of George Faint)

dock today you can see a mooring ring touching the mud. At one time it was a job to reach it in a dinghy! I can never remember any trouble shifting, berthing or leaving the Creek — whatever the weather.

With the rotary kilns coke was eliminated and the kilns were fired by coal. A lot of this coal was no good for anything else, for it had to be ground to powder before use. The barges were (with a few exceptions) good, well-found craft earning their crews a better living than they would have obtained ashore.

The majority of craft that loaded cement away were Smeed's, although I have known a few small motor craft to load; also some West Country ketches and on one occasion two of the London and Rochester Trading Company barges loaded for a special job down Channel. For a time some Irish craft used to load at Elmley Ferry; the cement was taken out by barge (a short trip) but probably paid poorly. We did one freight in the *Georgiana* but I do not remember what we were paid for it.

A busy time during the heyday of Murston Quay. Barges in the background turning to windward in a channel only about 3 barge lengths wide.
(Photo by a professional Sittingbourne photographer, probably Wrigglesworth)

The above view in 1979. 'Biddy's' still there, but not used as a pub; broken-down remains of the barge *Thomas and Frances* on the right; Linguria Maritime Shipbreakers in the distance on left; a scene of decline and desolation.   (Photo by Alan Cordell)

Skipper Henry Attwater Snr (starboard sweep) and mate Gladstone row the *Murston* through the London bridges. *Murston* was later used as a housebarge at Reading — and floated into a domestic garden during a time of floods. After further service as a garden shed (!) she was broken up about 1960. (Courtesy of Henry Attwater Jnr)

CHAPTER 6

WORKING THE LONDON RIVER

By Leslie Williams

I have read with interest all the books and articles about sailing barges, but there seems to be very little said on the subject of river barges and the really back-breaking hard work needed at times to get them about.

I was 14½ when I entered the firm of Smeed Dean and Co., just a slight lad at that time, and found that most of our work was to London up through the bridges. We were expected to go as far as Kew by any means other than a tug. This meant, for the mate, about six hours on the sweeps to keep way on if it did not blow too hard down river; you were on your own for the skipper stopped at the wheel. Otherwise you dredged with the anchor touching and you had to tend it all the time. We were once five tides getting to Wandsworth Creek from the Mudhole at Wapping. Then the spars had to be hoisted, another back-breaking job usually done by just the two of you. I have been told by a yachtsman that it was impossible for us to have done it, as it took six men to rig the . . . at Maldon. But we did it!

The 'London River' at Gravesend.   (Photo by Alan Cordell)

We also did a lot of work to the Surrey Canal. If the wind was down the Surrey Dock all the loose lighters blew down across your head and, with nothing to get a purchase on, it would take hours to work to the Canal entrance. Working up the Surrey or the Lea river we were towed by a horse and the mate's job was to go ashore and clear the towline of obstructions — you had to be pretty agile to do that.

The sweeps were also used to row round the bights in a calm, but if the tide was too strong you had to drop the anchor, to keep clear, and dredge. This meant 30 fathoms of chain at times and sometimes, with the anchor jumping over the bottom, you would lose the chain as you tried to heave it in. 'Iron Bight' at the bottom of Gravesend Reach was the worst place. Even running a line away in the dinghy was never easy, for you had to scull over the tide always, and Smeeds never supplied light lines.

I think now, in retrospect, what a boon a small outboard motor would have been to use with the dinghy lashed alongside; the cost would have been small and would have earned us many more freights a year.

Of course it was not a bad life and in those days (1920s) we took hard work as it came. It probably helped to be 45 years younger, I should not want it now!

CHAPTER 7

OF THIS AND THAT

By Leslie Williams

Windbound

I remember one winter lying windbound in the Lower Hope. We had left London three days before and I suppose skipper Jim Brooks began to get fed up with seeing me down the cabin, so he sent me up on deck to scrub the mats. As I rinsed them off they froze solid, so I put them on the hatches and went down the fo'c'sle. I lit a fire and cleaned my lamps and then lay back on the staysail (which was kept below when not in use). It was too cold for Jim to come for'ard and find me any more jobs, so I had a peaceful day. Without being big headed, I was always a bit smarter than old Jim. We got on pretty well most times and you never took charge if the skipper did not say you were capable. One mate I know had been in the firm a long while and his skipper was asked if he was fit to take charge. He said "no", so the mate did not get the chance. Later this skipper was telling skipper Tom Pearce of the *Youngarth* about it. Tom Pearce said "He is capable of taking charge isn't he?" The other chap said "Yes, but I didn't want to lose a good mate!" Tom Pearce did not think much of it. He said, "Someone had to give you your chance when you were mate, didn't they?". This incident was very unusual — most skippers were pleased to see their mates get on. My old grandfather had trained seven masters in his time, all good and competent men, as were most who sailed out of Milton Creek.

Smeed Dean was not a bad firm to work for and they did look after their barges, but we worked for almost nothing — which people who look back and think we had a perfect life seem to forget.

Little Alfie Lee on the bargeyard dished out the stores and rope, did the wire splicing, looked after the pitch fires and heated the tar and worked for as long as he was wanted with no fixed hours. I think he was paid labourers' money, about 28/- a week (now £1.40).

Up the Creek!

When I see some of the corners we used to work to, I wonder how we got there. Of course, we had a dinghy and a long line but this still had to be hove on the winch. I have known barges work up a narrow creek by running the kedge away, heaving up to it, dropping the main anchor, and running the kedge away again, perhaps for twenty times. I know this was done in the Navy, but we were only one man and a boy. No wonder I could sleep in those days!

Another trick I have never seen mentioned was peculiar to Milton Creek. In Smeeds we had to get our orders on which berth we were wanted. So in calm weather, as soon as we entered the creek, if one barge tied alongside another, the flood tide would roll them up the Creek in the channel. Of course, they would

A barge preparing to shoot Kingsferry Bridge about 1925. Her mizzen is already lowered and her mainsail partly brailed up in preparation for lowering her main mast.

(Photo by Colin Cordell)

touch the mud, but the barge that was afloat would pull the other one off. Meanwhile the mates would row up to the Lower Berth and go up to the village for orders. By the time they got back, the barges were still coming up the Creek; when ready, you would separate again and find your berth. They were a fine lot of sailormen who worked out of Milton Creek in those days — even in half a gale of wind straight out of the Creek it was unusual if you did not get up and done. Of course, the prevailing winds were westerly which meant you fetched some of the reaches.

Another thing that most of the books on barges never say is that some of the skippers were a morose lot and the mate was always doing something wrong, according to them. It was the worst thing for a mate, for it destroyed all his confidence in himself and if he did stick it long enough to take charge, he was never quite up to the standard of others who had been helped along -- who were the majority, thank goodness.

I have lain in the Swale, with one who was nervous, for a month waiting to go over to Southend. If the firm had not told him he would have to leave his barge if he did not have a go, we would have been there still! I left him as soon as a chance came along — he was a nice chap too.

But I preferred old Jim Brooks; he was lazy himself, but we always sailed if there was a chance. I did not mind getting wet in those days. He tried to push me along and asked three times for a barge for me before I got the *Emma*. I have a clock he gave me when I was married.

Bridgework

There seems to be some misconception about shooting bridges; so this was the drill for Kingsferry and Rochester Bridges, when you took on a huffler. You would sail right up to the bridgehole with all sail set; at the last minute the mate would drop the topsail and run aft while the huffler would let go the topmast stay and stand by the stay-fall. The stopper would be already off and the gear was then lowered. The mate would keep the mainsail clear of the wheel, while the skipper steered (there was a guard-iron to make sure the mainsail did not foul the wheel). As we always had the tide with us, we carried our way well through the bridge. We then anchored and hove up. It probably sounds more tricky than it was, for I never saw an accident, although we did not always get through without touching.

We have shot Kingsferry on our own at night, for I was a pretty good mate and always lowered the gear wherever we were. (Big Head?).

Ballast work

Ballast was loaded out of hoppers (or dredgers) at the top of Sea Reach. They were also called 'drudgers' or 'ballast engines'. Although not a well-paid freight, it was quick and clean. I was lucky in the fact that my ballast work was done in fairly tight barges, so that when you had pumped out the initial water you had nothing to worry about. We did quite a bit in the *Georgiana*, which was a good barge for that job as she had been built for beach work down Swin. I was her mate and she would carry about 90 yards of ballast. The *Emma* only carried about 60, so you can see that I was not much better off as skipper of her. You would lay above the dredger and drop down in turn on the ebb. You picked the breast chain up with your anchor and then sheered alongside. It took about 8 minutes to load into the fore and after holds. I had a theory that if you loaded some in the middle hold you eased the strain and carried a bit more — I do not know if it really made any difference but that is what I used to do. It was an exposed position but it was exceptional if you did not load. You had to be pretty smart at times or you could give yourself a lot of work. Fortunately most men at that time were, but I have seen one of Peters' men get his hand crushed on the rail — it was so cold it did not bleed.

Another chap had his head cut open as the shoot came down. It is a sign of the times that there was no first aid box aboard the dredger. Somebody tore a clean shirt up for bandages. At that time if you did not look after yourself, nobody else did — not much Welfare State then!

There were some London barges in that work — Scholey's, Cunis's and Covington's mostly, but there were also a few small barges in the last state of repair, in which the crew must have 'starved like tholes' (which is an old saying) for they were only small barges and sometimes would be three weeks between cargoes. The crew slept on bare boards and lived on bread and margarine mostly. But times were hard ashore as well. I made a living whilst I was mate. We never had to wait to unload. We once put out three freights in a week at Angerstein's Wharf at Charlton.

In the last barge I had, the *Bessie*, I went alongside the dredger every tide for a week and, as the P.L.A. had not been paid for the last few loads, I could not get loaded, so on Saturday afternoon I sailed back to the Swale. I had not earned a penny that week, my mate was fed up and so was I. I gave up barging soon after — at least ashore I could get the dole! As my old grandfather used to say: "There's no taste or smell to nothing!"

Dropping down through

Often, if we had loaded dust in the afternoon and the tide went about 10, we would push out from the dust wharf and wait for high water. I cannot remember ever coming down through at night with the bridge sail; this was usually done in daytime with another hand to help you, because you could see the set of the tide better in daylight. At night it was easier, and safer, to drop down behind the anchor. You could always get down and rigged — it used to take about 4 hours. I remember the landmarks: McDougall's Flour Mill below Battersea, the long drive down Chelsea Reach, Battersea Park, and the Embankment (with a night club and its kitchen close to the water). Then passing Westminster we would hear Big Ben strike about three times before we were clear. Over on the Lambeth side there was the Shot tower and 'Dewars Whisky' on another tower, showing a Scotsman with his kilt waving, done by lights. Next, we passed down through Waterloo bridge, then by the *President* and *Discovery* at Blackfriars, where we would look to see if any of our firm's barges were moored. Below Cannon Street there was a cold storage depot which worked all night. We would be coming now to where the bridges were closer. At London Bridge you had to pick your anchor up clear because of the stones remaining on the bottom from the earlier bridges. Once past Tower Bridge you came to a jetty where they unloaded bananas day and night. Once we were down to Wapping Old Stairs, we brought up and rigged; if we still had the tide down we got under way so as to get as far as possible. I suppose nearly all these places are gone, or altered — for the worse I'm afraid! I cannot remember ever working hard amongst the bridges or being in any trouble; but I do not know what I should make of it now!

Sittingbourne 1920

When I was a boy, Sittingbourne was more of a rural town than it is now. The High Street has not grown much apart from there being more banks, but what the shops sell has altered. At one time the three big hardware shops sold guns, which you could buy over the counter — you can imagine how us boys would look at them (and the boxes of cartridges) in the windows! Rabbit nets and snares would be hung in the doorways, also ice skates in winter, which shows there must have been a demand for them sometime. However, the winters do not seem to have been too hard as far as I can remember, although there must have been more snow at one time for there were plenty of snow ploughs about, owned by the Council. Plenty of animal foodstuff came up the Creek in barges and Sittingbourne had a market. As you went to school you would see the flocks of sheep and herds of cattle being driven through the High Street and it was also a common sight to see the old gipsy vans going through the town. Where Rolands' Garage is now was a brickfield — derelict, but the wooden hacks were still there. A stream ran down Crown Quay Lane; the water was drinkable . . . for it never killed me! As soon as you left the High Street you were usually amongst orchards and country paths led everywhere; hence a walk in the country was normal on Sundays. Once, when my wife and I were out for a walk before we were married, the first signpost we noticed said 'Sittingbourne 8 miles' — so we had a 16-mile stroll! Hale's (in East Street) made farm wagons. They would be finished off in front of the shop, then painted and lined in red by hand. The forge had three blacksmiths, with usually four horses at a time being shod — another show for us lads! There was a little shop on the corner of Crown Quay Lane that made harnesses and I believe they would make you a pair of leather sea boots; but when I started work afloat, rubber wellingtons were just coming in. Ballards, up by The Rose, sold sports gear and whips — the boy who lived there was the only one at my school who had a cricket bat. When we played cricket (up the 'Rec') with the school, we had his bat and another about a foot long! Our school (St. Michael's) was badly off for sports gear — there were just enough football shirts and shorts to go round and you found your own shoes or boots. We played in black and red (Sittingbourne F.C. colours) and we had a good team; I remember two of our best goalies — Moses Goldsmith and Hardy Coomber, both Milton boys. The regular roaming round the Creek, swimming and getting shellfish in the Swale, and picking up what was lying around in the country, meant that I had a pretty good boyhood. We were always short of money at home, for I lived with an aunt (a widow); but few were well off in those days. I expect the average wage right through the town was about two pounds a week. But Happy Days!

Elmley Ferry

To many (if they remembered it from their schooldays) Elmley Ferry would probably be the place from which James II made an abortive attempt to flee the country. But in its time it served to link the Sheppey village of Elmley and its Turkey Cement Works with Murston and Sittingbourne. At the turn of the century there was a large village at Elmley, with a pub, a church and a school; also at one time there was a coastguard boat and two cottages under Cullum Hill on Sheppey, which were the coastguard cottages. Smuggling was rife 150 years ago in this district. My own great-great-grandfather was the leader of one of the largest gangs in these parts and even today I could find the old smuggling paths across the marshes to the main road at Bapchild (my great-grandmother showed me them when I was about four). When I was young we always liked to go down to the Ferry; at that time there were two Ferrymen, Jack Carrier and Jack Wade. There were a set of barge blocks, a boat building shed, a duck pond, a pump, the Ferry Inn and two cottages. The Ferry Inn had no licence then, but you could buy soft drinks and tobacco. The water was the best part of a mile across at high tide but only about 20 feet at low tide. The Ferrymen worked three boats, which were moored along the causeway, so that it was easy to launch one of them at any state of tide.

With the closure of Turkey Cement Mills about 1904, the village of Elmley lost its purpose and the majority of the people migrated to Murston to work in Smeed-Dean's brickfields (which were expanding, as was the village of Murston). In my younger days many of the Murston men had been born in Elmley.

The Ferry was still useful. Smeed-Dean's mud-loaders would use it to get to the clay holes on Sheppey and at one time about 12 Gransden children would come down from the farm on the hill and go to Murston school. A van would pick them up at the Ferry and when they returned, about 4pm, they would take a sack of bread with them.

There was a cattle boat with two ramps, used when wanted at low water; it must have been a long job, but it did not seem to matter so much then. I have been over the Ferry many times when I was working on the sea walls, often we had a 1½ hour walk before we got to where we were working. The stones for facing would be brought by barge from Maidstone. It was alright in summer time, but pretty bleak in the winter; however, it was work, and better than the

Elmley Ferry House; it was demolished about 1960.   (Photo by Ferris)

dole, although our money was only 38s a week (paid once a fortnight). I knew a place where I could find oysters that came up from Whitstable — I used to fill my tin every day. I like them fried in butter (I cannot get them down raw!).

The Ferry was a pleasant enough spot and you could go swimming at any time, but it was a bit dangerous and several people have been drowned there.

The Ferry was in use until after the Second World War. I remember that soon after I came out of the Army, Jack Carrier died and the job was advertised. I thought about it, but I had a decent job and the Ferry was isolated. Anyway, I believe they decided that it did not warrant keeping and so they took the boats away.

Jack Wade lived in his cottage until the floods of 1953 when he moved to Murston and the cottages and Inn became derelict. About 1953 a chap came on the scene and said he had bought one of the cottages. He brought two mine sweepers round to the Ferry and began to claim everything in sight; he used to dump old cars and warn people away from the place, saying it was 'private property'. My foot! — it was as good as a public highway, but as nobody wanted to go there anyway it did not matter much. He is dead now and I believe the cars have gone for scrap, but the place is spoiled. The two long hards are covered with mud and one of the two channel marker posts is down (there are two buoys now to show where the channel is). The area is now a nature reserve and may be of interest to bird watchers, but not much use to us old watermen. I have seen a water colour of the place as it was 50 years ago; it looked lovely. I do not know who now owns it. There were many beauty spots on the Swale, at one time; Harty has changed little, thank goodness, since the time after the Nore Mutiny when a boatload of men from the British Fleet rowed round to Harty, stole a bawley and sailed to France. Both Elmley village and Murston are flat now; in a few years' time few will remember where they were.

Sea Reach

I am often reminded when I get up (which is usually at dawn, for I cannot lie in bed) of coming down Sea Reach early in the morning. This is because my garden lies E to W and I have only the marshes and the Isle of Sheppey between me and the rising sun. Of course, in Sea Reach you have the illusion that the sun comes up out of the sea. Looking back, it seems that it was unusual to have all the hours of darkness in the Reach. We would try to work our tides to suit our voyage. But even if you had a nice breeze you would rarely enter Sea Reach in the dark if you were going to meet the tide about Chapman Head. You would try to have all the tide with you, either up or down.

However, I can remember more about coming down than going up, perhaps because it was a bit more tricky, for the Swatch (which we worked) wanted a bit of finding in the dark. It was marked by a dim red light which was difficult to see in poor visibility. I have said somewhere before that you could find the Swatch by keeping the Chapman Head in your port snatch aft, but to do this you had to be far enough down. However, in those days you sensed where you were, except in thick fog. My practice, if caught at the top of the Reach in fog, was to sail into the Blyth sands, sounding till I could just lay afloat, and then let go. The big ships could not get at you then. One skipper I was with would not go on deck in a fog, for he imagined that he could see ships coming head first at him. It did not bother me, but any old sailor will tell you that you can visualise all sorts of things in a fog. I have willed myself to see one of the old galleons sailing by!

When you got in the Swatch after dark, you looked for the four flashes of Grain Spit because Sheerness (like Harwich) is well concealed from the west. If it was fine, and daylight, we would make what we called a short spit over and come inside the light. I would put my foot on the leeboard head to feel if it touched. I have never known any of Smeed's barges to go aground there (if the weather was rough you made sure you did not!) but I did see the *Flower of Essex* right on top of the Little Nore sands and another Essexman on the saltings at the bottom of Cod's Reach in the Swale. But this was after the War, when it was a job to get good crews for sailing barges. I will admit that in both places you would think you had water if you did not know better. As the old skippers used to say, 'Sea Reach is no harbour'. The tide runs so hard that when it is against the wind it makes a short steep sea and there is nowhere to run for shelter if you are caught, for sometimes you could not carry enough sail to go into the Medway. I do not suppose that the barges that were lost in the great 1914 gale would have been there if they could have got out of it. Thank goodness that on the occasions I was caught I was sailing light. Not that I disliked Sea Reach, for you could have a good sail without worrying about ships and if you had a stiff breeze you could hold yourself over the tide. We have run down from London at times and met the tide below Chapman Head. If we had enough wind we would creep along the Blyth sands and as the tide flowed get on top of them and run along the shore on Grain. But this was slow work and, although we often managed to get up to King's Ferry or outside Milton Creek, we never made it into the Creek, for the tide would be away and it was not worth chancing.

We could go home by train from the Bridge if we wanted to, or row the boat up to the 'Snapper' (just inside the Creek). We would go into the Creek on a day tide, if we could, for then our berthing orders were shouted out from the Lower

Leslie Williams as a barge mate in the 1920s.

Berth. A funny thing about getting our orders at times was that the first barge in the Creek would bring up off the Lower Berth and the mate go up to Charlie Shilling's for orders for all the barges (sometimes about 10 craft). By the time you got back the other barges were working by and you told them where to go. Obeying Sodde's Law, you would find that after doing all the work you would have orders for a wharf in McKenzie's Reach (near the top of the Creek), whilst all the others berthed further down the Creek! The only thing that you could say in favour of McKenzie's was that you usually swung round and loaded bricks away quickly.

A 'Milton Churcher'

When we were working in the Creek in rain and wind, we would often say 'it's a proper "Milton Churcher",' for that is the way the worst of the weather came. In my mind I can still see the showers sweeping across the marshes. Sometimes, by the time we got tied up, we were soaked through. No wonder we have aches now!

CHAPTER 8

REG PUTWAIN'S HALF-CENTURY OF SAIL MAKING

Extracted from an 'East Kent Gazette' of June 1949

For many years the centre of the thriving barge building district of the north Kent coast, Sittingbourne is now relegated to a near back seat in the nautical industries. A newer and more stable industry has taken the lead in the town.

Thames spritsail barges have the reputation of being faster than any other comparable sailing vessels in the world, whether loaded almost to water-level, carrying a large deck cargo, or sailing light. Those enthusiasts who make this claim have three undisputed factors to back their arguments — the magnificent seamanship of the barge skippers, the care which the old-time shipwrights put into their work, and last but not least the craftsmanship and skill of the sail-makers.

Sailing barges are still trading, but not many young men are attracted to the job of learning that seamanship from the older men and there are few shipyards now capable of building a new barge. Builders will repair a barge, or even convert one into a floating home, but no wooden sailing barge has been built since 1931.

Nevertheless, some of the old craftsmanship still survives. Sailmaking is an arduous profession, for a barge's mainsail contains thousands of square feet of canvas and is a hefty load to pull about the floor of the sail-loft. Yet Mr Reg Putwain of Crown Quay, who has been doing it since he was a boy — over 50 years ago — has never wished for a better job.

"My racing sails have won more cups and prizes than any man living or dead", he says with some justification. Records of the Thames and Medway sailing matches since Mr Putwain started his business in Sittingbourne are evidence of the success which his sails achieved.

Mr Putwain is very proud of his share in the victories of the barge *Sara*. In the Thames sailing matches she was first in the bowsprit class in four consecutive years — from 1931 to 1934. The following year she took second place, and then won again in 1936 and 1937. In the last race before the war, in 1938, she was fourth.

Her success in the Medway matches was no less conspicuous, for she won her class five times between 1930 and 1937. She had a perfectly setting suit of sails which were able to draw well up into the wind, and her record is certainly un-paralleled by any other barge, except perhaps the *Giralda*, 'champion of champions' (which was raced by the late Mr Arthur Coward of Sittingbourne).

Other names which conjure up for Mr Putwain the memory of many days hard work and exciting races are *Princess*, *Veronica*, *Cambria*, *Will Everard*, *Alf Everard*, *Lord Nelson*, *Queen*, *Northdown*, *Challenger* and the *Phoenician* (which was the last sailing barge to be built in Sittingbourne).

Most versatile of all the barges for which Mr Putwain made the sails was *Veronica*. In the staysail class of the Thames match she was first in 1933 and 1934 and then won the bowsprit class (beating *Sara*) in 1935. Back in the staysail class in 1936 she won again, and again in 1937 after transferring to the coasting class. Her record in the Medway matches was similarly unusual. She was first in her class during three consecutive years, sailing in the staysail, coasting and bowsprit classes respectively.[1]

Constant use of the sailmaker's palm has shortened Mr Putwain's right thumb, and his part in sailmaking now consists of cutting the canvas and supervising his one employee, 19-year-old Fred Inge. Fred, who has been with Mr Putwain for some years, has learnt much of the sailmaker's craft.

Probably the suit of sails which is now in the making in the sail loft at Crown Quay is the last one in which Mr Putwain will take part. It is for the barge yacht *Beryl* lying at Hoo. It is the owner's specification that all the sails should be white, although Mr Putwain says that he would prefer them to be dressed with the traditional red ochre.

Together the mainsail, topsail, foresail, mizzen, working jib and jib topsail embrace an area of 4,000 square feet, and there are hundreds of yards of hand-stitching in this 'suit'. Advantage of the hand stitching method is that the triangular sailmaker's needle parts the warp and weft and allows them to close again, but the machine's round needle goes right through. As a result the material is weakened.

The stitching of the *Beryl*'s sails is being done by Fred Inge. He and another apprentice, who now works in London, finished the mainsail and he is now engaged on the topsail.

Whitstable, renowned for 'divers, sailors and sailmakers', as well as oysters, was the birthplace of Mr Putwain. He was apprenticed to a sailmaker named Jack Kemp there and tells of the antagonism that existed between the religiously minded Kemp and a rival.

When he completed his apprenticeship he came to Sittingbourne in 1902. First he worked for the late Mr Boulden[2] and then for Messrs Burley Ltd. In 1907 he started work with Eastwoods, who had 60 barges at that time. After four years there he went to Canada for a few months, working in a tent factory in Toronto, but was soon back in England. He was with Wills and Packham Ltd. when they had 30 barges, until 1922, when he went into business on his own account. In association with Mr Spice, and Mr H.E. Andrews, of the Sittingbourne Shipbuilding Company, he now carries on in a sail-loft at Crown Quay the business which he started at Key Street.

During the war hundreds of awnings were made in the sail loft for the Services. The last suit of sails for a working barge was made last year for the *Varuna*, another craft which was prominent in the pre-war sailing matches.

Much of the work now is to do with the small racing yachts, such as the 'Uffa Aces', which are raced by the Whitstable Yacht Club. There again Mr Putwain's sails have met with great success and are in great demand.

---

1   In the period 1956-63 (i.e. after this article was written), *Veronica* and *Sara* raced in the same class. *Veronica* proved to be the faster barge, winning 12 1st prizes to *Sara*'s 1.

2   In Kelly's Directory for Kent, 1895, John Boulden of Crown Quay is the only sailmaker listed for Milton Creek; a 1908 Directory gives William Boulden instead. There must have been several more, but their identities were hidden under the names of their firms.

CHAPTER 9

CARGOES

By Alan Cordell

'Trust old Cordell to pick an easy one'.

It is alright, I know what you lot are going to say when you read this. But in my experience of life, it appears to me that people often get on by letting others do the work and taking the credit themselves. So I might as well climb on the band wagon!

The idea for this article (if you can call it that!) came to me when I saw a list of barge cargoes in 'East Coast Digest' (No. 3, Autumn 1972). This was submitted by Frank Willmott and had been compiled by that scholarly old barge skipper, Capt. Bill Kennett, during his half-century afloat. Now T.B.S.C. and I, between us, possess all of Bill's numerous records — they were kindly made available by his friend, Capt. Harold Farrington-House, and his niece, Mrs Irene Rhodes, when the old fellow died. So why not, thought I, use an extract from Bill's cargo books for this article? Thus, I offer you a facsimile of a double page of the *Sidwell*'s cargo book covering the period 3rd February-11th June 1921. And that gives me half my article!

The other half comes by courtesy of Jack Harvey, Richard Duke and Mike Taunton. Between them, they arranged for me to borrow the cargo books kept by Capt. Bill Harvey (Jack's father) when he was skipper of the stack barge *Bluebell*. Like Bill Kennett, who had the *Sidwell* for over a quarter of a century, Bill Harvey spent a similar period in the *Bluebell* and kept her in the hay trade right up until the war, when she was the last 'stackie' working to London. I give you two extracts from Capt. Harvey's records — a double page from his cargo book covering the period 20th June-12th December 1912, and a double page from his 'accounts book' for the period 3rd August-23rd November 1936.

The *Sidwell* extract shows that, like most Kentish 'brickies', she worked almost entirely between her home port (Murston) and the various wharves in London. Only occasionally would Bill 'go foreign' to perhaps the Blackwater or Colne and one such trip is shown at the foot of the page — a freight of imported oysters to add fresh blood (do oysters have blood? — someone tell me) to the oyster beds at Brightlingsea. Bill has often reminisced about that freight. At the time the *Sidwell* was a very leaky old barge and when Bill knew he was going to load oysters he said to his mate, "We're just the barge they need for this job — she leaks enough to keep the oysters alive!" A good joke, but in reality it could not have been very funny; on occasions when the *Sidwell* had a freight for the upper Thames where she had to lie afloat all the time, Bill could not leave her for more than a day or so — he had to stay aboard to keep her pumped out. Fortunately, however, the owners rebuilt her in 1922 and after that she was as tight as a bottle.

Date loaded	Place of Loading (cargo)	Consignee
Feb 3	Murston 3600	S J E Co
Feb 9	Wandsworth gas	Mr [illegible]
Feb 16	Murston / Mowbray	[illegible]
25	Battersea	S D & Co
Mch 2	Murston	W J Foxon
11	Camberwell	S D & Co
16	Murston	Gas Light [illegible]
21	Rotherhithe	S D & Co
30	Murston	Hampton U D
Apr 7	Battersea	[illegible]
12	Murston	[illegible] Hall
16	Greenwich	S D & Co
20	Murston	E W Moulton
29	Battersea	S D & Co
May 4	Murston	W J Foxon Deptf[illegible]
10	Battersea	S D & Co
14	Murston	Lane Bros H.S.
25	Battersea	S D & Co
30 & 31	Murston	F G Minter
June 9	Wapping / Moracco Whf	F Knowles

Capt. Harvey had an equally predictable existence in the *Bluebell* — hay from Harwich to London and manure back. Only two freights of stone broke the monotony during the last 6 months of 1912. An interesting aspect of this facsimile is the Customs stamp. Every barge had her cargo books inspected regularly, presumably to satisfy the Customs Authorities that the skipper had not found time for a few quick rum-running trips across the Channel!

A freight of hay was paying about £18 in 1912 and my second extract shows that this had only gone up to about £20 in 1936. So although the cost of living must have risen considerably in that time, the unfortunate bargeman, it seems,

Bill Kennett's entries in *Sidwell*'s cargo book, February 3rd to June 11th 1921.

earned roughly the same money. It is interesting to reflect that if you mention the word 'Queenborough' in T.B.S.C. company you usually evoke a loud groan because the place is so familiar; but the freight which Capt. Harvey took there in August 1936 probably broke his monotonous trading sufficiently to bring a cheerful gleam to his eye!

Well, Captains Bill Kennett and Bill Harvey, thank you very much indeed for all the donkey work you did years ago for my article. They tell me that justice is always done in Heaven (where you both are now), so I hope you are enjoying the managerial positions you richly deserve!

The *Bluebell* of Ipswich

Sailed ________________

Shipper	Quantity and Description of
Sailed from	Harwich Light June 2..
Sailed from	London with Manure June
Sailed from	Harwich with Hay and Straw
Sailed from	London with Manure July 8
Sailed from	Harwich with Hay and Straw
Sailed from	London with Manure Aug
Sailed from	Harwich Light Aug Aug
Sailed from	London with Manure Sept
Sailed from	Hares Creek Margolds Straw Sept
Sailed from	London with Manure Sept
Sailed from	Harwich Light Sept 2
Sailed from	Maidstone with Stone Oct 7 of
Sailed from	Harwich with Straw Oct
Sailed from	London with Manure Oct
Sailed from	Harwich with Hay and Straw
Sailed from	London with Manure Nov
Sailed from	Harwich Light Nov 25..
Sailed from	Millhall with Stone Dec 1
Sailed from	Harwich with Hay and Straw De

Bill Harvey's entries in *Bluebell*'s cargo book, June 20th to December 12th 1912.

Extract from *Bluebell*'s 'accounts book', August 3rd to November 23rd 1936.

CHAPTER 10

CEMENT TO TRURO
(Winner of T.B.S.C. Commodore's Cup for best log
submitted in 1978-79 Club year)

By Ron Dickenson

I have never believed in blaming gremlins, jinxes, spilt salt or broken mirrors for bad luck; nevertheless there are times when nothing goes right. Take the time when we carried cement from Murston to Truro, Cornwall, in the mid 1920s; I was third hand of the *Gertrude May* (skippered by Walter King with Fred Outridge as mate). We finished loading at 5 p.m. and tide time was 3 o'clock so we missed a daylight start. The small hours brought a flat calm and we had to 'poke' her out of the creek. Then, just as we got to the 'snapper' — fog. We went ashore on Turkey flat and stayed there. About two hours before low water she started to slide off the mud and she went right down into the channel (a weird experience) and lay there barely afloat.

As soon as we had water again, we went down the East Swale with a light westerly breeze which freshened during the night and when we were off the Foreland veered northerly. Quite nice; but as the sun rose the wind left us and a nasty mist developed, so we unlashed the sweeps and rowed her in under Dungeness (out of the shipping lane) and anchored in thick fog. This prevailed all day but after dark it cleared with a SW breeze and by morning it was blowing hard. The anchor did not hold too well in the soft sand so the skipper decided we should get a kedge out to steady her. During this operation we all three got a soaking. Walt changed his clothes and told me to do the same, but Fred kept his wet clothes on saying "We'll only get wet again". We kept an anchor watch all night (myself till midnight) and as far as I know, Fred did not take his clothes off so they must have dried on him.

During the next day the wind increased. Fred became more and more quiet and looked unwell — and he did not eat much. I turned in again at midnight after getting supper. Walt must have kept watch through the night by himself because at 4.30am he called me and said he was going to try for Dover as Fred was 'pretty bad'. *Gertrude May* was 'kicking her heels' and so getting the anchor away took some time. We finally made it, slipped the kedge and ran for Dover like a scalded cat, under fores'l and tops'l sheet. I went below to make a quick 'cuppa' and made Fred some Bovril but he could not drink much of it; he looked really bad.

Gertrude May was making good weather and nothing came aboard aft. We got the mainsheet block hooked and I paid out a bit of mains'l as we needed all the way we could get. She was really going now and, as we approached Dover, I could almost count the stones in the breakwater. Walt called me to the weather

The beautiful Sittingbourne coaster *Gertrude May*. Her final skipper under Smeed Dean, Hedley Farrington, moved to Colchester with the barge when she was sold. *Gertrude May* was destroyed by a mine in 1942 — Hedley fortunately survived but the mate did not.

(Photo by R. Stimson Jnr)

side of the wheel, to add my weight to his, and we were there. Walt might have underestimated the strength of the tide, for we took the entrance a bit off centre.

I have a vague recollection of rushing towards the wall on the crest of a sea and Walt's voice shouting encouragement to me. Then the sea hit the wall and came back on us. I suppose it knocked us away and into the harbour. As I looked forward the bitt heads and rigging only were clear of the water; everything else was submerged. Then it was over, and 'hop about then boy' as we sailed close to some other barges and dropped anchor.

Leaving me to stow the canvas and make things 'ship shape' Walt got Fred on deck and rowed ashore with another skipper. They got Fred to hospital with pneumonia and a temperature of 106°F. As for me, I had stowed the tops'l and fores'l and pulled the vang falls and mainsheet inboard before I realised that I was soaked from my chest downward. While ashore, Walt 'phoned the office for another mate. Meanwhile a force 8 raged in the Channel and we rolled water in one side and out the other. Our new mate arrived next day; he was Ted Wraight, 'Talking Tommy' as he was known,[1] and very aptly named as we were to discover! He just did not stop talking, even in his sleep. He was a barge skipper out of a berth.

The gale blew itself out in 48 hours and veered northerly and we resumed our journey once more. Walt nearly always went up and down through the Solent; I think he liked to have the option of stopping overnight. I forget if we stopped on this occasion but bad luck struck yet again as we cleared Portland Bill and met the tide out of West Bay. We were swept into the Race and the next half hour was hectic to say the least, being knocked this way and that and not enough wind to pull us clear. There was one redeeming feature, it stopped 'Tommy' talking!

However, all 'good' things come to an end and we carried on uneventfully until almost in sight of St Anthony, when the wind shortened and freshened. A nasty sea was running before we made our last 'board' into Falmouth and anchored near the *Cutty Sark*.

Next morning our pilot came aboard (it was compulsory to have him, much to Walter's disgust) and we made our way to Truro, where we discharged every bag of cement, dry.

We lay two days for a cargo up Channel. 'Tommy' used the time to see Cornwall, taking advantage of some tours by the local bus company. Walt gave me a few hours on navigation, so we were all happy. Then we fixed a freight of alum from Plymouth to Northfleet. Walt spent a lot of his 'off watch' time with me; he said "it's the only chance I get to —well speak!"

1   Why he was 'Talking Tommy' rather than 'Talking Teddy' is not known.

CHAPTER 11

CRACK SHOT NEW SKIPPER

By Hedley Farrington

In 1917 I left school at the age of twelve and a half to go mate with my father in the *Buckland*, the mate's money at that time being thirty shillings a week. After about a year my father was ill for some time and, when he was fit to return, it was decided that my brother Frank (being older) would be of more help to father. I was therefore shipped in the *Murston* with Henry Attwater, who until then had his wife as mate. I was still with him when peace was declared; we were lying in Brentford Dock, with the skipper at home, and I well remember the time as I went ashore to get a loaf and the locals were celebrating in the streets. I was roped in with the people and this was the first time I got the taste of beer.

After a time in the *Murston* I thought I would like to have a go at Channel work so I shipped in the *Persevere* with Captain Bill Gorf. He was a pretty hard case and I was only given a couple of months to stay by the other mates, but in fact I reigned for seven years. During the time we were at sea I either left or got sacked on a number of occasions, but when we got into harbour we had a drink and I got reinstated. One occasion was off Beachy Head; the third hand and myself were trying to get the flying jib off the stay out on the bowsprit. I was not doing it the way the skipper said so we had a few words; the only thing he could lay his hands on was the windlass handle which he threw; I dodged and it went overboard. If I had let it hit me and then caught it there would not have been such a terrific row!

We then transferred from the *Persevere* to the *George Smeed* and shortly after we fixed to do a freight of cement from Sittingbourne to Devonport in company with the *Gertrude May*. Being wintertime, the trip took about three months; we saw the Isle of Wight five times before we got into anchor, we had to keep going back to a roadstead for shelter. After arrival at Devonport the two captains went ashore for beer and when they came back I got the sack, so I packed my bag and walked up the dockyard. When I got to the dock gates I was stopped and kept in an office; the skipper said I had left in a foreign port. I was kept there until about eight that evening when the mate from the *Gertrude May* came with a note to say, 'Here is £1, go out and have a drink and report back on board again'!

During the time I was in the *George Smeed* I got married, that was in 1926 and our daughter was born in 1927. Things were very hard at that particular time; after one bad trip down Channel the remainder of the freight money after paying my share of the third hand's food left only twelve shillings and sixpence a week for my wife. I decided then to go and see the boss, Mr George Andrews, and he said that I could take the *Argosy*. We had a new pram for the baby and went to town and bought pots and pans, loaded the pram and went down to

The *George Smeed*.   (Photo by R. Stimson Jnr.)

McKenzie's Wharf (which was close to the Dolphin Cement Mill and also was Smeed Dean's top berth).

When we arrived at the barge, Harry Spice, her previous skipper, said that there was a rat on board that they could not catch. The new mate, who lived at Sheerness, said "Rats won't hurt you, I can catch them"; however I was not very happy about that as I detest the things. We sailed the next morning with a freight of bricks for Battersea Draw Dock and on arrival we berthed and got ready to discharge. The mate went ashore in the evening, so I made up a nice fire and turned in with a book. While reading I thought about the rat and, on hearing a noise, looked out and sure enough, sitting in front of the fire cleaning himself with his paws, was a big old rat. Now hanging in my bunk was an old twelve bore shotgun that I had brought with me from the *George Smeed*; I made a move to get this but disturbed the rat and he ran under the mate's bunk where we kept the pots and pans. I kept quiet hoping that he would come out to the fire again and after a time he kept coming so far then back again. I got fed up with this and made up my mind to shoot the next time I saw it.

This is what happened; as you know, the inside of the upright timbers in the cabin is boarded over with matchboard and the blast blew a hole right through this. Shortly after, the mate returned and laughed when I told him what I had done. He asked where the rat was and I replied that I reckoned I had frightened him to death. The next morning I called the mate to light a fire, he put his hand into the wood locker and shouted blue murder; the rat had crawled in and died minus his back!!

CHAPTER 12

COASTING WITH TOMMY PEARCE

By Chippy Wood

During my early years afloat as mate of Smeed Dean's little *Sam*, I think I went everywhere a river barge could go; to Weybridge; up the River Lea as far as Tottenham and the Surrey Canal as far as Peckham; and to all the creeks between Barking and Hammersmith.

After some time in the *Sam* her skipper — the popular Frank 'Pilot' Farrington — recommended me to Captain Tom Pearce of the coaster *Youngarth*. She was the last barge to be built by Smeed Dean (at Murston, 1913) and she was one of the biggest they had. In fact she was built specially for Tommy Pearce, who was the commodore-skipper of the fleet, and she could carry 150 tons to sea or 170 tons in the river. She had been named after Garth Doubleday, the young son of one of the firm's officials.

Tom agreed to give me a trial, although at that time (1923) I was only 16. When I joined her, *Youngarth* lay in Adelaide Dock, loaded with brick rubble for Felixstowe. Compared with the *Sam*'s, her cabin was an enormous palace! I could just reach her cabin top, which was white-enamelled. She had a cut glass door and drawer-knobs, a brass stove-funnel, a fitted carpet, a clock, a weather glass and a tell-tale compass hanging in the skylight.

I had just stowed my gear when the skipper came aboard and asked "Are we all ready?" I said "I think so", to which he gave me the encouraging reply "You don't want to think, you want to know". This sort of approach was typical of old Tom, and some of his earlier mates had disliked it. I remember an occasion a little later when I was whistling a tune as I was taking my trick at the wheel. Obviously my steering was not to Tom's satisfaction, because he said "If you can't steer and whistle, then stop whistling!" But I soon found that in reality Tom had a heart of gold and treated me as well as if I had been his own son. The one trip which my friends had forecast for me grew into a stay of several years.

We let go our moorings and I slacked out a bit of mainsail and set the topsail. The wind was out of the Creek and there were several barges turning up, which meant that we had to 'plumb' them about right. I had to drop the topsail twice, so by the time we reached the Creek mouth, I had hoisted it three times. I felt as though I had stretched several inches already! We sailed into the 'Grounds', through the East Swale, out to the Girdler (which was a lightship at that time) and through the Barrow Deep.

We unloaded in Felixstowe Dock and then received orders to load shingle home from Brightlingsea beach. For me this was the first of many such freights. In fact, several of Smeed Dean's barges were active in this Brightlingsea beach work.

The standard procedure was that the local workmen erected a withy[1] at the foot of the beach just where they wanted the barge's shrouds to be; they also left two wheelbarrows at the top of the beach, together with a shovel. We used to let go our anchor about 30-40 fathoms off the withy and sail in as far as we could. Then we went ashore in our boat, used the shovel to bury the barrows, and attached bow and stern lines to the barrow wheels. We then hove the barge in to the withy. If the wind was on shore, we made a stern rope fast to the bight of our anchor chain to keep her stern off the beach. All this might require several trips in the boat of course.

The workmen loaded us between tides by pushing wheelbarrows up planks.

We had an easy trip back to Murston and then loaded cement for Southampton. To my friends' surprise, I was still continuing as mate with Tom Pearce!

We did a lot of work down Channel — mainly cement for Southampton or cattle-cake (from Millwall) for Poole. Our return freights were usually china clay from Wareham to Queenborough or Battersea, or coke from Margate home to Murston.

For the Channel work we used to have our spars (hitchers, booms etc.) in spar irons each side lashed down to the rails, our light boards lashed down, our warps down the fo'c'sl (except for a big bass towrope which, for safety reasons, we kept on the main hatch just abaft the mast) and the fo'c'sl hatch lashed down. Our lamps and paraffin were kept behind the cabin ladder, so we never had need to go down the fo'c'sl. When turning to windward, the skipper always took her for the inshore tacks and I took her for the offshore ones. Light weather sails (staysail etc.) were stowed at nightfall, rather than risk complications in the dark.

The quickest freight we ever did down Channel was when we left Murston with cement for Southampton one Saturday afternoon and arrived back empty the next Saturday morning. In actual fact we were booked for a freight of coke home from Margate, but when we approached the harbour we saw two barges already loading. This meant a long wait for us, so we had a weekend at home and sailed back on Monday for our coke.

Our slowest trip down Channel lasted seven weeks, on an occasion when we took cattle-cake to Poole and brought china clay back from Wareham to Battersea. We had bad weather for most of the voyage and, on the way back, struggled into Dover Harbour at the start of the severe gales around Christmas 1926. We could not get ashore for food and our Christmas dinner consisted of corned beef pudding (with potato in place of suet), swedes and potatoes. For pudding we had duff (made the same way!) with jam.

On Boxing morning it fined off a bit. A brig lying near us lowered her boat into the water and her skipper and crew of four started to row ashore. In passing, they asked if we wanted anything, so Tom gave me a pound and I went with them. The brig's skipper and I landed near the eastern arm of the harbour and the skipper told his crew to keep the boat clear of the beach as we would not be long.

We knocked a butcher up and bought some meat, did the same to a baker for bread and found a dairy shop open, where we obtained bacon and eggs. Then we went into a pub and had a couple of pints each. You should have seen the wicked looks the brig's crew gave us when we rejoined them and they noticed our alcoholic breath! Just as I re-boarded the *Youngarth*, another gale sprang up and it was several days before we completed the passage. In fact, I let go our anchor at North Woolwich just as the ships' sirens were sounding the old year out and the new year in.

Of course, when you were up and down the Channel and East Coast so much, you had your sticky moments now and again. I remember once we were running past the Needles into the Solent before a gale of wind. In our loaded state, we were being pooped by the following seas. Tom and I were both at the wheel and we had lashed ourselves to the mizzen stay. An Admiralty tug came the other way, towing a destroyer on a very long towline. When the tug had gone past, the destroyer took a sheer towards us and it looked for a while as if we might have to gybe to get clear — and this could easily have brought our sprit down. Luckily, the destroyer then took another sheer the other way.

On another occasion we took coke from Greenwich to Murston and we had orders to get it there quickly, as the cement factory had nearly run out. Going down Sea Reach, it was blowing half-a-gale from the east and we were the only barge under way there (normally there would have been dozens). Off the Chapman Head a big sea hit us, washed our anchor chain back to the fore horse (the grating went over the side!) and distributed our stack of coke liberally round the barge. We had coke everywhere!

In all the time I was in the *Youngarth* I do not remember lying even a day waiting for orders. As Commodore-Skipper, Tom was then held in high esteem by the Smeed Dean management — in fact, as I said earlier, the *Youngarth* was built specially for him. Initially, she was to have been a 180-tonner, but before she was finished, the foreman shipwright realised that she would not be able to swing round in Adelaide Dock, so they shortened her by six feet and she could load only 170 tons in the river. To some extent this spoilt her for Channel work; she was just the wrong length for the Channel rollers and her rudder used to lift too far out of the water, making her a difficult barge to steer under some conditions, particularly when running before the wind.

When the *Youngarth* was built, Tommy was allowed to have some choice in the way she was designed and fitted out. Although she was a big barge and could easily have been flush-decked, Tom chose to have a cabin top to give more room in her cabin and a convenient place to stow light lines, fenders and other gear on deck.

Smeed Dean were a generous firm as regards the upkeep of their barges — we were never refused anything. We had three staysails (sometimes called jib-topsails), fine-weather, working, and a small one which we used to tack down low so that we could still carry it in strong winds when other barges were forced to stow theirs. We also had a normal jib, of course, and a balloon foresail which we used to set as a spinnaker when running. As regards the *Youngarth*'s hull, it was as tight as a bottle; we did not know what it was like to ship a pump.

One of Tommy's pet hobbies was modelling barges and other traditional craft in the authentic framed-and-planked manner. He worked on these when we were windbound or otherwise delayed and at times they graced the annual Arts and Crafts Exhibitions which Sittingbourne Co-operative Society used to run. In fact he was still exhibiting in his last years of retirement, during the late 1940s.

Unfortunately, Tommy's sailing career ended on a sour note. Together with the rest of the Sittingbourne men, we supported the bargemens' and brickfield workers' strike of the late 1920s; and because of this, Tommy (as Commodore-Skipper) came into dispute with Smeed Dean. The unfortunate result was that he relinquished command of *Youngarth*. I went with him into the *Victoria*, a smaller barge which had caused a sensation in 1897 when she capsized during a race — a most unusual occurrence. Later, the echoes of the dispute, plus Tommy's age, dictated a move into the *Vavasour*, a slow box of a barge engaged mostly in river work. Fortunately, however, he retired soon after this and Smeed Dean sold up anyway, so poor old Tom did not have to suffer this step down (which he took very badly) for long.

The *Youngarth* was sold to A.P.C.M. with the majority of Smeed Dean's barges in 1932-33 and went to work on the South Coast carrying cement from the Medina factory near Newport, Isle-of-Wight. She was later fitted with an auxiliary engine. After the Second World War she became a roads mooring barge at Greenwich and was eventually broken up about 1962.

When Tommy left the *Victoria*, I stayed for a while then served as mate of the *Alan Dean* and the *Maria*, also as skipper of the *Alpha* and the *Gratitude*. But by this time barge work was on the steep decline and I moved to the relative security of the Murston cement works.

Compilers' Note:
At the time in 1913 when *Youngarth* was nearing completion, former Sittingbourne man Mr George Sinclair (who was then living in London) visited Smeed Dean's yard. This was because his brother Alfred was one of the workmen there. George was so impressed with the *Youngarth* that he made further visits in order to measure her up and from these dimensions he built a ½-inch-to-the-foot scale model of her. Later, George moved to Exeter and today the model is one of the fine exhibits in the Exeter Maritime Museum.

1   Withy — a stake driven into the mud, sand or beach to serve as a marker.

CHAPTER 13

THE WINDFALL

By Ken Horner

As mate of the Maldon *Percy* in 1937 I sailed from Leigh to Sittingbourne light to go on Andrews' Shipyard[1] for repairs to covering boards and for new rigging chocks. At Kingsferry Bridge 'Doggy' Fletcher stepped aboard as huffler. Looking at her gear he said 'We'll wait for the bridge to lift, skipper', to my father. After a couple of trains had passed they let us through and we sailed to the Creek mouth; we were towed by Lloyd's small tug to Milton 'free'. The day after mooring on the blocks, one of Lloyd's lighter skippers came round and asked my Dad if I could go mate in Ellis and Andrews' *Valdora* for a freight of ballast for Lloyds; permission granted, I sailed that dinner time with skipper Ted Inge with Mr Andrews' nephew as passenger. Lloyd's tug towed us to the Creek mouth and we set all sail. There was a smart S.S.W. breeze and by joint agreement we went via the East Swale, saving a wait at Kingsferry. *Valdora* had no stem blocks, but a large bottle screw instead. This was to force Southern Rail to raise the bridge, as the gear was fixed. *Valdora* was reasonably fast (or there was more wind than I reckoned!) because we reached all round Sheppey and up to the 'Drudger' before low water and we even loaded on the same tide. After battening down, we were off down Sea Reach again. Having shipped quickly, I had no grub and no bedding so was looking for a quick passage. We tried the pumps going down Sea Reach and could not fetch water on either for'ard or after lee pump. I remarked to the skipper about the tight ship; he said she was well caulked with Sittingbourne mud outside and China clay inside! We anchored on the 'Lapel'[2] around high water, had a good meal (thanks to skipper) and turned in on the lockers ballast fashion — one foot on the cabin floor. If and when it got wet you pumped out a bit quick! Next morning we sailed up to the bridge and got towed through by Lloyd's tug right up to our unloading berth. We uncovered hatches and moored up twenty-four hours after I had joined her. The skipper paid me the enormous sum of £2.10s. before she was even discharged or measured out — the easiest ballast freight I ever did. A mate's share of a ballast freight to Leigh from the 'Drudger' was about £1. Averaging three freights per fortnight, mates in ballast barges never married!

Whilst on the shipyard at Sittingbourne in the *Percy*, I helped Ellis and Andrews out on two or three occasions as they could not get mates. If my recollection is correct, I sailed in the *Leslie* (skipper Sid Court) from Leigh to Kemsley Dock light; then back to Leigh loaded with ashes; then back again to Milton Creek light. Sittingbourne skippers were a friendly crowd and not a cutthroat outfit as rivalry with Essexmen has sometimes indicated. Ellis and Andrews' skippers that come to mind are Bill Kennett (a very friendly old gentleman) and

Two craft which visited the Sittingbourne Shipbuilding Company's yard for maintenance work in the 1940s. *Trilby* (in the foreground) was rebuilt and motorised there. The exercise was a miraculous feat — she was lengthened, deepened and widened! In the background is the *Verona*. (Photo by A.S. Bennett)

his mate Dick Chambers (an old ex-skipper) in the *Sidwell*; Bill Barnard and son in the *Swift*; and Chris Freeman in the *Monarch* who, when trading to Leigh, would turn out at any hour of the night to help Essexman or Kentishman alike to moor up or get under way.

Also whilst *Percy* was on the yard, I remember the many laid-up barges in the Creek, most of them Wills and Packham's. They were pretty little barges, clean, with all gear close-stowed and not a rope's end adrift or anything untidy round the deck. *H.T. Wills, Samuel Bowly, Five Sisters, Sir Wilfred Lawson, Henry & Jabez, Edinburgh, Llandudno, W & P* and *Ebenezer* are the names that stick in my mind.

Compilers' note:
We thank Essexman Ken Horner for allowing us to include this article; and we are delighted with his view of Sittingbourne men!

1 Andrews' Shipyard — same thing as Sittingbourne Shipbuilding Company's yard (Andrews owned it). This was also sometimes called Harvey's yard, after the surveyor.
2 Lapel — area of shallow water, giving good anchorage, between Queenborough and Sheerness.

Mercy at Beaumont Quay, Essex, about 1905. (Photo by Bill Kennett)

Jimmy Toms (skipper of the *Mercy* for several years) was a devout Salvationist, as were his wife and children. Pictured here is the Toms family about 1918 in uniform. Mabel (second from right in back row) later married bargeman George Faint. Percy (back row) became mate of the *Georgiana* when his father took charge of her. (Courtesy of George Faint)

CHAPTER 14

THE LOSS OF THE 'MERCY'

By Alan Cordell

The late Captain W. Kennett, of Sittingbourne, was one of the town's most respected bargemen. He left school in 1889 when he was ten years old and took a job selling bread rolls; at the end of the first day he was paid a halfpenny and one stale roll — needless to say, he only kept the job one day! The next few years were spent working for a newsagent, the London, Chatham and Dover Railway, and later for a tobacconist. Then he started barging, as mate of Smeed Dean's stumpy *Derby*, in 1895.

He served as mate in several of Smeed Dean's craft, often trading to small ports round the Essex coast. One harvest-time when he was in the *Levitt*, he took a cargo of flints to Beaumont Quay, in the Walton Backwaters. All the local labourers were harvesting, so skipper and mate had to unload the barge, for which the consignees paid 9d. a yard. When Smeed Dean's manager heard this, his comment was 'Preposterous!' — he only used to pay crews 6d. a yard for unloading their own barges.

The accompanying picture shows the *Mercy*, a 95-ton barge built at Murston in 1896, lying at Beaumont Quay about 1905. The original photograph was taken by Mr Kennett — he was her mate at the time. Skipper J. Toms, who for many years was a side drummer in the Salvation Army at Sittingbourne, can be seen standing against the windlass and Mr Wade, manager of the coal and corn store in the background, stands on the quay. The lady and her young son lived in a nearby farmhouse — Mr Kennett recalls that the lad spoke such broad Essex that the Kentish crews had a job to understand him! In the picture, it can be seen that the barge's anchor is bowed — this was to avoid getting it entangled in the weed in Beaumont Cut, the narrow canal which craft had to negotiate before reaching the quay. It is interesting to note that the quay is built from the stones of an old London Bridge. The store (demolished about 1965) displayed a stone bearing the following inscription —

"This Building and Quay was Erected by the Governors of Guys Hospital 1832 —

P. Harrison Esq., Treasurer.

The stone used in the Quay formed part of London Bridge built about 1176".

This stone is now built into a small plinth on the quay.

Amongst his memories of Walton Backwaters, Mr Kennett recalls the little sprittie *Gleaner*, built specially to work up Beaumont Cut, and the two well-known hufflers[1] Jack Scone (who huffled to Kirby) and David Lay (who took you to Landermere or Beaumont Quay). Landermere, Mr Kennett maintained, acquired its name from the smugglers, who used to say 'Land 'em 'ere'! David Lay lived in one of the row of picturesque cottages which still stands today near Landermere Quay. Another of these terraced cottages bears a plaque saying that it was the early home of Sir William Gull, physician to Queen Victoria. Unfortunately, the glorious image is left slightly tattered by a recent book (serialised in an evening newspaper) which names Sir William Gull as the man responsible for the terrible 'Jack the Ripper' crimes in 1888. Sir William is buried in the churchyard at nearby Thorpe-le-Soken.

Mr Kennett left his berth as mate of the *Mercy* to take charge of the handy little stumpy *Garfield* and later the *Monitor*. It was not long, however, before he found himself back in his old barge *Mercy*, but this time as skipper. Here it is worthwhile recounting how the craft came by her name. Mr G.H. Dean, a director of the firm of Smeed Dean and Co. Ltd., was one day driving his horse and dogcart along Crown Quay Lane, Sittingbourne, towards his works. He passed under the railway bridge just as a train went over the top and his horse, being a high-spirited creature, bolted. Swerving suddenly, it drew one wheel of the dogcart into the ditch, which bounded the lane, and threw Mr Dean into the adjoining meadow. Beyond a severe shaking he was unhurt and, in remembrance of his escape, decided to call the new barge which was being built *Mercy*, because it was a mercy he was not killed. Mr Dean had a belief that a providence watched over him at all times, guarding him from danger. This providence does not seem to have guarded the barge as well, because Mr Kennett lost her in a gale down Swin in 1918. I reproduce now Skipper Kennett's story of the disaster. Apart from inserting punctuation and making one or two minor word changes, I have left the report as Skipper Kennett set it down. For a person who left school in 1889 at the age of ten, I think the grammar is astonishingly good.

Report of foundering of sailing barge Mercy, *May 23rd, 1918, 5.30 a.m., near Swin Middle light vessel in 3 fathoms. Whitaker Beacon bearing N.E., Swin Middle light vessel E.S.E.*

We had loaded ballast on Colne Point on Tuesday 21st (about 95 tons) for Lloyd's Paper Mill, Sittingbourne, and had anchored off to wait for sunrise (not allowed to move before — war time regulations). It was almost low tide when we weighed anchor in the early morning of the 22nd. The wind was south, moderate, and we set all sail, including staysail. By the time we got to the Bar Buoy the tide was at flood. We reached down to the Wallet Spitway on the starboard tack and had to make several boards to get to the Swin Spitway. We now had the tide in our favour and made a good stretch up on the port tack, but had to make two boards to windward on the starboard tack in the S.W. Swin. We expected to fetch up on the port tack after passing the Maplin Lighthouse, but unfortunately the wind westered and freshened and we had to lower the staysail and stow it over the stem blocks and still beat to windward to the West Mouse Buoy. I then decided to stretch over to the East Swale on the starboard tack as it was nearing high tide (about three-quarters of an hour to go) and a nasty sea was making. We were making good way and were just below the West Oaze Buoy when we had the very bad misfortune to break the connecting bar of our port leeboard. I thought the leeboard would hole our side and was forced to go about on to the port tack so as to secure it more easily. I had a difficult job getting the runner fast to the preventer[2]. We hove the fan as far as it would come and I managed to get the head above the solid chock, get a snorter[3] through the link hole and make fast to the connecting shackle. The mate, being a good lad, sailed the barge.

The wind was still freshening and it was high tide, so there was no alternative than to anchor off the edge of the Maplin Sand. We kept our board over to the edge of the sand, then came round on to the starboard tack and were preparing to take sail off and anchor when we were struck by a terrific gust of wind. The vang hook straightened out and the sprit went out with such force that the leech rope of the mainsail broke at the main brail bridle. The sail went in two halves from bridle to throat and the topsail blew to ribbons. The tide was now ebbing and we ran off with the foresail and anchored just below the Blacktail Spit, paying out thirty fathoms of cable (our best). The wind had now increased to gale force and a very heavy sea was running. I paid out another ten fathoms of cable to ease the strain on the windlass, which left us with twenty fathoms (not first class condition).

We then made everything as secure as possible and spent the rest of the ebb, the next flood and two hours of the next ebb on the cabin top. During this time we were pounded with heavy seas except when we were swung straight up on the flood tide; the seas then ran much longer and we rode them fairly well. Our anxiety was our boat, which was continually running up by either quarter, although on a very long painter. After high water we fortunately swung down quickly. At about two hours ebb (which would be about 1 a.m.) on Thursday 23rd, the wind and sea moderated slightly and we were more hopeful of riding it out. Watching for an opportunity, we unbarred the cabin hatchway to get down and get a fire alight for a cup of tea, having had nothing for fourteen hours.

We got down alright, wedged the cabin hatch from below and got the fire going. Then we had our worst calamity — we were struck by a tremendous sea which actually came down the cabin funnel and put the fire out. The next minute we were broadside to the sea — our cable had parted. With much difficulty we managed to get on deck and secure the cabin hatch, but what a plight we were in — drifting down broadside in the dark, no lights anywhere (except the Mouse), no anchor bent to let go, our only sail was foresail and mizzen, and the boom defence from Barrow to Maplin lay below us. The sea was breaking broadside over us and watching for a chance, I finally got for'ard and released the down-haul from the foresail. I got to the fore halyard and was almost washed over-board to leeward but just managed to get hold of the lee rigging. Making another attempt, I got to the halyard and was able to set a bit of the foresail and so get head down before the wind and sea. We gathered way and were lucky to get to the nor'ard of the boom defence. I then managed to completely set foresail and mizzen. I fortunately saw the Maplin Lighthouse and after hauling up under the shelter of the sand in Abraham's Bosom, I lowered the foresail and stowed the mizzen. I managed to get our second anchor secured to the broken chain — luckily, a shackle was already in the ring of the anchor. This took considerable time and we drifted away from a sheltered anchorage, so I had to get to windward again. By the time I got into three fathoms we were abreast of the Swin Middle light vessel, with the Foulness Sand to windward. We anchored there paying out about sixteen fathoms of our remaining cable. Fortunately it held and we were riding head to wind and sea with a sheltering sand to windward (wind-west). We had deepened in the water considerably and, on unbarring the cabin hatch and going down into the cabin, we found 1ft. 6ins. of water in the well. We got two pumps going and pumped till we were exhausted, but could not make any impression — in fact, it was gaining, so after all our effort we were sinking.

Sidwell, 1939. She was named after Sidwell Drake, a member of the family of brickmakers for whom she was built. Bill Kennett loved her more than anything else in the world.

(Photo by George Osbon)

It was now coming daylight and, seeing the Government Patrol (steam trawler) about half a mile off, we called his assistance by distress signals. We then pulled our boat up, baled her out, got a breaker of water in her and packed up a few provisions and the ship's papers, cargo book, etc. We had a good new boat (fourteen feet long, six feet beam) with three good oars and a sail and spars already lashed in her. She had a long painter which I intended to pass round the mizzen mast, wait for water over the sands, and sail for Brightlingsea. We then saw that the Patrol Vessel had got steam up and was getting her cable in, which took some time (we were told later that they had been riding on eighty fathoms). She then came within a barge's length astern of us; we got in our boat and went aboard of her. The Captain asked me what suggestions I had for saving the barge, so I asked for four of his men to man the pumps, to which he agreed. I left my mate on the trawler and went back on board the barge with the four men, but she was pitching and lunging heavily so we got back in the boat and returned to the trawler. The barge sank shortly after — about 5.30 a.m. The trawler's captain and crew were a fine lot of fellows — they loaned us dry clothes and gave us a much-needed meal with plenty of fresh fish. They dried our clothes and later took us to Brightlingsea. I left my boat in charge of the Customs Authorities, giving to them and an Admiralty official a report of the position of the wreck, then trained home via Colchester, Liverpool Street and London Bridge.

It didn't take long for Smeed Dean to find Captain Kennett and his mate another barge — this time they took the *Spurgeon* (which many years later became the Thames Barge Sailing Club's first Club barge). It was just a week after the foundering when they ran down by the same spot with a cargo of flints for Foulness Landing. *Mercy*'s spars were sticking forlornly out of the water and the Patrol Vessel was still close by. Her crew were amazed when they saw who was sailing *Spurgeon* — they wanted to know why Skipper Kennett and his mate were not having a month's convalescence!

Captain Kennett always maintained that *Mercy* could easily have been salvaged, but she was blown up about a year after the sinking.

After taking two or three more of Smeed Dean's craft, Captain Kennett eventually settled in the *Sidwell* and stayed with her for nearly thirty years. She was actually owned by H. Andrews, an official of the firm, and when Smeed Dean sold out in the early 1930s, *Sidwell* went to the newly-formed partnership of Ellis and Andrews. During the Second World War, *Sidwell* was engaged on ammunition work in the Medway and her mate was (of all people) Mr Chambers, under whose command Mr Kennett had served when he started his 'apprenticeship' in the *Derby*. Eventually, Captain Kennett and the *Sidwell* retired together in 1946.

Today, *Sidwell* lies derelict at Temple Marsh, Strood, after many years' service as a housebarge and a Sea Scouts' Headquarters. Captain Kennett also had a long, useful and well-earned retirement before making his last passage (to the Better Land) in 1969 at the age of 90. He now rests in Sittingbourne Cemetery.

1 The full story of the hufflers in Walton Backwaters is told in 'Down Tops'l' by Hervey Benham.
2 Preventer — a length of chain which barges carry, rigged between the top of the leeboard and one of the deadeye shackles. This prevents the leeboard from being lost if, as in the case of the *Mercy*, the connecting bar breaks.
3 Snorter — a specially designed length of chain, with a small link at one end which will go through the large link at the other end.

CHAPTER 15

DEATH OF THE 'SAM'

By Ron Dickenson

I have given considerable thought as to the date that this event took place and I think it must have been the winter of 1925-26 or 1926-27 (it happened so long ago and I have only memories to go on).

Anyhow, I was mate of the *Sam* under skipper Frank 'Pilot' Farrington at the time. I have a copy of F.G. Willmott's 'Cement, Mud & Muddies' in which *Sam* is listed as having carried 85 tons of cement. That must have been a good few years before I joined her — she was in my time a leaky old thing only suitable for cargoes which could not be damaged by sea water.

We loaded flints at Hollow Shore Wharf in Oare Stray, Faversham, one winter day. The tide went about 4 p.m., so it was coming dark as we blew out of the creek under half mains'l and fores'l with a strong wind S.W. and dropped anchor outside the creek. There was another barge to windward of us but it was by then too dark to see who she was. The sky looked as if someone had kicked it. The wind increased by the hour until at about 8 p.m. 'Pilot' decided to lower the gear down because she began to 'drag her anchor'. We were 'making' a drop of water as usual and so tried the pumps every hour or so.

At about low water (10-11 p.m.) the strength of the wind increased to a howl. We were 'jawing' about nothing in particular, then 'Pilot' said, "listen", and jumped for the cabin ladder. A faint call came again as we scrambled on deck and there, almost alongside, but blowing to leeward as though they had no oars, were two men in a boat, rowing like mad-men. As they swept past, one of them threw the painter. 'Pilot' caught it and we held them and pulled them alongside. The men were 'all in'. When we had secured their boat 'Pilot' asked them below. They were the crew of the barge to windward. They had been ashore, being Faversham men, and had tried to get back aboard and were caught by the sudden increase in the strength of the gale.

There is no doubt at all that their lives were saved by the fact that *Sam* was to leeward of them and that we heard their call. Had it not been so they would have been swept out to sea where no rowing boat could have survived that night.

We sat for an hour or two and the wind eased a bit so they decided to 'have a go at it'. With the flood tide to help them, they got back to their barge, while we watched in case they had to come back. Again my memory fails at the name of the other barge, but I think it must have been one of the Cremer's.

Frank and I slept on the lockers as best we could for what was left of the night and at day break, the wind having eased considerably, we hove the gear up and just below low water we ran out of the Swale. We were bound for Small Gains ('Oyster') Creek, Canvey Island. As the next flood tide came the wind freshened to strong again and (being S.W.) it caused a nasty sea as well. We were

Barge *Murston* at McKenzie's Wharf, 1907. In the background is the Dolphin Cement Works. (Photo by G. Goldsack)

making a long and a short tack up past the cliffs of north Sheppey and kept as near inshore as was prudent. We were on the pump now almost continuously and the water came up brown, showing that it was in the hold, washing about among the flints.

Sam was making heavy going of it now, getting low in the water and 'dabbing down' to leeward in the heavy puffs. 'Pilot' said "We'll take her in to Queenbro' " and, as an afterthought, "if she'll make it". I knew what he meant as we opened the harbour but in she went. We pumped until we were almost on our knees and poor old *Sam* had hardly enough way to come round. Frank put her ashore above Queenbro' Causeway and we finally got the water under control. Then the skipper went ashore to report and I kept 'jogging' on the pumps.

We were told to "bring her home", which we did. Her freight was transferred into the 'stumpy' *Vincent* and we were told to move into the *Murston*, then having a re-fit on the yard.

I am informed that *Sam* did some time in the mud work after this; I suppose a regular 'Blackwall Caulk'[1] would help to keep her afloat!

As far as I am concerned, she died that day at Queenborough. She certainly never left the Swale again, as a working barge.

Compilers' Note:
One reference book indicates that the ailing *Sam* was eventually sold (for £8.10s!), but 'Pilot' used to say that her hull was finally used as a basis for a new wharf when Smeed Dean extended their Marsh Berth about 1930. Certainly two other Smeed Dean barges — *Florence* and *Monitor* — were used in the initial construction of the Marsh Berth about 1918. They were possibly followed by *John Bright*.

Perhaps, a few centuries hence, they will be dug up and marvelled at!

1   Blackwall Caulk — mud forced naturally into a leaky vessel's seams, so keeping her relatively watertight.

CHAPTER 16

WHY DIDN'T YOU LOSE HER, SKIPPER?

By George Faint

After many years as a mate and skipper in Smeed Dean's fleet, I was eventually forced to look for a living elsewhere when the Milton Creek work folded in the mid-1930s. I took charge of one or two Colchester barges and then had a couple of seasons as master of the yawl *Thalassa*, owned by Alan Baker, who was director of the East Anglia Flour Mill at Colchester.

At the beginning of the war in 1939 I returned to barging because my job as a yacht master had gone. I took over Goldsmith's *Cetus*, a big wooden 200-ton coasting barge. She had only fairly recently come off the yard, where she had been given an extensive refit after being towed back from Germany. The visit to Germany was entirely unexpected, as about a year previously *Cetus* and other Goldsmith's barges were off Yarmouth when it came on to blow and, as they could not be got into harbour, the crews were taken off and the barges left at anchor. The gale proved so severe that they disappeared and were thought to have foundered, but they were eventually found off the German coast, damaged, but still afloat.

I did a few uneventful freights in *Cetus* and then at the end of November took a cargo of oilcake to Yarmouth. There was no return freight available so I got ready to sail light for London. Being war time there were Naval Regulations in force, one of which prohibited sailing at night. This meant that to make a long passage it was necessary to sail at first light in the morning, which I did. My mate was a young lad with little experience, so I did not bother with the bowsprit and left it stowed up, as there was a fair wind. By dark we had reached Orfordness and anchored there for the night.

On going below I noticed that the glass had fallen a lot and was still falling rapidly. During the evening the wind started to freshen, the sea got up and the barge began to roll heavily. About midnight it was blowing hard straight on shore and I was not very happy. I decided, in spite of the sailing regulations, to get under way and stand off shore for a few miles, until I could get a slant into Harwich. With great difficulty the mate and I got the sails on her, broke the anchor out and got sailing.

No sooner had *Cetus* got clear of the land than the wind wester'd and flew round to the N.W. The sea began to build up more than ever and, with the barge heeling over so much, the boat filled and went, taking the davits and quarter boards with it. The wind being now in the N.W. I regretted leaving Orfordness, especially as we were now being blown out into the North Sea with prospects of another trip to Germany. I decided to come round and head back for the shore, which (after a struggle) I managed to do. Soon, the topsail blew clean out of the bolt-ropes and shortly afterwards the mainsail tore in half, when the leach rope parted halfway up. If this was not enough, the mizzen (mast and all) then went over the side and had to be cut clear.

By this time I was not sure of my position, as the tremendous wind was accompanied by torrential rain, thunder and lightning, and through it all I could not make out the dimmed Orfordness Lighthouse. *Cetus* now was in a bad way, taking it green and making water. I stood in towards the land under the foresail, the only sail left, until I reckoned we were near enough and then let the anchor go. The anchor roared out, taking all its 60 fathoms of chain, setting the windlass on fire in the process! Luckily it held.

It was now 2.30 a.m. and after lashing the sprit down I went below, where I found 2 feet of water in the hold. The pumps would not work, as the violent motion had stirred up the muck in the bilges, which choked them when we tried to pump out. I decided that the only thing to do was to send for assistance, so I fired off distress flares. There was no answer to my signals and we hung on (the only thing we could do) and eventually the Aldeburgh Lifeboat arrived at 9 o'clock in the morning. The distress signals had been sighted by the Clacton Coastguards who reported them to Aldeburgh.

The lifeboat wanted to take us off and I was sorely tempted, as I had had enough and felt like pulling the plug out and leaving her. However, the weather had fined down and I thought "I've never lost a craft yet and I am damned if I'm going to start with this one". I asked for assistance into Harwich, but the lifeboat refused and went away.

About an hour later the lifeboat returned and agreed to tow *Cetus* into Harwich and after some argument they also agreed to put a man aboard to help get the anchor in. They had wanted me to slip it, but I was not having it as the anchor and chain were new and I wanted to use them. *Cetus* was brought into Harwich and the lifeboat left me anchored in the Stour. The cost of this assistance was later settled for £400.

Not having a boat, I had to hail a launch to get ashore, where I reported to the agent and bought some food. We spent the next two days in clearing up and getting pumped out after clearing the blockages. As I had received no orders from the agent and the weather had settled in fine with a northerly wind, I decided to sail for Grays. I set what sails I could, jury-rigged a jib for a topsail and set up the bowsprit. *Cetus* made quite a smart passage considering her condition (she looked a wreck) and we fetched up at Grays.

I was chaffed about trips to Germany and when I reported to the office, where they were thinking of the costs of another extensive refit to *Cetus*, I was asked "Why didn't you lose her, Skipper?"

Compilers' Note:
We are pleased to record that George's great work was not in vain — *Cetus* is still afloat today (1979) as a housebarge at Otterham Quay, Rainham, Kent.

CHAPTER 17

A SAILORMAN BORN

By Ron Dickenson

How can a man suddenly become something he has never been before; and I mean just step into it as though he has been doing it all his life?

It was late Summer 1945 and I was a Sgt. Royal Engineers I.W.T. stationed at Marchwood Depot (opposite Southampton Dock). The R.E's had converted an L.C.T. (Landing Craft, Tanks) into a sucker-dredger and passed it on to I.W.T. for delivery to Richborough in order to dredge the gut there. I had already been detailed to form a crew and go with the vessel under a Captain R.E., IWT, (who shall be nameless). Late on the evening before departure he sent for me and I found a very worried man waiting. He had received his Admiralty instruction for navigating a 'swept channel' from Southampton to Richborough, a channel swept by the Navy and (hopefully) clear of mines.

Captain X showed me his instruction and admitted that as far as chart navigation was concerned, he did not know his ankle from his elbow. I helped him get rid of his bottle and sent him to bed with a warm glow of confidence.

Next day we got the odd bits and pieces aboard and cast off about 4 p.m. We cruised down to an Admiralty buoy off Ryde. At daybreak a Navy cutter came alongside with instructions for us to get on our journey. Our route proved to be one quite familiar to me — Nab Tower, Looe Channel, Beachy Head, Dungeness then in to Hythe and hugging the coast round the Foreland. My crew were good watermen, but that is all they were; and I found that once they had nothing to steer by, they started 'writing their name' in the wake. After trying one or two I became resigned to a 'do it yourself' situation.

Then a lad came on to the bridge with a mug of tea and some chow.[1] I knew that the chap had never worked afloat before the war — he had already told me; but as he stood behind me, obviously interested, I said "That black line is called the 'Lubber Line' and represents the ship's head; do you think you could keep it where it is?" He said he would like to try. Watching the wake, I finished my meal in comfort and then said "You told me that you had never worked afloat". He again assured me that he had not, but continued to steer a faultless course till I relieved him. That lad and I had the wheel between us for the rest of the voyage. We anchored in Pegwell Bay that night and went up the river next morning. Oh, I did not give the lad's name did I? It was Sapper Eric Farrington-House, grandson of old 'Webby'[2] and brother to Harold and Perce. He was born in the (now famous[3]) old house in Eastbourne Street, Sittingbourne.

A surprising lad was young 'Ike'; he made a good mug of tea, too! He grew up and began his working life when sailing barges were becoming things of the past and that is probably the reason that he did not follow family tradition.

Ron Dickenson views the broken down cabin top and deck of the *Gladstone* in Milton Creek, 1979.
(Photo by Alan Cordell)

1   Chow — Army term for food
2   'Webby' Farrington was one of Sittingbourne's best-known bargemen at the end of the 19th century. He regularly took cement from the Murston works to France in his barge *Monday* — and is reputed to have done his fair share of smuggling. He had seven sons, all of whom became bargemen.
3   This house, no. 36 Eastbourne Street, hit the newspaper headlines in the early 1970s. The local council wanted to demolish all the houses in this and other nearby streets. But owner-occupier Harold Farrington-House steadfastly refused to move out. Eventually no. 36 was the only building left standing — changed from a terraced house to a detached mansion in 5 acres of grounds! Old Harold died in 1976, happy no doubt that he had beaten the system.

CHAPTER 18

MEMORIES

By Harold 'Jack' Butcher

The Great Gale of 1914

Some literature which I read recently revived one of my memories of the local barge *Yieldsted*.

I saw her go out of Sheerness harbour as I was coming in on the afternoon of 29th December 1914. This was just before the great gale that took 8 lives and caused the loss of 5 Sittingbourne barges, *Eliza, Ada Mary, Frank* and *Ruth* (of Smeed Deans) and one of Burley's, a stumpy sailed by old Joe Dean and his mate. I cannot recall her name, but she sank in Sheerness Harbour, just outside Queenborough Spit. The *Yieldsted* was near Chapman Head and of course had to bring up at dusk that night, as did all the others, as no navigation was allowed during the war below Chapman Head after dark; that is how they came to be caught in that westerly gale. The *Yieldsted* was saved that night by her skipper, old Jack Hambrook ('Scranny Jack' as he was known) — a superhuman effort standing on her forecastle hatch tending her chain as she dragged down in between the other craft.

I was in the *Mary Ann* at the time, coke loaded, and rode it out under the West Shore in Sheerness; when daylight broke next morning there was a picture of sunken barges up the Medway. Saltpan Reach claimed several Rochester craft, also some Government-owned craft. The *Ruth* drove into Southend Pier. Skipper Teddy Wyles and his mate were drowned — their bodies were picked up at West Mersea; the *Frank*'s crew, Lou Pilcher and his mate, were both found in the cabin when she was raised, like Ginger Houghting and his mate in the *Ada Mary*.

One of Smeed Dean's little stumpy barges, the *Eliza* (Bert Aspin skipper) dragged down the river until she hit the sands at Shoebury and sank. He and his mate sat up on the throat of the mainsail (as it was above the water after she sank) until taken off by the Southend lifeboat at dawn. Old Bert (dead now since 1948) always said his life was saved by the cat, which was tucked inside his coat as they climbed up to the throat of the sail, because it kept him warm until they were taken off. His cottage, which was only a few yards from where I live now, was always full of cats. I once counted seven when I went to visit him.

A few more remarks about Sheerness Harbour during the 1914-18 war — nearly all freight was carried by sailing barge and lighter from the Medway towns — ammunition, dockyard stores, the lot. A huge boom was laid across Sheerness Harbour, with a gateway that could be closed when the occasion arose. All sailing barges, no matter where from, were towed in by two tugs that were chartered for the job, the *Kite* and *Kestrel* from Messrs Knight of Chatham. Long strings of barges, sometimes a dozen, were towed in under the West Shore and their Customs Clearance examined by the Naval Authority. Even a barge with house refuse had to have Customs Clearance (a Transire we used to call it) when coming out of London, but when leaving Sheerness you had to make your own way out of the gate and if you had no wind it meant rowing with sweeps, as the tide on the ebb would be inclined to set you in towards the Dockyard.

That is just what all those barges were doing that had come away from Milton Creek after having had their Christmas at home on that December afternoon. It was an absolutely flat calm, the water like glass, and those chaps were struggling to get out of Sheerness on the last of the ebb, out to the Grain Spit to catch the young flood up the Swatch. We in the *Mary Ann* never had enough wind to get across the harbour into Queenborough. That calm was broken by a whisper of wind about 6 p.m., then a gust which seemed to come from nowhere and before 9 o'clock it was blowing a whole gale, which developed into a force 10 or even more as the night wore on. Those barges, brick loaded, nearly level with the water, must have had a hell of a time when the flood tide made up river against the gale. It was surprising that more were not lost.

Channel Barging during the First World War

The five or six years preceding the 1914 War were, in my opinion, the peak years of the sailing barge. The decline set in after the war mainly because of the development of the lorry as a means of transport; that might not have come about as soon as it did but for the war. This may be only my opinion but I think that the barge might not have disappeared as quickly as it did had it not been for the development of the internal combustion engine which the war hastened.

The Thames and Medway barges did not suffer as much as the coastal craft when war burst on the world in August 1914. The restrictions on night sailing and entering of ports between the Humber and Falmouth, where a spritsail barge could nearly always be seen, had its effect at once and for a period it was a very lean time for the big craft. As ships poured into London the Government used ketches and sailing barges for storage. The big craft were loaded with all sorts of cargo and during the early days of 1915-16 they lay about buoys in tiers of half a dozen. One barge, the *Dominion*, had a cargo in her for months, so did the *May* and *Emma* (not the Ipswich and Maldon ones — these two splendid sailing barges belonged to Weymouth and very conspicuous they were in any company, being kept up more like yachts than barges).

It was a common sight to see ships in their war-time dazzle paint lying at anchor in the Thames, especially in Long Reach, St Clements, Northfleet Hope and Gravesend Reach, with some of the big coasters alongside taking in cargo overside to ease the pressure on the docks. Then, as the number of men in the army in France grew, the problem of supplying both the British and Anzac troops began to be felt so the sailing barge was brought in. The coasters lying at buoys up and down the Thames were unloaded, overhauled and given a Board of Trade survey. They were fitted out with a set of international code signal flags, a medicine chest, extra life saving gear and then started trading to the French ports of Calais and Boulogne. There were only a few at first; but when it came to 1917 it was a common sight to see dozens lying in the Downs off Deal waiting to be given clearance by the Dover Patrol to cross the Channel.

They were all there, barges that in my boyhood days at Brightlingsea had seemed like ships; the nine big ironpots of E.J. & W. Goldsmith of Grays, whose names all except one ended in 'ic', all of 250 tons; the wooden craft of the same firm, *Cetus, Perseus, Dominion, Cecilia, Dreadnought, Ardwina* as well as the other class of 180 tons; the black sailed barges of W.R. Cunis of Woolwich (*Glenmore, Normanhurst*); the '*Glens*'[1] built by Little of Rochester; Samuel West's Gravesend fleet; all took part. Then as the work developed the barges of the Thames were brought in; barges that had not been below the Nore in their life were to be seen lying alongside the quays of Calais and Boulogne. The colours of nearly every firm that owned barges were represented. Goldsmith changed their tricolour flag to blue, white and blue and, for obvious reasons, the *Germanic* became the *Lais* and the *Teutonic* became the *Maymon*. Cargoes were mostly fuel, coke, coal, pitch and cases of 'don't know' materials listed on the manifest as H.M. Stores. The traffic began to go both ways in 1917-18. Ridham Dock had been taken over by the Government and barges were unloading there with shell cases, ammunition boxes and all sorts of materials for the factories to repair and re-use.

I came across the *Sara* of racing fame in Calais, for at that time she had a special job as a coaling depot to the I.W.T. tugs which were used to take lighters of stores up the canals as close to the lines as possible. The tugs used to come alongside to refuel and when the *Sara* was empty, she would sail to England to load coal and return to her berth. Some outstanding characters came out in this work. Captain Tommy Harker, skipper of the *Oxygen*, was one; he made some fantastic passages, in appalling weather, running coal from Hull to the French ports. Poor Tommy, he bought his own barge after the war, the *Challenge*. She was cut in two in mid-Channel with a cargo of Guernsey stone — Tommy, together with his wife, mate and third hand were all lost.

Smeed Dean had only two barges on this work at the time, the *Persevere* and the *S.D.*, 'Sudden Death' was the latter's nickname. She used to be ketch-rigged but in 1914 she was re-rigged as a spritsail barge. She was a huge barge of about 280 tons. Her master when war broke out, Captain George Winn from the *Persevere*, did not like the ketch rig so it was agreed to re-rig her. Mr George Andrews, who was manager of Smeed Dean at that time, once told another skipper that one day he would have the unhappy task of going round to George Winn's wife to tell her she was a widow. Fortunately he was wrong and George, who did not know when it was time to lie windbound, left the *S.D.* and went into another big coaster — the *Leonard Piper*. This barge must claim to have been as near the enemy lines as any barge for having loaded a cargo for St Valéry -Sur-Somme, she was met by a tug at the mouth of the River Somme and towed to her destination. The poor old *S.D.* was caught by a German submarine while bound for Le Havre or Cherbourg with a man named Dorrell as master. The crew were ordered into the boat and time bombs were placed in the forecastle and the cabin, putting an end to the *S.D.* The submarine towed the boat for some time towards the English coast before casting them adrift and I believe that they were picked up off Beachy Head. For years their boat lay at Elmley Ferry; it was a really big boat and the 'Muddies' used it to ferry themselves over to the island opposite where the mud hole was. It was from here that every day, as the tide suited, one or two barges loaded mud for the cement works at Murston.

We now come to early 1918 when the ports of Calais and Boulogne were threatened by the German push after their forces, released now from the Eastern Front following the Peace Treaty with Russia, were concentrated on the west.

Last respects for Monty.   (Courtesy of Harold Butcher)

The barge trade, which had now swelled into hundreds of craft, was pushed further west down the French Coast to Le Tréport, Dieppe and Fécamp. This brings us to the origin of the photograph which was taken near Dieppe. At that time the docks were crowded with spritties of all sizes, even the little *Phoenix* of Faversham with sixty tons of coke. The crews occupied their time (while waiting to unload) maintaining the gear and barges with whatever materials they had — painting, scraping, oiling spars, etc. On this particular day in late June or early July 1918 my schoolboy chum, who at the time was mate on the *Gothic*, decided to scrape down the top-mast and give it a coat of raw linseed oil. The drill as I knew it was to unshackle the top-sail halyard from the head-stick, shackle on your boatswain's chair, lash a bucket to the chair with your scrapers, sandpaper and file to sharpen the scrapers, and then get a third hand to heave you to the top of the topmast. You then swung yourself round the mast as you scraped each fleet, as we called it, sandpapered down each section as it was finished and then got yourself heaved up to the top again to paint the topmast with raw linseed oil.

How Monty fell is a mystery. He may have slipped out of the boatswain's chair; an easy mishap which I have done more than once, or he might have fallen while shackling the chair on to the halyards. I do not know, it was over 60 years ago, but fall he did and when he hit the deck there was no hope for Monty Patrick of Brightlingsea. At that time I was mate on the *Sportsman* and we arrived in Dieppe the day after the funeral. I soon heard the story as the crews were aware that we came from Brightlingsea and knew Monty. It was decided to bury him in the little hillside churchyard, the Mariners Church I think it is called. The Port Authorities were very good, the Harbour Master of Dieppe appears in the right hand corner of the photograph, next to the under-taker. A Military Chaplain officiated at the service; in fact it was a Service funeral as such. Captain Francis (his skipper on the *Gothic*) stands at the head of the

147

grave holding a wreath. Next to him on his left is the little third hand and on his right is the skipper of the *British Oak* who had taken care of the funeral arrangements.

Monty was an orphan who lived with an aunt at Brightlingsea and had planned to marry on his return to England. The photographs were sold for whatever one cared to give for the benefit of the little girl back home. We played, fought and started work together and when I found the photograph and looked at those young men around the grave, many of whom I knew, I wondered how many, if any, are alive today.

An Unpleasant Voyage

The sailing barge *Hydrogen* (240 tons burden) left Milton Creek on Friday, 9th April 1922 on one of her usual trips to Goole. Loaded with 200 tons of cement, she carried as crew Captain A. Coward, myself (mate) and a lad who had never been to sea before, by the name of Miles, who during this particular voyage had the most remarkable escape from being knocked bodily overboard I have ever witnessed.

After getting clear of the Creek (which dries out completely at low water) and passing through Kingsferry Bridge (the only bridge between the Isle of Sheppey and the mainland) we proceeded down the Swale into the Medway and out of Sheerness into the Thames Estuary, having had a fine fair wind to assist us in this narrow and difficult piece of water. The wind was S.W. and we squared off to run down the Swin Channel. We passed between the Buxey and Gunfleet sands and into the Wallet. Evening saw us off Harwich, wind failing and tide coming up against us, so we anchored in Harwich rolling grounds (and they were well named, too!) Owing to contrary winds, calms, etc., we did not get a start from there until Wednesday, the 14th, very early in the morning, and the wind now having come away from the S.W. again. Running away along the Suffolk and Norfolk coasts all day Wednesday, wind freshening and glass falling with some wet in the wind at times, we passed through Yarmouth Roads and Cockle Channel and hauled the wind on our course to the Humber. Now we began to feel the weight of the still increasing puffs, having hauled the wind seven to eight points.

Our freeboard was 12 inches from water-line to deck and so we had got ropes, spare spars, etc., lashed on the main and fore hatchways. There were no watches; if the hand (there were only two who could steer at the time) away from the wheel could find time from the numerous jobs to rest his legs or eat, well that was his watch below. Our third hand was not much use, being new both to the sea and ships, and he was also sea-sick, but he kept about just the same. Tea-time on the 14th and we were scudding down by Cromer with the head of the topsail down and two reefs in the mizzen. The glass was still falling rapidly and the wind still increased, giving promise of a very 'nice' night, as rain was falling wholesale now. As we approached Cromer we felt the force of wind and sea still more and, as the old ship had got her lee rail buried, things were not exactly comfy about the decks; but we shipped no heavy water (the wind was off-shore) and we hauled up to hug the coast as close as possible. It became clear to us that we were in for a very dirty night — it was blowing a gale of wind southerly. To leave the Norfolk coast, where we had a bit of shelter, and run across the Wash (or Deeps as we call it) to the Humber, meant running to a dead lee shore, and the Humber wants a bit of finding on a dark night — thick with rain, with a gale of wind to make matters worse — so we decided after a bit to heave to, as best we could, and dodge backwards and forwards under the Norfolk shore.

I would here like to point out the relative disadvantages of a sprit-rigged barge and a ketch-rigged vessel. When it comes to heaving to, a ketch-rigged vessel can reef down 1, 2, 3 or 4 reefs and even if she has only got a third of her mainsail or less set, it can be set smart, so it will not fight. But not so the spritsail barge — as soon as you start the sheet and begin to gather in the brails, the mainsail hangs in baggy folds and, if you reduce sail by about a third (when you are head to wind or close to the wind), it fights and flogs something awful and all one can do is to get all brails (viz. peaks, main, middles and lowers) as tight as possible. I would also point out the advantage; in fine weather one man can set the whole suit of a spritsail barge's sails in a very short time.

Well, as the night came on, it gave all it promised and a bit more and for 17 hours we were off and on, fo'c'sle battened down, head and shoulders into every sea we met. During the early hours of the 15th our first tripper, who had been helping to work the heavy lee-boards up and down as we wended from one tack to the other, thought he would find a spot out of the wind and rain a bit. So unbeknown to either the captain or myself he went forward, got on the fore hatch, and stood under the lee of the foresail (which was bowlined to windward). We were hove-to on the starboard tack at the time and wanting to come round on the other tack; I went forward to let go the foresail bowline and jib sheet to get a bit of way to come round.

Thinking this lad was aft on the quarter, I let go the foresail and in the darkness could see nothing; but I heard a frightened yell and I knew in an instant that the foresail had hit him as it went to leeward. I never expected to see him again, but on rushing to leeward was surprised to see him picking himself up out of the lee scuppers on the port bow. Our rail was less than two feet in height, the fore hatch coamings were almost as high and the foresail swept the hatch; so I have never been able to understand why he was not bowled clean over the side that night.

Next day the weather moderated somewhat and we decided to lay a course for the Humber. But the wind had by this time gone further westerly, so we could make only slow progress. However, after another day and a night of wallowing about in the Wash, we passed in by Spurn Head early on the Friday morning and sailed up to Hull on the flood tide (which was running at a tremendous rate, being heavy spring tides). Wind failed us as we approached Hull and so we had not much control. When we got abreast the Railway Pier we let go the anchor and I have seen windlasses smoke when the chain is running over the wooden barrel; but this morning ours burst into flames, an occurrence I have only seen once. It was the usual custom for sailing vessels to tow up to Goole as the tide is so heavy in the Ouse that a tug was very useful to round you head down and hold you against the flood while you sheered into the lock. However, this was a Good Friday and there was not going to be any more towing until after the Easter Holidays.

After the captain came back from reporting and imparted this news, we decided we would try and sail to Goole on the next flood, as we did not relish four or five days at anchor in Hull Roads when we might be tied up in dock. We knew the Humber fairly well, as we always sailed empty to Keadby (up the other river, the Trent) but we had never sailed up loaded. We started off again on the young flood and all went well. We kept clear of the many sandbanks as we had got a commanding breeze, and we passed out of the Humber into the Ouse. The flood tide was now running at a tremendous rate and it would soon be dark, so we decided to anchor in a hole that we knew of where the vessel would lay afloat on the low water, so as to have the daylight tide next morning for getting into Goole docks. The Humber sloops and keels had to do this sort of thing, so we were not doing anything unusual.

We rounded head down upon tide and slacked off sheets and wangs to ease the anchor all we could while we brought her up; but as soon as the anchor touched bottom she tore out 30 fathoms of chain before the cable broke at the 30 fathoms' shackle. We had still got our sails set (trying to ease her down to the anchor) when this happened, so we sheered over to a sandy patch and checked her on this until we got the second anchor ready and brought her up. On the first of the ebb tide we dropped down to where we judged our lost anchor and chain was lying, brought up again, and turned in to our bunks to wait for low water, when we were going to sweep for our lost anchor.

Now we had had no sleep since leaving Harwich (at 1 a.m. on Wednesday morning) and it was now Friday night, so we were very tired and were soon asleep. After what seemed about five minutes (but was in reality an hour or two) we woke to find our ship right down by the stern, and on scrambling on deck found she had taken a sheer to the bank and now lay all adry to the mainmast. Her head was right up on the stone wall and her stern down in the river, with the water on deck aft. We were making no water and so could do nothing until the flood came again. So as it was getting daylight we decided to go off and try and sweep our lost anchor on the slack low tide.

Our lucky star was shining for a little while just then, for we swept the anchor with a wire buoyed at one end with 4 lifebuoys and the other end on the boat. The wire swept under the fluke and we brought the end of the wire to the buoys, rove the end through the eye of the wire and gradually worked it down, so that it was jambed tight over the fluke, buoyed it, and went back to the barge as the tidal bore was making up the river below us; a bore in the Ouse and Trent is quite common on heavy spring tides.

We had to wait only a few minutes before the bore reached us and whipped us round while her head was still on the wall. The tide flowed very quickly and as we lifted off the river wall, we went for'ard to heave up our anchor and, upon looking down the fo'c'sle hatch, were surprised to see the water coming over the floor. We shipped the pumps; the water did not gain at all, and it was not long before we were able to gain on it.

Well, we hove up and sheered over to the opposite side of the river, as it was flat and sandy mud on that side. At first we were going to pick our buoys up and get our lost anchor on board, but we thought we had better get on the shoal to ascertain the damage if we could. Soon we had the pumps going again, and the three of us pumped her dry; we thought she had only strained on the steep wall, which wooden craft often do and take up again after they have floated. We laid on that flat all the ebb, and could see no more damage outside. We thought all was well as we had cleared her of water before she grounded, but that Saturday night, when the flood made again, the water flowed into her fo'c'sle as fast as it flowed outside. We stayed at the pumps until the water put the lamp out for'ard

Hydrogen in all her splendour about 1910, when she was nearly new.
(Courtesy of Harold Coward)

and sheered her in on the shoal as far as she would go, nipping down aft to grab what we could before she dropped. When the water was nearly up to the fore part of the main hatch, she went down head-first; we ripped the tarpaulins, so as to sink her where she was in shoal water, in case on the last lap she sheered off into the channel.

Soon she was under; it was 9 p.m. on Saturday night and blowing a gale of wind again with rain. We in our small boat had to find our way to the edge of the marshes, miles from anywhere — prospects of a very pleasant Easter now! How she was raised and repaired would make too long a tale, but what had actually happened was a large piece of limestone rock had stuck in her bottom and stopped there while we pumped her dry, but on grounding on the opposite shoal it had been forced up. We found it inside (lying feet away from the hole) after she was raised and that piece of stone now adorns my garden path as a memento of my most unpleasant voyage.

1 *'Glens'* — a fleet of several barges all of which had a name beginning with *Glen* eg *Glenbury*, *Glenavon* etc.

CHAPTER 19

FINAL DAYS OF THE BARGE ERA

By Leslie Williams

My memories of barging spanned about 20 years, from the time I went away with Grandad on his *Unique* (at the age of eight) until I was forced off the water at 28. I saw the decline of the sailing barge in a few short years. When I was small, Grandad would take me away whenever he could. He had stopped my parents taking me to Canada — I do not know how and he did not talk about it; I believe I was to follow later, which I never did. As Grandad was a widower, I had to stay with relatives to go to school — not that I had an unhappy childhood, far from it; I was always fond of reading and I think I could have got on if I had help, but that was unheard of in those days.

My cousins and I were always round the Creek, which at that time was full of barges. Unlike today, none of it was fenced off and you were allowed to walk anywhere. Vandalism was unknown; of course somebody was about day and night because barges were moving every tide, for they always loaded away and never loaded in the same berth as the one in which they had been unloaded. Grandad was nearly always corn-loaded for Filmer's Dock. This was not very long after World War I and things were still tight for food. Grandad usually had something for us to take home, one time it was haricot beans and on others it was tinned meat, for he was always in the London dock work. I remember when I was away with him once, he came back aboard with a jar of preserved ginger, which was pretty expensive then; and I have known him to have a coal locker full of 1lb tins of corned beef. He used to keep all his tea packets so that if he got hold of any tea (I know he got hold of about 10lb one time!) he could say he had bought it. I do not think that one would have worked! I remember years after, when I was married and on the dole, I brought some apples home for a pie. Grandad was living with us, and he got on to me for stealing. I said "What about all the stuff you had aboard the *Unique*?" He said "It was given me". I said "Well, the farmer gave me the apples!"

Once when we lay in the London docks in a fog, the mate and myself went out in the boat and filled it with timber, which at that time was not supposed to be touched. The police were pretty hot, but once it was aboard and out of sight, they did not bother. Even ashes could not be thrown over the side, but of course, we just used to wait for night time.

As I have said before, I left school at 13, for I was supposed to have T.B. If so, it cured itself, for I never had any treatment. I doubt if it was true and anyway, it got me away with Grandad. Sail seemed romantic to me at that time, which I suppose it was, and there were plenty of ketches and schooners about. However, I realise now that the crews were on starvation wages, even an A.B. on a P. & O. Liner only got £2 a week.

In Sea Reach, with a fair wind, the sailing ships would drop the tug and set all plain sail; but it was a poor barge that could not run away from them. I saw the last British barque, the *Garthpool*, loading in Long Reach. We sailed close to her and what struck me was the amount of wire rope in her rigging. I think this was her last freight before she was sold.

In the docks, I would look at the ships from all over the world and wish that Grandad would give me the money to go out east and back; for I had read all the stories of the Pacific in the 1800s. At that time I had the illusion that Grandad was wealthy — I believe all grandchildren think that.

We lay at Woolwich one time and somebody shouted out — when we went on deck we found a body under our quarter. It was enough for me — I dived down the cabin again. I believe the mate held it till the police came along. I did not want any tea and it was some time before it was out of my mind. There never seems anybody more dead than when drowned. I heard that when Tich Wood-fine picked one up, he went through the pockets! I can believe it and although I think I could now, I certainly could not when I was younger.

Although it seems longer, I only had a year with Grandad. When he was doing well, he gave me 4/- a week pocket money, but he bought me other things during the week. If I went ashore with the mate, Grandad paid for the cinema and fish and chips. We always had plenty to eat aboard. If we lay at North Woolwich, Grandad would put the engineer of the Billingsgate boat ashore on their way up. I believe he lived handy, and we always got a box of fresh haddock in return. At other places, such as Leigh, Grandad would come aboard with a bucket of fish. Fresh fish is worth eating — no comparison with frozen.

North Woolwich, where we often used to lie, was not a big place ashore. The ships in the dock loomed over the few streets that were there. There was a big pub, the 'California', and a few shops. One (a shoemaker's) was run by a Dutch-man and he had lived there about 50 years. Grandad showed me a knife he had bought off him (for 1/-) worn down to about half, but it still cut. He would make you a pair of leather sea boots for £5, but only the old skippers bought them after rubber boots came along.

There was a fish and chip shop which fried in dripping; if we brought up there about 9 p.m., one of us would go ashore to get some for supper.

At Starvation Buoy (at Woolwich), where the Essexmen lay, one barge was permanently on the collar, as we say, i.e. head to the buoy. The owner lived aboard, I believe he had an interest in another barge and probably lent money to the neighbouring barges, for they lay for weeks at a time. When this chap wanted water, he would take two boats ashore at Sankey's Wharf, fill one up with water, tow it back and bail it out into his tanks; this would last him a month.

Over on the other shore, under the Arsenal, there were a few barges which did a bit of Government work at times; the *Edward VII* was one. They rarely seemed to do any freights — most of the time the crews were on the dole (signs of the times). If they only had three freights a year the crews still stopped in the barges; they were good bargemen too. Still there was no other work. I think that if you went for a job and offered to work for nothing, you would not get a start at that time!

Things were not too bad in a large firm, but the big money had finished with the end of the First War. When I started work, freight rates had already been cut

'An affinity with the water'! The Milton-built *Bedford* deep-loaded, with water sloshing along her lee deck.
(Courtesy of F.G. Willmott)

three times and work went by seasons. Timber in the Surrey Docks was summer work (after the ice had cleared in Scandinavia). Corn was a winter job mostly.

To my mind, working with a barge that was almost always loaded gave you an affinity with the water that you do not get with a light barge. It is easier to step straight into a boat (for one reason) rather than to clamber up and down the side. In retrospect, everything seemed so easy, considering the places we went to with no mechanical means. Of course, we must have worked hard at times (and got into trouble!) but human nature forgets all those things.

I am pleased that I was able to see some of the barging scene before the rot set in. It was a good school to build character and self-reliance, which few jobs today seem to do.

CHAPTER 20

BARGEMAN'S YARNS

By Leslie Williams

Grandad used to say that he had a mate with him once, Len Cherrison, I believe. They had been fog-bound for a week and were running short of food (they had some potatoes, but not much else). The mate wanted some chips, but had no fat to fry them, so he fried them in linseed oil — thinking no doubt, that as it was a vegetable oil it would be alright. But also, linseed oil boiled three times makes varnish. Anyway, he ate them and then complained of a sore throat; and I do not wonder — it might have killed him!

When 'Pilot' Farrington was single he was always broke; he would often leave Murston with nothing in his pocket. If he was given money for the tow above bridges he would spend it. Anyway, they lay somewhere up the Thames and he and his mate 'Tich' Woodfine were broke and hungry. 'Pilot' had his gun away and there were plenty of swans about, so one evening 'Tich' enticed a swan close with a piece of bread and 'Pilot' shot its head off! They pulled the body aboard and plucked it — then there was the question of what to do with the feathers. They finished up with burning them and I wonder they were not caught, for there is nothing worse for making a smell. The police were pretty hot at that time, but they got away with it and dropped down to Battersea to load. 'Pilot' would earn enough to grub himself home by helping barges down through the bridges. I believe we were allowed 6 shillings.

One of our mates, when lying in the docks, stole a box of apples. His skipper was ashore. The mate had been spotted and a policeman was down the cabin almost as soon as he was, but the policeman made the mistake of not arresting him straight away. Instead he locked him down the cabin. While the policeman went to get help, the mate ate all the apples and broke the box up and put it on the fire. When the police came back they had no evidence and could do nothing!

When 'Snowy' Hubbard was mate of the *Vavasour* they lay on one voyage in Ipswich Dock. 'Snowy' liked his beer and was also as strong as an ox. Going back aboard one night he passed a Dutch boat with a coil of new rope on the hatches, so he nipped aboard, picked it up and started to take it to his barge. He ran into a policeman round the first corner and as soon as 'Snowy' saw him he said, "Just the bloke I wanted to see — I found this coil of rope on the quay and was just taking it to the Police Station". They carried it down to the station and took 'Snowy's' name and his barge's name. The next day the Dutch skipper came round and gave 'Snowy' a pound for finding his lost rope!

'Snowy' was really caught once. He was on the dole and went down Lloyd's foundry and stole some brass. He did not get it home as he was stopped round near the Creek by a couple of detectives. But he almost got away with it, as it took four policeman to lift it into their van. Although the Magistrate said at first it was impossible for one man to have carried it, I am afraid he got three months.

Once when he was watching some men putting up telegraph poles he asked the foreman if he could have one for firewood. The foreman, joking, said "Yes if you can carry one"; but he did not know 'Snowy', who just put one on his shoulder and walked off with it!

Once when 'Pilot' Farrington was mate on the *Youngarth* during the first War, they came out of the docks bound for Yarmouth. On the way they called into Queenboro' and the skipper went home for the night. Bob Tyler was the third hand and both 'Pilot' and he were broke. After tea they raided the skipper's copper jar for enough for a pint and went ashore. As luck would have it they met a mate from a Goldsmith barge who owed 'Pilot' a pound, which he paid. This meant they had plenty of money for beer and they drank it all up. The next morning the skipper came off and they got under way. 'Pilot' and Bob were still drunk and hardly knew what they were doing. Outside the harbour it was fine, so they were told to bring the big jib up and set it, which they did — upside down! 'Pilot' said later he wondered why the sheets were too short! There were many bawleys about and they called out to Tom Pearce, "Haw, Haw, Haw, what have you got there? — a lot of farmers, skipper?" It was then 'Pilot' realised something was wrong and said, "I'd better set the jib again". Tom Pearce said, "Let it be and show what a lot of fools I've got on board!" — but he let him set it properly later on. 'Pilot' said later they must have drunk about 40 pints the night before!

In the later part of my sailing days under Smeeds, all we were doing was running light for dust and there was always a crowd of barges at Camberwell. All the skippers would go home until their barges were loaded. Bill Duparque was the foreman of the vestry, a good old boy really, he would always pay 2/- to borrow your boat. The men were allowed to pick all the tots[1] out of the dust and it made their money up. I believe they were paid £3 a week at the time. The *Toots* was an unrigged barge of Cunis's that lay in the slop berth and loaded the contents of road drains, which took about a week to load. One weekend Frank Taylor, mate of the *Grace* wrote this gem:—

> Baa Baa Duparque
> Have you any tots
> Jam jars and bottles
> And old iron pots.
>
> You give two bob for trimming[2]
> Except for a certain few
> And they get half a doller
> For . . . . crawling round you.

It was one fine day at the vestry
We had just gone under the shoots
When along came Baa Baa Duparque
And stepped aboard the *Toots.*

He set the pumps a working
The fumes came thick and strong
We all cried out with horror
But he smelt nothing wrong.

Baa Baa Duparque
Have you any tots
Jam jars and bottles
And old iron pots.

We stuck this on the door of his office on Monday and then hid round the corner to see what he would do. He read it alright and then tore it down, saying "Bloody lot of fools"; he could have been right!

I was talking to an old boy at Whitstable a year or two ago; he knew Grandad and a lot more of the old skippers. He said that when he was working afloat as a boy he had a row with the skipper and left him in the Tyne. He got a passage in another barge as far as Yarmouth where he had to go ashore and live rough until he picked up a barge which took him to Harwich. After a day or two he picked up yet another barge, which was going to London; and then had to find one going to Whitstable. It took him a fortnight to get home from the Tyne. He said he was 13 at the time and had been third hand in the *Edward*. I said "Good Lord! She was only about 90 tons," and he said "That's right." When I saw her last I would have thought twice about going round the Island[3] in her. She was stumpy rigged and used to run chalk from Long Reach to the Surrey Canal.

One of the queerest things I saw was when I was mate of the *Buckland*. We had orders to load sugar for Filmers — we were to load in the Surrey Docks. We locked in and were making our way to our ship, when we passed a ship loaded with timber which had a 10 foot list to starboard. She suddenly came upright and then settled down with a similar list to port. The strange part of it was that she was not being unloaded. All the crew came rushing on deck, including the mate, who was just shaving. He brought his razor with him, which would have been the only thing we would have saved if she had gone right over. This was in calm water — it would not have been so unusual at sea.

When 'Taffy' Taylor was mate with Ebby Shrubsall in the *Aberdeen* (about 1923) they had orders to load out of a ship in Northfleet Hope. It was dark when they went alongside and there was nobody to take their ropes, so Taffy got up on deck somehow and went to make a rope fast. As he stood up, he felt two hands on his shoulders; when he turned round he saw a bear standing over him! He says he does not know how he got back aboard the barge! At daylight when the crew turned out, they laughed — the bear was as tame as a kitten. Of course, they would not have let a dangerous animal run loose.

When Grandfather's Uncle Jack was mate of a collier, the crew were having a drink in a pub at Sheerness. The landlady had a dog in the bar and she was saying that all he did was sleep and he would not eat his food, even though he was only a young dog. Uncle Jack said "We are coming back here, let us take him away with us and see if the sea air does him any good". The landlady agreed and they took the dog and left Sheerness that tide.

At first the dog did not show any interest, but after a couple of days he began to come round for food at meal times — which he did not get! They gave him some water, but not much else. They took about ten days to get back to Sheerness. When they took the dog ashore he went bolting up the road into the pub, made a fuss of his mistress and then ate everything put in front of him. The woman was awfully pleased to see him so full of life and the crew were on free beer all that trip. They told her it was the sea air that did it — it was, the dog did not get much else!

I am too fond of animals myself to care much for this yarn.

Once when I had the *Bessie* I loaded 80 tons of glass at Queenborough. It was the middle of the summer and my brother-in-law came away for a trip with us. We left Queenborough with a light wind easterly and rounded the Spit at low water. About four hours later we were in Gravesend Reach — as we came up to Tilbury we saw two ships in collision. One was a Dutch vessel with a deck load of garden produce, of which most went over the side. The river was full of tomatoes, melons and cucumbers! I sent the boat away with all our buckets, which were soon filled; I would not have bothered if it had not been flood tide and therefore salt water! We washed the stuff in fresh water and had fried tomatoes all that trip!

When I was young it was common to see people drunk and asleep on the footpath, which reminds me of two yarns.

My Grandad, when a young man, had gone ashore to work on the building of the first Lloyd's mill at Sittingbourne. He was living in Shakespeare Road at the time and had been working all night. His wife had bought some herrings the day before and as Grandad was coming home from work he was thinking how nice they would be for breakfast. He was passing through St Michael's churchyard when a drunk put his head out of an open grave that had been dug and said "What's the time?" Grandad, who was startled, said later that he felt all his hair stand up straight! But he recovered enough to say, "I don't know what the time is, but it is Resurrection Morning and you're the first one out!"

When I was mate on the *Buckland*, I was just over 14 and we were lying at Bell Wharf, Leigh. Skipper Bill Barnard went to the pub and I walked to Southend to the cinema, as there were none in Leigh at the time. I saw 'The Monkey's Paw', by W.W. Jacobs. I do not know if readers are familiar with the story, but the mother calls the only son, who has been killed, back from his grave. I can still see now the wreaths being pushed to one side and a hand coming up! I did not see a soul as I walked back along the shore and, although I was not exactly scared, I was not very comfortable either! Good job I did not hear anything strange!

The *Aberdeen*   (Photo by R. Stimson Jnr.)

Grandfather's relationship with the directors of his firm, Wills and Packham, was generally very good. However, there were occasional spots-of-bother, for example at the time of the bargemen's strike of 1890. He was on strike with the rest and spent some of his time helping in a local soup kitchen. When the dispute finished he went down to his barge, lying near Crown Quay, and was quietly pottering around when Mr Packham appeared. A few cross words were exchanged about Grandad's participation in the strike — and he was sacked on the spot. So he packed his belongings in a bag, left the barge, and made his way to Crown Quay Lane, where he met none other than Mr Wills — who re-engaged him immediately, adding, *"I'll* tell you when to go!"

1 Tots — bones, old iron and other items of modest saleable value; hunting for them was delightfully known as 'totting'.
2 Trimming — trimming cargo.
3 The Island — Isle of Sheppey.

CHAPTER 21

MORE BARGEMAN'S YARNS

By Alan Cordell

One dark evening, a barge was bound for a wharf at Battersea. When she arrived, the wind and tide conditions were such that it was not possible to shoot her alongside immediately, so the crew anchored her some 20 yards out in the stream. They were just preparing to run the dolly wire ashore in the boat, so they could warp her in, when they were spotted by the night-watchman. He decided to give her a hail:—

"What barge is that?"
"Evening".
"No, I said 'What barge is it'?"
"Evening".
Pause.
"Oo's she belong to?"
"Knight".
Pause.
"You'd better clear off — I haven't got time to mess about".
(Story by courtesy of the late Bill Kennett).

The traditional bargeman's method of coaxing wind out of a flat calm by tossing coins over the side has been described in an earlier chapter. On that occasion, the *Yieldsted* was dismasted when her 'reckless' skipper, Jim Fenteman, threw two pennies over the side — and conjured up a gale!

A similar incident befell the *Martin Luther* and the *Buckland* when they were in company with each other off the Chapman Head Lighthouse in Sea Reach of the River Thames, about 1927. They had drifted up on the flood tide (with no wind) all the way from Grain Spit and, eventually, the fed-up teenaged mate of the *Buckland* — 'Jock' Kennett — decided it was time to bribe the Wind Gods. His contribution was a halfpenny, which was duly committed, with a 'plop', to the deep.

Nothing happened for some time and at length skipper 'Bony' Rossiter went below to get his tea, leaving 'Jock' in charge on deck. 'Bony' was just tucking-in nicely when he suddenly heard the wind piping up and felt the barge heel over. Springing up the cabin ladder, he arrived on deck just in time to see the *Martin Luther*'s sprit come down in what was now a force 8 wind from the south-west.

'Bony' and 'Jock' quickly dropped the topsail and brailed the mainsail up to the sprit. Then they put the *Buckland* about and ran before the wind back down Sea Reach. Half-an-hour later the storm blew itself out and they were becalmed again. But by this time they were below Southend pier (ie. more or less where they had started from); and as the ebb tide was coming away, they had to anchor. So a whole tide's work had been lost.

Meanwhile, the out-of-control *Martin Luther* had blown ashore, fortunately without any further damage occurring. But, understandably, 'Jock' Kennett never told the *Martin Luther*'s crew what caused the whirlwind!

(Story by courtesy of Albert 'Bony' Rossiter and 'Jock' Kennett).

Back in the 1930s there was a time when some Sittingbourne barges were bought up by a big London firm. Their skippers were given instructions to report to their new management the next time they were in London.

So one skipper, who had a reputation for his quick wit, duly turned up and was introduced to his new boss Mr Bridges. The following exchange took place:—

Mr Bridges: "Hello, skipper, I hear from your last firm that you're a bit of a flyer". (Meaning a fly-by-night).

Skipper: "No, I'm the captain of a barge, not an aeroplane".

Mr Bridges: "Well, don't try to cross me".

Skipper: "Don't worry, I never try to cross bridges — with a barge, it's easier to go underneath 'em".

Mr Bridges: "This report says you wet your cargo on your last trip. How did that happen?"

Skipper: (resting a hand on Mr Bridges' shoulder) "Well chum, if you think about it carefully, I believe you'll come to the same conclusion as I have — it was caused by water!"

(Story by courtesy of Albert 'Bony' Rossiter).

One night during the bargemen's strike of the 1920s, skippers A, B and C were on picket duty at the wharves owned by Smeed Dean below Murston Quay.

A little after midnight they heard footsteps approaching and, in the moonlight, could just perceive skipper D coming down the path with a kitbag over his shoulder. He was obviously intending to take his barge away on the 1 a.m. tide.

"Where are you going?" barked A, as he sprang out from behind a stack of bricks, armed with a heavy iron bar.

"Home" said skipper D as he about-turned and hurried off back towards Murston.

A little later the trio made out the silhouette of barge E sailing away from Murston Quay. As she approached them, A and B started to discuss ways and means of stopping her.

"Don't worry", remarked C, "When she gets outside the Creek, she'll meet the west tide and have to anchor".

"So what?" said B. "She'll be able to get under way again in a couple of hours".

"No she won't", C said, "I knew she was due to sail tonight, so I threw her windlass handles in the mud. They won't be able to get their anchor up again!"

Next morning, as the jaunty trio prepared to go off duty, they spied barge E's crew rowing up the creek in their boat.

"What are you doing up here?" shouted C.

"We've come back to get a couple of windlass handles", came the bad-tempered reply, "Somebody's pinched ours".

(Story by courtesy of Albert 'Bony' Rossiter).

Wood's *Excelsior* was reputed to have been the handiest barge working to Milton Creek. The prevailing wind is such that it was 'right on the nose' for barges sailing up Ballast Wall Reach, so much tiring and painful work with the setting booms was required to help them to windward along the narrow channel. But *Excelsior* used to accomplish the task fairly easily; she was inherently handy and her apple bows and raking stem enabled her to 'bounce' off the mud at the end of each tack and fill off on the new tack without much bother.

Around 1927, *Excelsior*'s career came to an end when she was laid to rest at Wood's Wharf (see Chapter 22). Later, her ailing hull was sold for one shilling and sixpence to a man who wanted to dismantle her for the wood and ironwork. Shortly after starting work, he was rummaging around in her cabin, and found: one shilling and sixpence! So she was a good bargain.

The presence of a rat, or rats, on the barges was a common and, to most bargemen, nauseating problem. Vast numbers of these creatures lived in the brickfields, dining splendidly on the tasty rotting food in the large mounds of London refuse ('rough-stuff') which was brought down by barge and used, after sorting and sifting, as fuel for the brick-burning.

Stories are occasionally told of the right royal battles which were fought between rival teams of rats — especially Burley's v. Smeed Dean's, because they lived near each other! The survivors would then sometimes board a barge loading for London, in search of more food, and finish up getting off at the other end to do battle with the Big City rats!

Hedley Farrington and Taffy Taylor had their own lethal ways of dealing with rats, as described in other chapters. But when kindly old Bill Kennett had one living aboard the *Sidwell* he took a much more benevolent view. Asked one day by fellow-bargeman George Faint how the rat was getting on, Bill said "Oh — he's alright; the only time he annoys me is when he comes in my bunk whilst I'm asleep and nibbles my toenails!"

CHAPTER 22

A MILTON CREEK RAMBLE

By Alan Cordell

On 20th July 1975, a party of ten Society for Spritsail Barge Research members set off at 11.00 a.m. for a Milton Creek walk. The first stop was at the historic Crown Quay, where barges were built back in the 1860s and 70s, and which later became a Wills and Packham lay-by/timber wharf. Next, the party viewed the same company's barge yard with the sheds, where *Olive May*, *Olive Mary* (later called *Arcades*), *Raybel* and *Phoenician* were built, still standing. A further short walk took the party to the site of White's yard where many famous racers, including *Vectis, Clara, Victoria, Dreadnought* and *Beatrice Maud* were built; unfortunately the place is no longer recognisable as a barge yard — it is an aggregates depot instead.

Continuing down the east side of the Creek, the desolate and overgrown Adelaide Dock was visited. Fifty or more years ago there would have been a dozen or so barges loading or discharging in the Dock. Just to the north of the Dock is the site of Alf Wood's old barge yard. A few charred timbers in the mud were all that remained of *Wye, Monkwood, Nashenden, Loualf, Alliance* (large), *Alliance* (small), *Phoenix, Donald A* (ex *The Portage*) and *Jessie*. The ruined remains of Smeed Dean's barge yard and cement works were seen next, with the sunken hulk of *Thomas and Frances* still lying at the cement works quay. Another half-mile of walking brought the party to the derelict hulk of the *Gladstone* (built 1867), which had been lying in that spot for fifty years. After a picnic lunch, some of the party boarded the hulk and strolled round her deck, no doubt imagining '. . . the wheel's kick and the wind's song . . . and a grey dawn breaking' (to quote from Masefield).

To get to the west bank the party re-traced their steps to Sittingbourne, making a quick visit to the Dolphin Sailing Barge Museum on the way. Here, the *Fanny Maria* (ex *Frances*) was just floors and frames while the hulls of the *Veronica*[1], *Saxon* and *Nellie Parker* had obviously seen better days, although it was not permissible to go on board to check their condition. A bit of footslogging was saved on the west bank by travelling on the Sittingbourne and Kemsley Light Railway to get from Sittingbourne to Kemsley near the mouth of the Creek. This little narrow-gauge railway is a delight to the historian, archaeologist and steam enthusiast alike. It operated from the turn of the century to about 1969 carrying pulp and other paper-making materials, plus shift workers, for the Lloyd's (now Bowater's) papermills at Kemsley and Sittingbourne. Now it is run by a group of amateur enthusiasts and, hauled by picturesque little tank engines, gives pleasure to hundreds of weekend trippers.

From Kemsley Down station, the party walked south along the sea wall to 'The Mud Hole', where in days gone by Burley's barges used to load mud for the

Remains of the *Dauntless* near the Creek Head about 1960. One of her skippers, 'Ike' Mannering, named his house in Staplehurst Road after her. On the right is the bow of *New Hope*. These barges have now disappeared. (Photo by Alan Cordell)

The last barge to survive in the group just outside Adelaide Dock was the *Jessie*, pictured here in 1960. She was burnt for her ironwork and bottom planking some three years later.
(Photo by Alan Cordell)

The bows of the *Baltic* protruding from the saltings of 'The Mud Hole' below Churchfield Wharf, 1961. She looks similar today. This barge was the subject of a thrilling rescue in November 1907 when she belonged to Keep, of London. Bound for Newlyn (Cornwall) with cement, she missed the harbour entrance in bad weather and grounded on the rocks of Mousehole (St Clement's) Island. For technical reasons the local lifeboat could not be launched and *Baltic*'s crew were rescued just before she sank by six local men who went out in their crabber. They were all awarded cash and a '*Baltic* medal' for their bravery.

The *Baltic*'s mate turned disaster into success by marrying the Mousehole Harbour Master's daughter and settling in the village.

Baltic herself was raised and repaired, and sold soon afterwards to C. Burley. Her sailing career eventually ended about 1935 when she was damaged in collision with a steamer.

(Photo by Alan Cordell)

Dolphin Cement Works a mile up the Creek. There was evidence of three old barges here, two almost completely buried. The third, which has been identified as the *Baltic*, had her bows and most of her foredeck showing. A little further on the party saw a huge graveyard of barges (mostly Burley's) just above Churchfield Wharf. *Carisbrooke Castle, Genesta, Ninety-nine, Scud, May, Ventura, Lizzie, Pomona, W.B., Edith, Our Boys, Vectis, Sydney* and *Sportsman* all finished up here. *Pomona* was still fairly complete, but the rest were just remains of floors and frames.

Walking further, the party came to the wharf once owned by Woods, another Sittingbourne brickmaking firm. The bones of four of their barges were still visible here: *Strathmore, Emma and Sarah, Harmony* and *Excelsior. Harmony* is interesting — she went on the blocks for repairs around 1920, but never came off again; although very silted up, those blocks are still visible beneath her today.[2]

On the final stage of the walk, the party saw the sites of Eastwood's Wharf, now used for unloading sand from motor barges, Gransden's Wharf and Shrubsall's (later Eastwood's) barge yard. In the period 1868-1901, Robert Mark Shrubsall built some fast racing craft here (like *Pastime* and *Gazelle*), and from 1902 to

Two of the many derelict barges near Churchfield Wharf, 1950. The *Our Boys* is seen from the deck of the *W.B.* Murston Quay is in the background. (Photo by Alan Cordell)

All the Churchfield Wharf hulks except the *Pomona* were burnt for their ironwork in 1952 — she was sunk deeply in a soft patch of mud and would not burn. This photo was taken in 1960 and she looks fairly similar today. (Photo by Alan Cordell)

Thomas and Frances at Murston Cement Works Quay, 1957. She has since gone to pieces a lot, as seen in the 1979 view in chapter five.   (Photo by Alan Cordell)

1908, Eastwoods built some of their 'county' class barges (eg. *Northampton, Bedford, Hereford* and *Wiltshire*) at this yard.

It is interesting to note that yesterday's rubbish is today's gold and the Sunday pot-hunters were out in force digging over the old brickfield rubbish heaps in search of jars, bottles and pots. Even some of the S.S.B.R. party succumbed to the temptation and went home distinctly heavier than they came!

1   *Veronica* was the most successful and famous racing champion of all time. At the end of her useful life she was given to Dolphin Yard. Some people thought she could be preserved as a static exhibit ashore — but sadly, she was cannibalised for parts and then dumped in a Medway Creek.

2   See Compilers' Note

Compilers' Note:
The barge hulks on Wood's Wharf were partially broken-up for their wood and ironwork around 1932. This resulted in the loss of all direct identifying features, i.e. names, ports of registry, scrolls, official numbers and registered tonnages. Hence identification has been attempted by making enquiries amongst several folk who knew the hulks before the breaking operations.

Most are agreed that the two barges at the NE end of the Wharf are *Emma and Sarah* (nearest the Creek) and *Strathmore* (nearest the seawall). The latter is in fact the bow half only — she was cut in halves in the Thames by a steamship about 1923 and the stern section was not brought back.

There are two likely ideas about the pair of hulks at the SW end. One of our 'identification team', an old bargeman (now dead, unfortunately), gave the opinion that the barge on the

Gladstone at Murston; she has deteriorated slightly since this photo was taken in 1956. She was abandoned at this spot about 1928 after being damaged in collision.

(Photo by Alan Cordell)

blocks is *Harmony* and the adjacent one stern-on to her is *Excelsior*. However, two local residents who played on these craft as children, say that *Columbus* is on the blocks, *Harmony* is the one stern-on nearby, and *Excelsior* was broken up to the NE of the wharf and its other hulks. If so, she must have been broken up completely, because there is no trace of a barge in this position now (although her floors and bottom could be under the mud, which has built up considerably over the years).

Another theory which was published some 15 years ago agrees on 3 of the 4 names, but gives locations which do not match the known evidence.

In the above article, the 'old bargeman' theory was used because it represented the best state of knowledge at that time (1975). The 'local residents' theory came later.

CHAPTER 23

A GLIMMER OF HOPE

By Alan Cordell

Leslie Williams' depressing but accurate appraisal of Milton Creek (1970s — fashion) in the earlier chapters prompts me to start this chapter with a big moan. (Did I hear someone say 'Typical'?!)

During the course of researching this book, I followed up a clue from historian Frank Willmott of Rainham and recently found the grave of Sittingbourne's most successful racing-barge builder, Robert Mark Shrubsall, in the yard of Milton Congregational Church. Robert was very famous in the last quarter of the 19th century and his prolific output of about 70 fast barges included at least 9 racing champions — as named in Chapter 1.

When Robert was laid to rest in 1901 he joined several other barge builders and skippers who were already buried in the same churchyard. No doubt at that time the church was thriving and the grounds well-kept.

But what has happened now? The church is no longer used as such and, with the typical contempt which modern society has for things it should respect, the churchyard is used as an unofficial rubbish tip. So we have the disgraceful situation of Robert Mark Shrubsall, Sittingbourne's most illustrious barge-builder, and several of his distinguished contemporaries resting in a rubbish dump. People of Sittingbourne — you should do something about it.

However, having got that off my chest, let us look at something brighter — conservation.

Undoubtedly the most successful local conservation effort in recent times has been that related to the Sittingbourne and Kemsley Light Railway, which runs alongside the Creek. This little narrow-gauge line was built around the turn of the century[1] and later extended for conveying goods and staff between Ridham Dock and Lloyd's paper mills at Sittingbourne and Kemsley. When Bowaters (the current owners of the mills) decided to go over to road transport — about 1969 — it was fortunate indeed that they allowed a group of amateur enthusiasts to continue operating the Sittingbourne — Kemsley section of the line. Now the charming little trains (drawn by steam tank locomotives) of the Sittingbourne and Kemsley Light Railway give pleasure to thousands of trippers each summer.

Burley's Barge Yard has always figured high in the interest of the marine historian, because the upright timbers in the forge are made from the tillers of old barges — and they still carry their intricate carving to prove it. (The forge would have been built around 1890, when barges were exchanging their tillers for wheel-steering). Also, the forge, sail-loft, repair berths and blocks all nestle together in a fairly compact and tidy manner — by Milton Creek standards, that is! When Burley sold their last motor barge in the mid 1960s, the yard became disused and derelict.

Robert Mark Shrubsall and family's headstone, Milton Congregational Church Yard.
(Photo by Alan Cordell)

An after dark view of the Creek Head through an arch of the light railway viaduct, 1962. Lloyd's Wharf, with lighters alongside, is a blaze of light. (Photo by Alan Cordell)

The light railway in a commercial state, 1966. The loco is the *Alpha*.   (Photo by Alan Cordell)

Around 1969-70, an organisation was set up with the aim of leasing, restoring and opening Burley's Yard as a working 'folk' barge museum. Fortunately, the local firm of Bourncrete (who by this time owned the site) proved very helpful and agreed to a lease at a 'peppercorn' rent — a very public-spirited action in view of the potential development value of the land. So at Whitsun 1970, Councillor Buckey formally opened the new venture, which was called the Dolphin Sailing Barge Museum (after the former Burley's Dolphin Cement Works — which had made Dolphin Brand cement — nearby). The museum people took the opportunity to tell the assembly that Milton Creek was reborn and the future of the yard was bright.

But, in actual fact, it soon became evident that the operational methods at the museum were, to put it mildly, unusual. The less said about this the better, but it came as no surprise to the nautical world when, after a few troubled years, the museum was closed and the site started to revert to its derelict and over-grown state.

However, salvation was just around the corner. In 1978-9 a nucleus of power-ful London-based barge organisations and knowledgable barge owners encouraged and guided the museum officials into reorganising and re-opening the yard. This time (in May 1979), Col. Donald Dean V.C. performed the ceremony. Col. Dean was a very appropriate man to do the job, because of his interesting connection with barges — Smeed Dean's *Donald* was named after him when she was launched in 1898, and after Col. Dean won the V.C. in the First World War, *Donald* was renamed *V.C.* to commemorate the honour. Features of the re-opening ceremony were the sunny weather and the presence of several barges including the fully-rigged, dressed-overall *Victor*.

At the time of writing (June 1979) it is too early to make predictions about the yard's future. But, on the surface at least, it is giving a good impression; important staff changes have been made, both the sail loft and forge contain

Burley's Barge Yard, about 1948. Hulk of the *Fanny Maria* in the foreground; astern of her is the *Scud*, which had finished trading a year or so earlier. On the left is one of Burley's lighters sitting on the repair blocks. Behind the barges are two buildings; the larger is the sail loft, which has now been preserved as part of Dolphin Yard, and the smaller has been demolished. Behind the lighter is the shed where the *Charles Burley* and possibly other sailing barges were built.   (Photo by Arthur Bennett)

Burley's Yard, derelict and overgrown, in 1978, after a few years of operation as the Dolphin Sailing Barge Museum. The large building is the sail loft, the small one is the forge.
(Photo by Alan Cordell)

The re-opening of Dolphin Yard in 1979, by Col. Donald Dean V.C. Some powerful London barge organisations, together with the original founder Tony Ellis, helped rescue it for a second time.   (Photo by Alan Cordell)

high-quality exhibition material and the barges *Revival* and *Oak* are being re-rigged there. If the management and publicity proves to be good and the wasteful blunders of the previous era are avoided, then the Dolphin Sailing Barge Museum (or Dolphin Yard as it is more usually called) might successfully lead the way to an improved Milton Creek.

One project which has made very steady progress in recent years is the Court Hall Museum in Milton High Street. This very attractive old building dates from 1450 and has served at various times as a court hall, a prison and a school. At some point in history it was joined on both sides to rows of terraced cottages which in 1958 became due for demolition, and obviously the Court Hall (which was empty and disused) was threatened as well. But fortunately some interested local citizens contributed enough money to ensure that it was saved and restored and it opened under local council guidance as a museum in the early 1960s. About 1970, the responsibility for running the museum passed to the Sitting-bourne and Swale Archaeological Research Group, who have made really good progress with it. Most of the town's history is represented — in particular the museum has a fine model of a papermaking machine. Milton Creek and its barges are fully covered, and included in this book are photographs of the museum's fine pair of paintings showing the Creek in 1866.

Bearing in mind the obnoxious odour which often emanates from Milton Creek and pervades the town, it is heartening to hear a rumour that a group may be set up to conserve the Creek. Certainly there is no doubt that if the industrial effluents were cleaned up and the old barge wharves dredged, the Creek would

The *V.C.* (formerly the *Donald)* leaves Milton Creek loaded on her first voyage under her new name, about 1920. A bit of hard 'sore shoulder' work is being done with a setting boom on her starboard bow. She finished her days as the housebarge *Annabelle* at Chelsea, and was broken up about 1976. (Photo by Ferris, courtesy of George Faint)

Four ex-bargemen at the re-opening of Dolphin Yard: left to right — Ron Dickenson, 'Chippy' Wood, Les Williams and George Faint.   (Photo by Alan Cordell)

Milton Court Hall in 1956 when it was joined to cottages on each side. Whilst this photo is historically interesting, the Hall has a better appearance now that it is detached and surrounded by lawns. (Photo by Alan Cordell)

make an ideal marina (with sheltered moorings and a good rail service to London). In fact, the owners of the land bordering the Creek could make a fortune, bearing in mind the demand for yacht moorings these days. Well, look at the effluent-free Conyer Creek nearby!

I have a beautiful picture in my mind of Adelaide Dock, Murston Quay and part of Murston brickfields laid out as a yacht marina. The yachts float in crystal-clear water and the gas works is of course suitably screened, landscaped and camouflaged. The charming Murston Old Church, which has stood near the Creek for 800 years and has been derelict since the middle of the 1870s (when the new church was built half-a-mile away), is embraced in the scheme. Described by Arthur Mee in his book 'Kent' as 'a gem of beauty', the church is restored for use as a yacht-chandlery and the now overgrown churchyard is laid out as a floral garden. Cordell's scheme also restores the 'Brickmaker's Arms' (on the Creek bank) to its original function as a pub. It served the brickmakers, cement mill workers and bargemen for nearly a century; in future it can serve yachtsmen.

And what about that old idea, first aired over half-a-century ago, of a lock at or near the Creek mouth? With water locked in, the Creek could take on a permanently attractive appearance and it could be in use at all states of tide. It would be possible to have regular motor launch trips up the Creek, suitably timed to fit in with the runs of the light railway trains down the Creek (or vice-versa, of course). A word of caution on this idea, however — the permanent high water level would obviously inhibit the use of the Dolphin Yard blocks (if they are

A COUNCILLOR makes a perfectly workable suggestion concerning clearing waste land, but it is shouted down by his fellow councillors.

Instead of bickering among themselves, Sittingbourne councillors should have done a little more research into the project, which would have given the answer to several problems.

One, the council would probably be able to get a government grant for the work.

Two, jobs would have been found for the local unemployed at reasonable wages, not just a dole supplement.

Three, the area would be vastly improved.

Once Milton Creek was famous for its oyster beds and barge building. Now it is a silted up, rubbish encrusted, foul smelling open sewer.

For the council's information, the creek was mentioned in a recent government report as being heavily polluted and in urgent need of attention.

As for a certain councillor's remark of "I don't see how it would help and I don't think anyone would be interested anyway", quite a few people are interested in seeing Sittingbourne and area cleaned up!

Kent is known as the Garden of England. If the present situation is allowed to continue, Milton Creek will become known as the cesspit of that garden.

L. D. HARRIS

Eastwood Road,
Milton.

I WELCOMED Cllr. Morgan's letter published in your paper. At least one member of our council takes note of public opinion and is prepared to offer his help.

Unfortunately, again the text of his letter dealt with minor things. No one disputes that the odd house can make a street seem unkempt, and that a coat of paint works wonders. I sincerely hope that volunteers are found to carry out this admirable restoration work.

Volunteer labour will never be enough to deal with the major cleaning up operation that this town really needs. I strongly suggest that Milton Creek heads Cllr. Morgan's list.

It would take time and money, but Milton Creek can again become a true asset to the town. Dredging and landscaping are the first priorities. Perhaps a river-type lock could keep out silt and allow clear water to flow. The former quay-sides could be converted into a yachting marina. Boat builders should be encouraged to bring their industry to the town. Ships chandlers could supply the ever increasing boating fraternity. Maybe even a decent restaurant and public house could appear on the scene.

A pipe dream? Perhaps, but any improvement would be better than the present polluted mess.

L. D. HARRIS

Eastwood Road,
Milton.

Letters to the 'East Kent Gazette' 1972. Great minds . . . and all that?

A beautiful painting of the picturesque Creek Head in 1866, on display in Milton Court Hall Museum.   (Photo by Alan Cordell, courtesy of Swale Archaeological Research Group)

ever restored for use, that is) and might cause problems for the shipbreakers at Churchfield. But perhaps compromises could be made, so this and the other ideas above might be worth a thought from those who eventually take up the fight for the Creek — be it a new conservation group, the Dolphin Sailing Barge Museum Trust, the Sittingbourne Society, the Sittingbourne Sailing Club, or all four.

In actual fact, the Sittingbourne Sailing Club provides a small glimmer of hope in this direction. They lease an area of land from Blue Circle Industries (formerly A.P.C.M.) at Murston and their sailing dinghies and caravan H.Q. add a touch of cheer to an otherwise dull wilderness. But, of course, dinghies can be hauled out of the water after use and so the pollution is no great problem for them. For the cruising yachtsman, keeping a boat in the Creek is just not 'on' at present. In fact, a small lighterage firm which was based at Murston Quay until recently has moved away because of the foul state of the water.

But let us be optimistic and hope that one day someone will have good reason to write a book about the Beauty of Milton Creek!

1   It was initially just a short railway connecting Lloyd's Sittingbourne paper mill to their wharf near the head of the Creek.

'A gem of beauty' — the surviving chancel of Murston Old Church, 1956. It looks the same today.   (Photo by Alan Cordell)

The square-rigged ship on the memorial stone of John Brunger.

(Photo by Alan Cordell)

CHAPTER 24

AROUND THE TOWN

By Alan Cordell

Without wishing to depress the reader, I have to start this chapter by saying what fascinating places cemeteries and churchyards are! Many of Sittingbourne's nautical stories can still be discovered by looking closely at the local burial grounds; the only trouble is that these stories often turn out to be sad ones.

If you walk along the path leading through St Michael's churchyard, right in the town centre, you will see the stone marking the grave of Captain John Farrington (a well-known local name, this). The stone tells us that John 'lost his life in falling overboard' on 18th September 1845 at the age of 58.

If you then walk for another half-mile to Sittingbourne cemetery, you can find several gravestones which portray a veritable wealth of nautical history. These are in the old (south) end of the cemetery and, taking them in chronological order, we start with the memorial to William Walter Henry Port, who, the stone tells us, was drowned in the Regent's canal on 27th July 1882. Reference to contemporary files of the 'East Kent Gazette' show that William was the young mate of the barge *Myrtle*. He went ashore for the evening, which was a common thing for bargemen to do when their craft were moored in London. Shortly after nightfall he returned, descended into the cabin, spoke briefly to the skipper (who had turned in) and went out again. On the following morning, William was not in his bunk and, sadly, his body was found in the canal later that day. It was concluded that he must have tripped into the canal in the dark.

Next is the stone for 19 year-old James Henry Cleaver. This has a barge carved on it and tells us that poor young James was 'killed by a falling mast' in 1896. My search in the files of the 'East Kent Gazette' revealed that James was mate of the Smeed Dean barge *Russell*. He was severely injured by her falling mast when her forestay broke as the gear was being lowered whilst shooting Kingsferry Bridge (the bridge did not lift for barges until the 1930s). He died from his injuries a day or so later. At the subsequent inquiry, barge owners were reminded that they should take great care to maintain their barges' gear in good condition.

Another stone displays an anchor and records the death of George Ost (Mariner) in 1900. It also adds that an older member of the family, James Ward Ost, was drowned in 1889 and interred at Flushing. Back in the last century one of Smeed Dean's foreman shipwrights was named Ost; but whether he was a member of the same family, I do not know.

For more than half a century, the best-known firm of stonemasons in Sittingbourne was Millen and Chrisfield, later renamed F.J. Millen. (Fred Millen, who followed his father Samuel into the business, was a distinguished Sittingbourne F.C. full-back and captain before the First World War. He was known as the 'Sittingbourne Colt' for his fast and alert style of play. He later became an official

The spritsail barge which marks the resting place of Richard Rayner.   (Photo by Alan Cordell)

of the Club). This firm produced, amongst other things, a nice 'line' in gravestones bearing a full-rigged ship. One of these records the death of a member of the Glandfield family (which was another local 'nautical' name), and one also marks the grave of John Baker Brunger who (it tells us) was drowned on the 7th April and found on the 6th May, 1901, age 25 years. Reference to a contemporary 'East Kent Gazette' again gives us the full story. Young John was the master of Smeed Dean's *Whitehall* and fell overboard whilst sheeting her mainsail home in the Jenkin Swatch. A Sheerness boatman found the body floating off the Cant[1] a month later; it was identified only by rings and pocket contents. At this inquest it was stated that John left a young widow, but fortunately, no children. It is interesting that the widow, Rosina Jane, joined him in 1959, ie. no less than 58 years later. *Whitehall*, by the way, was named after the residence of George Dean (which is now offices for Swale Council in Bell Road).

Moving on in time, we note another stone displaying a carving of a spritsail barge (these must have been made to special order, I should think). It tells us that Richard O. Rayner was drowned in 1906 at the age of 21. According to the 'East Kent Gazette', Richard was mate of the Wills & Packham barge *Samuel Bowly*. Whilst she was under way in the Swale, a rope which Richard was hauling on broke and he fell backwards over the side. At the inquest, the *Samuel Bowly*'s master said he was very surprised that the accident was fatal, because Richard was a strong swimmer. In fact, he had been swimming in the Thames at Twickenham when the barge took a freight there only a few days earlier. A heart-touching final note on this tragedy appeared in the 'East Kent Gazette' exactly one year later — when Richard's mother remembered her son's death via the 'In Memoriam' column.

Moving on a few years again, it is now worth noting the memorial to Frederick Chapman R.N. 'who lost his life on *H.M.S. Vanguard*, 9th July 1917, aged 39'.

My final stone of interest in Sittingbourne cemetery is that recording the death of Jimmy Toms, who is mentioned and pictured in an earlier chapter. As well as being skipper of several local barges (including *Mercy*, *Gore Court* and *Georgiana*), Jimmy was a devout side-drummer in the Salvation Army. In fact, whenever possible, he used to leave the barge and go home to Sittingbourne on a Sunday, so as to do his bit in the band. Jimmy left a directive that the Salvation Army coat-of-arms should be carved on his gravestone and this was done when he died naturally in 1953 (at the age of 83). A Salvation Army friend of mine is aware of no other carving of this type, except on the grave of William Booth — the founder himself.

Moving on to the burial ground of Milton Congregational Church, the memorial stones to the illustrious barge-builder Robert Mark Shrubsall and the prize-winning barge skipper William Wood are mentioned elsewhere in this book. Another stone worth noting here is the one for Stephen Taylor, who was also a very successful barge builder and died in 1869.

Other nearby burial grounds could probably reveal more history; but time and space is limited. So to finish this section, here is a sobering thought: these memorial stones, which seem so fascinating today, in contrast represented much grief and distress when they were put there all those years ago. This is particularly so in the cases of unfortunate accidents at sea.

Well, now let us move on to something more cheerful — the local sports teams; and let us start with the main one — Sittingbourne F.C. For many years this Club was held together by the finance and goodwill provided by the local barge-owners and brickmakers; indeed they rescued it from financial disaster and extinction on several occasions. Mr Jabez Wills (of Wills & Packham) and Messrs G. Goldsack, F. Hyland and H. Andrews (all of Smeed Dean) were active Club officials at various times and it was they who were partly responsible for some of the Club's survival and success stories.

Formed by a group of amateurs in 1886 (from the ashes of the earlier Sittingbourne United F.C.) the Club quickly grew in stature and started to field one or two part-time professionals during and after the 1898-99 season. They competed initially in the Kent League, then, after winning the Kent Senior Cup in 1902 and the Kent League in 1903, they competed in the stronger South-Eastern League for several seasons. During this period before the First World War, Sittingbourne (often called 'The Brickies') had many outstanding players. Amongst them were the fair-haired halfback Fred 'Snowball' Chandler, who played in the first team for no less than 11 seasons before emigrating to Canada in 1911; and winger Gosnell who played for Sittingbourne, (briefly), for Newcastle United (where he won two league championship medals and two F.A. cup runners-up medals), and for England, all in the period 1904-10.

When reformed after the First War, the Club had several mediocre seasons before, in 1922, they came back with a resounding bang. Due to some extensive reorganisation within the Club, and deep involvement from the local industrialists, that year marked the start of a glorious part-time-professional era. In the next

The Grove — home of the Gore Court cricket and hockey clubs. The cricket club was in fact founded by George Smeed and many years later the Smeed-Dean-Andrews partnership secured The Grove for the club.   (Photo by Alan Cordell)

nine seasons, many eminent professional footballers were attracted to the Club by the offer of supporting jobs in the local industries. Under the almost continuous captaincy of centre-half Bill Dickie (formerly of Chelsea and Stoke City) the Club appeared in the Kent Senior Cup Final no less than 5 times during that period, winning twice (in 1929 and 1930). The 1929 cup-winning team was, in fact, graced by an international — left-half Plum, who had played previously for Charlton Athletic and England. Sittingbourne also stepped up from the Kent League to the Southern League for three seasons and home gates of 3,000 people at the Bull Ground were quite common.

During this long period of professionalism, a local amateur footballer appeared in the team for a while and later moved on to make very good. He is well worth a mention in this book because, he, George Watson, was a member of the family which owned the watermill in Chalkwell Road (just north of the railway line) and also the Milton hoy[2] barges *Constance*, *Hope* and *Orient*. George moved away from the town and played as an amateur for Corinthians (who were a leading amateur club of the day) and for Charlton Athletic. His crowning achievement came when he was selected for the England amateur team in the early 1930s. George was also a very fine cricketer.

But, to get back to Sittingbourne F.C., the expense of running such an accomplished team eventually became too much and the retirement of Bill Dickie in 1931 coincided with the reversion of the club to mainly amateur players. They did, however, usually field one or two experienced part-time professionals to steady the team, such as the ex-Arsenal, Portsmouth and Ireland full-back Mackie, who appeared for a season or two in the late 1930s.

In 1936 the Club celebrated its Golden Jubilee. Bill Dickie, then aged 42 and resident in the town, turned out with his team of old-timers from the Sittingbourne sides of the '20s, and they fought a 2-2 draw with the existing Sitting-bourne 1st XI. The game was followed in the evening by a re-union dinner at the Bull Hotel.

Since the Second War, Sittingbourne teams have been mainly amateur, competing in the Kent League. There was, however, a spell of total part-time professionalism for more than a decade from the mid-1950s to the mid-'60s. One 'big-name' player during this era was the ex-Liverpool and Wales goalkeeper Cyril Sidlow, who spent a season or two with 'The Brickies'. Southern League soccer again came to the town for a few years, with the same result as before — financial disaster. There was one player who served for most of this period, halfback Harold Brockington, and he may have equalled or even surpassed the long-service record set by 'Snowball' Chandler half-a-century before. Also like 'Snowball', who obtained a Kent Senior Cup winner's medal in 1902, Harold picked one up in 1958 when Sittingbourne won the trophy for the fourth and last time.

With the decline of the local barge, brick and cement industries and the general loss of interest in live football in the south, Sittingbourne F.C. has declined also. The Bull Ground's grandstand and extensive terracing (trimmed in the Club colours of black-and-red) was put there in the palmy days, but now sees only about 130 spectators at a home game. The loss of public interest in live entertainment and activities in the south of England over the last 15 years has indeed been quite startling.

Edward Lloyd Ltd, owners of the local paper mills and also a fleet of barges, lighters and tugs, used to run a works amateur football team. Lloyd's F.C. ('The Papermakers') were very prominent in Kent League football between about 1930 and 1952 and their greatest success was winning the Kent Amateur Cup in 1950. Like some of Sittingbourne F.C.'s amateurs, a number of Lloyd's players represented Kent over the years and one, Tommy Hopper (who was with them for many seasons) went on further to gain England amateur international honours. Also in a similar manner to the Town Club, ex-Football League players were sometimes persuaded to join Lloyd's (but as amateurs) by the offer of good jobs in the paper mills. In fact, some Sittingbourne F.C. players moved to Lloyd's for the same reason. Getting back to Tommy Hopper, he was (I believe) the only locally born footballer to play at international level apart from George Watson mentioned above. He left Lloyd's in 1947 to join Bromley, with whom he won an F.A. Amateur Cup winner's medal in 1948, then moved on to Canterbury City and Faversham Town. Tom died at the early age of 56 in 1972; by that time he was resident in Faversham and he was buried in Ospringe churchyard on the outskirts of the town. I am not sure whether the 'East Kent Gazette' mentioned his passing, but in any case (I am told) the 'Faversham News' did him justice. Lloyd's, later renamed Bowater-Lloyd F.C., declined sadly and rapidly in the 1950s and 60s and they now play only in local football — but their superb ground gives evidence of their wonderful earlier years in the Kent League.

As with marine tragedies, there is evidence in Sittingbourne cemetery of two unfortunate fatalities amongst local footballers. At the north end of the site is a grave with a flower vase in the shape of a football; it marks the resting place of 13-year-old Donald Whibley who, the inscription tells us, died naturally in 1937 and was 'A great little sport'. Donald was, in fact, the son of eminent Sitting-bourne F.C. left-winger Jack Whibley, who played for the Club before the First World War and came back again to finish his career there in the mid-1920s. The

Garfield House in Park Road.
(Photo by Alan Cordell)

intervening years were spent playing league football for Crystal Palace, who gained promotion during Jack's time. It may have been some consolation for the sad loss that Jack had two other sons who became accomplished sportsmen. Nearby is a grave which has a full-size football mounted within an arch in the headstone. Here rests Stewart Young, the 23-year-old Sittingbourne Reserves goalkeeper, who was unfortunately killed in a motoring accident in 1938. I know this spot well — my late relatives are waiting next-door for me to join them!

Several of the cricket clubs in Sittingbourne are very well-known, including Bowater-Lloyd and (in particular) Gore Court C.C., who play at a picturesque ground (called 'The Grove') which was given to the town by the Smeed-Dean-Andrews partnership. Gore Court also run ladies' and mens' hockey teams, which play at The Grove, and they used to run (before the First World War) a football side as well. These Gore Court teams, plus a pub, a road and a Smeed Dean barge were all named after George Smeed's mansion Gore Court House. This was demolished many years ago, but the park in which it stood is now King George's Playing Field. The present pavilion was, in fact, previously the Gore Court House stables.

Leading out of the town south towards the above-mentioned Gore Court road and park was, and still is, a road named (not surprisingly) Park Road. Standing in this road is a fascinating building called Garfield House, which was built for Daniel Wills, co-founder of Wills and Packham. In the typical individualistic way of those far-off days, Daniel had some elegant high turrets styled into the roof, so that he could look out over the other Sittingbourne roof-tops and see his barges sailing up Milton Creek. The present use of the building as offices is something of a mundane contrast to its earlier grandeur!

Other buildings in the town with nautical connections are the former iron-work foundries — Littlewood's (Milton Hill) and Gardiner's East Kent Iron Works (Frederick Street)[3]. 'Nautical' buildings still visible by the Creek are:

The remains of Littlewood's original iron foundry building on Milton Hill, 1979.
(Photo by Alan Cordell)

Wills & Packham's office at Crown Quay; the former Wills & Packham barge-building sheds (now warehouses for The Quay Cold Storage and Wharfage Co. Ltd.); the old warehouse at the now-infilled Filmer's Dock; the White Hart pub nearby; the former Burley forge and sail loft at Dolphin Yard; the derelict remains of Burley's Dolphin Cement Works; and at Murston, the former Brickmakers Arms public house and the Blue Circle brickworks and offices.

It is interesting that the names of several barges were in fact taken from local buildings — the *Gore Court* and *Whitehall* as mentioned above, *East Hall* and *Cryalls* (named after farms), *Brightside* (named after the owner's house — which has since been demolished — in Borden Lane)[4]; and there was even a barge called *Sittingbourne* afloat way back in the last century. Other craft took their names from farms and places in the surrounding countryside, such as *Bexon* and *Yieldsted*.

The situation was sometimes reversed, of course, and houses have at times been named after barges. I recall a second house named *Garfield*, after the barge, and others called *Dauntless* and *Favorite*. Harold Butcher, long-serving mate of the *Hydrogen*, chose this name for his house; which meant that his skipper, Arthur Coward, had to make do with *Gen-Hydro*!

1 Cant — the shelf of mud, causing shallow water, which extends out from the north shore of the Isle of Sheppey.
2 Hoy — a vessel engaged in the trade of delivering the fuel and provisions for the town — coal, vegetables, etc. She would normally work on a regularly scheduled and advertised shuttle-service to London. Merchants would be able to book their goods on to her as required.
3 The former East Kent Iron Works buildings are now operated by Medway Fabrications Ltd.
4 The site is now occupied by a terrace of five houses known as 1 to 5 Brightside.

June in commission as a sailing-barge-yacht during the 1930s.

(Courtesy of Arthur Bennett)

Surrey, derelict and sunk at Lower Halstow, 1961.

(Photo by Alan Cordell)

CHAPTER 25

HALL OF FAME

By Alan Cordell

What does one start with in a chapter like this? The racing champions? The giants? The film stars? The last survivors? The war heroes? Or the famous men?

A very difficult question to answer; but it seems to me that nothing can quite equal the glamour of a film star (especially a feminine one, like a barge!) — so we will start there.

This particular bit of glory goes to two barges built by Eastwoods during the brief period (1902 to 1908) when that firm occupied Shrubsall's former yard near Prentis' Quay. At that time their foreman shipwright was Alex Styles (a Lower Halstow man)[1], who launched ten barges into Milton Creek, nearly all being named after counties. The two which were later immortalised for posterity on celluloid were the *Surrey* (launched 1903) and the *Wiltshire* (launched 1908).

Surrey was built specially small so that (with one leeboard removed) she could go through the lock from the River Thames to the River Wey at Weybridge in Surrey. Eastwoods had one other barge which was small enough to do this — the *Landrail*; built by Ambrose Letley at Lower Halstow in 1894, she could even go through the lock with both leeboards in place. So these two barges worked mainly at the task of taking bricks from Eastwoods' works at Milton, Otterham, Lower Halstow, Conyer and Shoebury to their depot at Weybridge. They were so small that their cabin tops were extended to the quarterboards to give more room in their cabins, and for this limited work they were rigged — not surprisingly — as stumpies.

About 1934 Twickenham Film Studios were looking for a suitable small barge to feature in the film 'Beauty and the Barge' and they arranged to charter the *Surrey* from Eastwoods. She was temporarily re-named *Heart in Hand* and skipper Dick Virgo and his mate were employed to take her to the various locations. The film was a comedy, starring Gordon Harker, Judy Gunn, Jack Hawkins, Margaret Rutherford and Ronald Shiner and contained picturesque shots of the barge at Lower Halstow, on the non-tidal Thames and under way in the Thames.

After the filming, *Surrey* regained her true identity. But unfortunately the Weybridge brick barge trade soon died out — eliminated in all probability by the growing use of motor lorries. So the poor *Surrey* was laid up at Halstow and her derelict hull still lies there, forlorn and sunk, to this day.

In 1937, Pinewood Studios started work on a glittering musical called 'Sailing Along'. The leading part in the film was taken by one of the stage and screen superstars of the day — Jessie Matthews. Other well-known names in the cast were Barry Mackay, Jack Whiting and Alastair Sim and the barge selected for the job, again by arrangement with Eastwoods, was the topsail-rigged *Wiltshire*.

The sailing-barge-yacht *Five Sisters*.
(Photo by Joseph Hines)

Location shots were made showing the barge sailing in the lower reaches of the Thames and moored in the upper reaches. Skipper Jack Wheatley, from Rainham, was employed (together with his mate), to put the barge where the film director wanted her. There is no doubt that Miss Matthews and the *Wiltshire* made an eye-catching pair, particularly during one song-and-dance routine on the main hatch.

The film was released in August 1938. Some of its hit songs (such as 'My River', 'Trusting my Luck', 'Your Heart Skips a Beat', etc.) were also recorded by Miss Matthews on disc.

Wiltshire was, in fact, the last barge built by Eastwoods. After the filming (for which she retained her own name) was completed in 1937, she went back to her brick work in the Thames and Medway. She was later taken over by the Government for ammunition lightering and other tasks during the Second World War. Neglect and mishandling eventually caused her to sink in Stangate Creek. She was moved out of the main channel and today all that can be seen of the once-proud *Wiltshire* are a few timbers covered in seaweed and barnacles, sticking out of the mud at about the half-tide level. A sad end indeed!

Both of the above films are in the library of the National Film Archive, Soho, London, and occasionally they are brought out for a public showing.

Having dealt with the film stars, it seems fitting to write next about the local barges which became the subjects of books. First of these by a long way was the *G.A.M.C.*, which had been built at Sittingbourne in 1869. Shortly before the First World War she was bought by a man named Cyril Ionides, who was faced with the problem of the expense of bringing up a growing family whilst indulging in his favourite hobby of big boat sailing. Cyril's solution was to sell his house and yacht, then buy the *G.A.M.C.* and convert her holds so that she became a comfortable sailing home. At that time the upkeep of a barge was relatively cheap and so Cyril was able to meet his objectives. He renamed the barge *The Golden Hope* and, to make her somewhat easier to handle at sea, converted her to a 'half-sprit' rig (in other words, she had a standing gaff instead of a sprit). Cyril (assisted by one Arnold Bennett) eventually wrote the book 'A Floating

Home' (published by Chatto and Windus, 1918), in which he described his conversion work and subsequent voyages. (Cyril disguised the barge's identity in the book, calling her *Will Arding* before conversion, and *Ark Royal* after). *The Golden Hope*'s address in the 1912 Mercantile Register really sets the imagination working — 'The Waste', North Fambridge, Essex. It is believed that she finished her days in the 1940s as a houseboat in the Blackwater and was then burnt or broken up. She was, as far as I can trace, only the second barge to be converted to a sailing-barge-yacht and it was many years later before the idea really caught on.

Next in this distinguished line was the small barge *June*, which was built by Taylor in collaboration with the Burham Brick, Cement and Lime Company at Murston in 1869. She was one of the series of barges owned by the above company which were named after the months of the year, the days of the week and the four seasons; and her work was mainly in the brick and cement trade on the Medway, Thames and other nearby waterways (particularly from the owners' works at Burham).

Around the time of the First World War, A.P.C.M. bought up the B.B.C.L. Co. and *June* continued in similar work for her new owners until 1933. Then, in keeping with A.P.C.M's policy of going over to tugs and lighters, *June* and most of her sisters were offered for sale. A young barge enthusiast, Arthur Bennett, bought her and had her holds professionally converted so that she became a sailing barge-yacht. Until the Second War came, Arthur and his wife Dorothy lived aboard and sailed the *June* all over the accepted 'barge-waters' — Kent, Essex and Suffolk — and in 1939 Arthur set down the whole story in his fascinating book '*June* of Rochester, Topsail Barge' (published by Edward Arnold in 1939, reprinted in 1949).

Conscription into the services meant that Arthur had to leave the *June* laid up in Conyer Creek for the period of the Second War; and this enforced neglect made her unfit for recommissioning when hostilities ceased. So today, *June* is reduced to just floors and frames mouldering in the Conyer Creek mud.

Five Sisters was launched from Wills and Packhams' yard in 1891 and was also a typical small Milton Creek topsail barge. She was named after co-founder Henry Packham's five daughters and was owned by Wills and Packham for most of her working life, being engaged in the usual local trades — bricks, sand, wheat, coal, etc. She was eventually sold away and in 1947, when she was laid up in Milton Creek, naval officer Tom Larken and his wife Peggy bought her for conversion to a sailing-barge-yacht. The great virtue of the scheme was that as and when Tom was posted to the various naval depots he could (within reason) take his home with him. Hence *Five Sisters* became well-known in London, Gosport, Yarmouth (Isle of Wight) and even as far afield as France, Belgium and Holland. The fact that this small barge was able to make long open-sea passages at an age of 60 and over pays tribute to the men who built and maintained her. After the Larkens sold up and came ashore to live (about 1965), Peggy wrote a book about their life and voyages in the barge ('*Five Sisters*' by Peggy Larken, published by Robert Hale 1970, revised 1977). At present (June 1979), *Five Sisters* is still afloat as a housebarge in the River Hamble, Hants.

Last but not least of our published book subjects is the *John & Mary*, launched from Alfred White's yard in 1897. She was built for the Faversham firm of Horsford and her working life was mostly spent in trading to and from Faversham

On the right is the *Phoenician*, the last barge built at Milton Creek, in Ipswich Dock about 1977. Lying outside her is Thames Barge Sailing Club's *Centaur*. Both barges are now sailing-barge-yachts. Whilst *Phoenician* is the bigger barge, she was given a narrow stern so that the lock gates at Lowestoft, where she regularly traded, could close behind her.

(Photo by Peter Ferguson)

and Oare. At the end of the Second World War she was bought by D.H. ('Nobby') Clarke who had her fitted out as a sailing-barge-yacht at Conyer. 'Nobby' did some fairly extensive cruising with *John & Mary* in the late 1940s and early 1950s and then spent several years living aboard her as she lay in a static condition at Brigg in Lincolnshire. This is not a good situation for a wooden vessel to be in — the topsides and decks tend to dry out, causing leakage problems if and when she goes to sea again. So when 'Nobby' decided to sail her south once more in 1958 he had plenty of difficulties to overcome en route. The story of *John & Mary*'s refit and hair-raising voyage is told in the book 'East Coast Passage' by D.H. Clarke, published by Longman in 1971.

John & Mary later became a housebarge at Twickenham and was finally broken up at Brentford around 1976.

Statistically, it is almost incredible that the four books written so far about barge-yachts all feature craft built at Milton Creek. But even so, this is not the end. Some years ago, Arthur Bennett showed me the draft of his forthcoming book 'Us Bargemen', which describes his adventures with his second barge-yacht, the *Henry*[2]. Although built at Grays, Essex, in 1904, she was rebuilt by the Sittingbourne Shipbuilding Company during the 1940s.

Milton Creek built about 500 barges all told and the racing champions of the Thames and Medway are mentioned elsewhere in this book; but as this is the 'Hall of Fame', let us name them again. Shrubsall built at least nine:— *Anglo-Norman, Laura, Early Bird, Whimbrel, Godwit, Britannia, Gazelle, Pastime* and *Dunstable* (named *R.G.H.* when built).

Another of Shrubsall's barges, the *Mary Jane*, was owned at Southend and was quite successful in the annual regatta matches there before the First War.

White built five champions of the Thames and Medway:— *Clara, Nelson, Queen, Vectis* and *Dreadnought*.

Wills and Packham built the very fine coaster *Phoenician* in 1922 for the famous Essex barge owners Horlocks of Mistley. (It was undoubtedly a compliment to Wills & Packham and Sittingbourne that such a distinguished Essex firm should order a new barge from this yard). *Phoenician* did them proud — 9 first prizes in 10 outings in the Coaster Class between the wars!

Burley owned the fine coaster *Northdown* (built at Whitstable, 1924) and she was a regular competitor during the 1920s and '30s; she lifted the Medway Championship (Coaster Class) in 1929.

Alexandra, Annie Lloyd, Alice Lloyd, Bessie Hart, Charles, Maria and *Nellie Austen* were match winners from unidentified local builders. (It is probable that Stephen and John Taylor built some of these).

Whilst the above-named craft are the ones which actually won championships, many other local barges competed over the years, sometimes with distinction.

After racers, how about giants? The barque-rigged *Esther Smeed*, launched at Murston in 1868, was the biggest sailing barge of any type ever built. And the *Olive May*, launched by Wills and Packham at Sittingbourne in 1920, was the biggest spritsail barge ever built (as well as being the only one ever launched with an engine already installed).

How about long life? The *Favorite*, built at Sittingbourne in 1803, was still afloat as a housebarge at Chiswick Mall in 1966, by which time she was the second-oldest floating vessel in the world and the oldest in Britain. There were ideas for preserving her; but then, possibly due to being struck by a passing vessel,

Olive May (on right) lying alongside *Will* in St Katharine's Dock, about 1977. *Will* (formerly *Will Everard)* is one of the four biggest identical steel spritsail barges ever built. But contemporary registers show *Olive May* as slightly bigger.　　　　(Photo by Alan Cordell)

Favorite racing in 1928 — note the crew-man out on her bowsprit. The early 'Red Triangle' emblem can be seen in her mainsail; later, the topsail barges carried a bigger emblem in their topsails. Skipper of the *Favorite* at this time was Bill Chapman who, being completely bald, was known as 'Hair-Oil'. One of his sons named his house in Hawthorn Road after the barge.
(Courtesy of Gordon Wansbrough-White)

Lady of the Lea in Filmer's Dock, 1948. She was the last sailing barge built (in 1931), but looks like one of 100 years earlier! She is still afloat as a sailing-barge-yacht.
(Photo by Alan Cordell)

she sank and had to be broken up. Poor owner Gordon Wansbrough-White rescued just one possession from the wreck — a record of Paul Robeson singing 'River Stay Away From My Door'!

Favorite (a curious spelling, but possibly correct in 1803) was originally swim-headed and budget-sterned (ie. shaped like a lighter) but, as and when major repairs were needed over the years, she was modified into the now-conventional stem-headed and transom-sterned shape.

An early owner of the *Favorite* was Sittingbourne merchant John Huggens (he may even have built her), but she eventually found her way into Smeed Dean's fleet. To create a bit of fun, they raced her in 1928 (when she was 125 years old!); but she was a slow barge and nobody was surprised when she failed to pick up any trophies. However, as the longest-lived barge of all time, *Favorite* did not need other honours!

It is interesting to reflect that whilst *Favorite* was one of the earliest barges built, Milton Creek had a visit in 1948 from the last barge built. She was the small stumpy *Lady of the Lea*, built at Rotherhithe in 1931 for H.M. Government specially to do ammunition work from Waltham Abbey on the River Lea to the Woolwich Arsenal dockyard. She was sold in 1948 to a private owner who moored her in Filmer's Dock for a few months whilst arranging her conversion to a sailing-barge-yacht.

Who were the last sailing survivors owned locally and working to Milton Creek? Well, the very last were the *Maria*, *Pimlico* and *Victoria*, owned by Ellis

Maria bringing a freight of ballast up the Creek, 1949. Kemsley Mill can be seen in the background. *Maria* was burnt at Stoke Creek, River Medway, about 1967.   (Photo by Alan Cordell)

Pimlico on Crown Quay blocks, 1949. She is still afloat as a houseboat at Borstal.
(Photo by Alan Cordell)

Victoria leaving the Creek, 1949. She later became a housebarge and eventually a 'weekend retreat' at Wrabness, Essex.
(Photo by Alan Cordell)

Ninety-Nine laid up at Churchfield Wharf, 1961, shortly after finishing her trading career. She was later moved to the 'barge graveyard' above the wharf and burnt. She was for many years a Medway cement barge and came to Milton Creek as a motor barge when bought by Burley in the mid-1940s. Her unusual name commemorated the fact that her keel was laid at a Frindsbury yard in 1899. (Photo by Alan Cordell)

and Andrews, and working in ballast and general cargo until 1950. (It seems that *Victoria* redeemed herself after her fatal capsize in a private race in 1897 — mentioned elsewhere — by putting in a very long span of local service). The last brick-and-cement barges working (until about 1947) were Burley's *May, Charles Burley* and *Scud*, and A.P.C.M.'s *Dunstable*. In fact, *Dunstable* also had the distinction of being the last local sand barge — she was in this trade until about 1940. Formerly the *R.G.H.*, she was rebuilt in 1927 and renamed to commemorate the absorption of Smeed Dean into the Dunstable Cement Company. This firm was also known as the 'Red Triangle Group' because their emblem was a red triangle which, as far as the barges were concerned, was added to their sails and bowboards. The Murston works still traded under the name of Smeed Dean, however, until being sold completely to the A.P.C.M. (now Blue Circle) around 1932-3. Sand was an essential commodity in brickmaking; it was used to prevent the clay from sticking to the moulds and all the local brick firms had one or more barges engaged in this work from Leigh sand hill. When *R.G.H./Dunstable* was rebuilt, her sides were specially reduced in height in order to make her more suitable for sand work — the crew did not have to throw the sand so high!

The disappearance of these sailormen left the following motor craft as the last vessels owned and working in Milton Creek: the tugs *Elizabeth Murre* (Bowater) and *Cromford* (A.P.C.M.) with their respective fleets of lighters; and Burley's motor barges *Queen Philippa* (which also towed lighters), *Charles Burley* and *Ninety-Nine* (these last two being former spritsail barges). All these craft finished

Charles Burley at Burley's Yard (now Dolphin Sailing Barge Museum) in 1960. She finished work about 1964 and is today derelict near Maldon, Essex.   (Photo by Alan Cordell)

in the early 1960s, leaving only a few craft owned elsewhere to occasionally bring in cargoes as described earlier in this book.

Sittingbourne barges were well to the fore as war heroes at Dunkirk. The full-size barges *Ada Mary, Beatrice Maud, Burton, Monarch* and *Spurgeon* (there may have been others also) took part. *Beatrice Maud* was amongst the sixteen barges which actually went on the beach — she rescued many soldiers. The other four named above had supporting roles. Also at Dunkirk was the small East Coast barge-yacht *Nancibelle*, built by the Sittingbourne Shipbuilding Company in 1930.

I think the above paragraph is a fitting conclusion to the meritorious deeds of the Sittingbourne craft. How about the men? Well, as Leslie Williams says elsewhere in this book, Milton Creek bred many fine seamen, most of whom could have won honours had the opportunity arisen for them. But this author is going to mention just eight, with apologies to those for whom the opportunity did not arise.

It is impossible to trace the skippers of all the Sittingbourne match-winners, and in any case, many of these barges were sailed by men from elsewhere. Only four local match-winning men can be traced: William Wood (buried in the yard of Milton Congregational Church) sailed *Bessie Hart* to first place on the Thames in 1866; Arthur Coward (whose life story is told in an earlier chapter) won the 1897 Queen Victoria Diamond Jubilee Thames Match with *Giralda*; Ernie Britton likewise 'came good' on the big occasion by winning the 1937 Coronation Thames Match (Staysail Class) with the *Dunstable*; and Hedley Farrington ('Pilot's' brother) — who left Sittingbourne during the early 1930s to live in

The fine coaster *Beatrice Maud* — a Sittingbourne-built Dunkirk hero. She is still afloat today as a sailing-barge-yacht.   (Courtesy of Walter Dowsett)

Colchester — won several events with the Essex barges *Memory*, *Mirosa* and *Redoubtable* in the barge-yacht matches of the 1960s and '70s. Hedley has, in fact, won first prizes at every venue except the Swale, and is still alive in Colchester today.

In addition to the above four locally-born racing skippers, Harry Munns — a 'foreigner' who moved to the town — must also be mentioned. Born at Erith in 1841, Harry was almost certainly the greatest racing skipper of the last century. Between 1863 and 1898 he sailed many well-known champion barges, including *W.H.D.*, *Anglo-Norman*, *Conqueror*, *Early Bird*, *Majestic*, *Gazelle* and *Haughty Belle*. Indeed, during this period he was champion skipper no less than 13 times on the Thames and Medway, with many 2nd and 3rd prizes also to his credit. An 1899 'River and Coast' magazine printed an article describing him as the 'Archer of the Thames' and giving his address as Sittingbourne. In fact, Harry had then just moved to the town to finish his working days as the ship's husband to Lloyd's fleet of barges, tugs and lighters, and he remained in Sittingbourne until his death.

Next there are the medals-for-bravery winners; let us start with the accompanying extract from an 'East Kent Gazette' of 1916 which gives token to the bravery

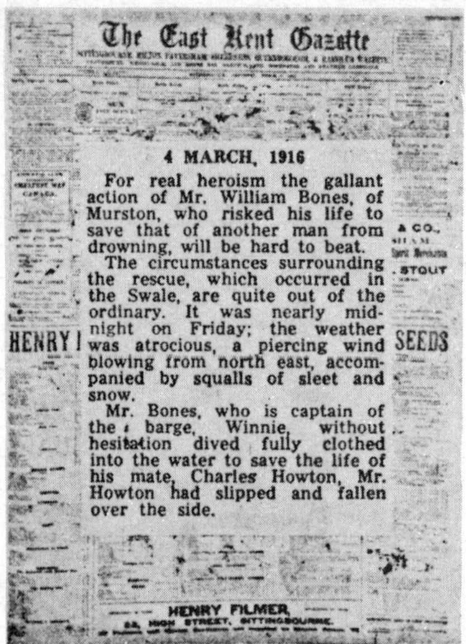

Extract from the 'East Kent Gazette' describing the bravery of Bill Bones.

of Bill Bones, who was presented with a commemorative medal at Sittingbourne Town Hall. Bill later gave up the water and did well as a building contractor in North East London.[3]

Close on Bill's heels was Harold 'Jack' Butcher, still alive in 1979 and still riding his bike — at the age of 85! Harold came to Sittingbourne from Brightlingsea in 1912 (ie. he is the ideal mixture — a Man of Kent and an Essexman all rolled into one!) Immediately after the First World War, Harold had a short spell in the Merchant Navy and during May 1920 he was an A.B. aboard *S.S. Athenic* bound home from New Zealand to London. Whilst in the region of San Salvador (Central America — near the Panama Canal), a distress call was received in the middle of the night from the American cargo-liner *S.S. Munamar*, which had struck a reef and was in sinking condition. *S.S. Athenic* steamed to the spot and launched three rowing lifeboats, with Harold as stroke oar in one of them. Harold's barge experience brought him to the fore in this exercise — his boat was the first to reach the wreck and the first to return on a second trip. The total complement of 50 passengers and 30 crew were rescued by the three boats with, as Harold says, "only a broken bone or two". Harold's participation in this exercise brought him promotion to quartermaster, but nevertheless, after one more deep sea voyage he returned to barges as mate of the fine coaster *Hydrogen*, working with Smeed Dean's fleet. Harold forgot all about the *Munamar* incident until one day in 1922 when Smeed Dean's manager told him to turn up at a special Council meeting at Sittingbourne Town Hall — the American Embassy were going to present him with a medal. This was certainly a wonderful honour and the 'East Kent Gazette' went to town on it. Only Harold's wife Grace, who was presented with a silver teapot, knocked the icing off the cake; she stood the teapot in front of the fire, melted a hole in it — and threw it away!

Last but by no means least of my local award-winners is another versatile Kentexman (combination of Man of Kent and Essexman — Cordell terminology!).

Also 85 this year (1979), he rides his bike even better than Harold Butcher —
Harold says so! The man in question is George Faint, who was born and brought
up on the remote Horsey Island in the Walton Backwaters of Essex. George's
family were almost the only residents of the island (his father looked after the
farm there) and, as it was surrounded by water, George had no early schooling.
Around 1906 the family moved to Beaumont Quay and George was sent to try
to catch up with the other children at school in Thorpe-le-Soken. He says he did
not succeed! In 1908 he went afloat as mate of the locally-owned *Gleaner*, and
later transferred to the *Valentine* (owned by Green at Brantham). However,
Smeed Dean's *Mercy* and *Jane Mead* were working regularly to Beaumont Quay
and Jimmy Toms (skipper of the former) persuaded George that he had a better
future with the Kent firm. So George soon became mate of the *Mercy*, lodged
with the Toms family in Sittingbourne and later married Jimmy's second daughter
Mabel.

George went on to become skipper of several Smeed Dean barges and when
the firm finished he moved elsewhere — seeing service with Sully, Paul, Cranfield,
Goldsmith, Francis and Gilders and Bingham.

Now, to get to the point (about time, you may say!); in the late 1930s,
George had a couple of seasons as skipper of the yawl *Thalassa*, owned by Alan
Baker, who was director of the East Anglia Flour Mills at Colchester. In 1939,
Thalassa competed in the Fastnet Race. George brought her home second, and
the skipper's prize of a fine clock still adorns his 'nautical' flat in Sittingbourne
today; a prize to be proud of indeed!

To conclude this final chapter, it has to be said that the decline of Milton
Creek has been very severe and sad. But it is doubtful whether any other port,
however thriving today, can produce a record which would seriously challenge
the great honours (outlined above) won by Milton Creek and its men in the past.

1 Alex moved to Chalkwell Road, Milton, to be near the barge yard. He later moved away
   to Rainham (Kent) and died there in 1956, at the age of 86.
2 The book 'Us Bargemen' was published by Meresborough Books in 1980 and is still
   available at £6.95 (plus 70p postage).
3 It is thought that Bill was responsible for the names of Sittingbourne Avenue, Borden
   Avenue, Faversham Avenue and Kent Road, in Enfield.

POSTSCRIPT

CHANCE IN A MILLION

By Alan Cordell

In June 1979 I formed the opinion that Leslie Williams and I had finished compiling the manuscript of this book. So, with a sigh of relief, I sent it off to our admirable young typists.

But in the spring of 1981, whilst still working on maps and photographs, some stunning news filtered through to my home in Twickenham via an efficient branch of my grapevine. The information was in fact so incredible that I was nearly floored with shock and amazement! And having collected my thoughts, I just had to grab a pencil and add a Postscript to the earlier work.

The essence of the story was that the nearby Kingston Archaeological Society had found two small cement tablets, marked *'Barge Yieldsted'*, under the floor of a riverside house. *Yieldsted*? — ye gods! that was only Grandad's barge!

Wasting no time, I 'phoned the Society representative, Mrs Hall. She proved very helpful, and was as keen to learn about the *Yieldsted* as I was to learn about the tablets. She explained that four tablets in all had been found, and each measured about 4″ x 2½″ x ½″. Whilst *'Barge Yieldsted'* had obviously been inscribed on two of them before the cement had set, the others merely bore the word 'Sample' written on them in pencil.

A bargain was quickly struck. She would bring the two tablets to my house so that I could inspect and photograph them; and in return I would give her the considerable amount of available information on the *Yieldsted* (the result of 40 years' research) and show her my 'barge museum' housed in a Second World War air-raid shelter in my garden.

Mrs Hall and her family arrived with good news — I could keep one of the tablets. So an interesting morning was had by all and the 'museum' gained a valuable exhibit — I reproduce a photograph of it here.

Now what is it all about? In other words, how, why and when did those tablets get under a floor in Kingston? Well, of course, the solution must be a matter of some conjecture, but I have tried to form a theory about it, based on the following facts:—

1. The tablets were found under the floorboards of Picton House. This is an historic building (dating from 1740 and overlooking the River Thames) which was recently rescued from threats of demolition, mainly by the efforts of Kingston Archaeological Society. It has since been restored and renamed Amari House. Whilst obviously a beautiful dwelling in an earlier era, it is now an elegant block of offices. At the back of the house is a wharf which was regularly used by spritsail barges in the days of barge trade.

The cement tablet found under a floor in Kingston-upon-Thames.   (Photo by Alan Cordell)

2. The *Yieldsted* was in commission from 1870 till 1930. For most of that time she worked in the Milton Creek (Sittingbourne) brick and cement trade to the wharves in and around London.

3. Grandfather Jim Fenteman was skipper of the *Yieldsted* from about 1887 till 1903, and part-owner from about 1895 till 1930. His home during his whole lifetime (1855-1939) was always in Sittingbourne.

So it seems pretty likely to me that when the floorboards of Picton House were last renewed, the *Yieldsted* was lying at the nearby wharf. Perhaps one of the local builder's merchants wanted to see what her brand of cement was like when set — how strong?, how hard?, etc. So some samples were made up (in tobacco tins, maybe?), and the *Yieldsted*'s crew decided to write the barge's name on two of these and leave them under the Picton House floor as a memento (and puzzle!) for a later generation to discover. For good measure, the ones without inscriptions were left there as well after the merchant(s) had been satisfied.

It has been suggested that perhaps cement companies supplied sample tablets anyway. But, in 40 years of research on barges and their cargoes, I have never seen one; and, even if they did, it is unlikely that they would inscribe some of them with the name of a barge. No, a much more feasible solution is that those tablets were made up and inscribed by the *Yieldsted*'s crew and left as a memento.

Now to the burning question: did Grandad do it? After all, other people also sailed in the *Yieldsted*, including that popular, tobacco-chewing old salt 'Scranny Jack' Hambrook, who was her skipper for the last 20 years of her trading life. Well, I was only four years old when Grandad died and so my memory of him is very faint. But fortunately I have some older relatives who knew and remember him well; one of these, my cousin Denis Fentiman (note how some branches of the family spell the name with 'i' in the middle instead of 'e'), says that Grandad often used to reminisce about his various ports-of-call and Kingston was frequently

The Haven.
49. Ufton Lane.
Sittingbourne.
Kent

Nov 6/1938

Dear So & D & my two Boys
We was pleased to hear from
you and You was all well
I am pleased to tell You we
are both fairly well I was
a bit queer last week I had
got some more sugar but
I have cut down my food
a bit and feel a lot better
We are glad You like Your
job it is a nice change
for You
Madge has come to London
as a nurse to Children at
Hilburn it is at a place where
they take Children in for
the day whilst their Mothers
are out to work She thinks

Sample of Jim Fenteman's handwriting.

mentioned. Moreover, Denis produced for me a letter which Grandad wrote (to his son Dick — Denis's father) in 1938. The front page is produced here; and if we compare the circled areas with the writing on the tablet (particularly the up-strokes on the 'i' and 't'), we find there is a remarkably strong resemblance. In fact, I am fairly confident in saying that it was indeed Grandad who inscribed those tablets.

Let us suppose that I am right (for once?). Then what are the chances of a man leaving a secret memento under the floor of a house 60 miles from home — and his grandson moving into that area and being on the spot to pick it up 80 or more years later?

One chance in a million, perhaps?

APPENDIX 1
SPRITSAIL BARGES BUILT AT MILTON CREEK

(Extracted from the 1912 Mercantile Register, which does not identify the builders of the registered craft; however, the following list classifies the barges built at Milton Creek under their builders as far as could be determined from other sources.)

Built by Burley
C. & B. 1876, *Charles Burley* 1902, *Dorothy* 1898, *F.B.* 1877, *Laurence* 1896, *May* 1893, *Stanley* 1890, *Sydney* 1889, *W.B.* 1877.

Built by Eastwoods
Bedford 1905, *Berwick* 1906, *Cheshire* 1903, *Edwin* 1903, *Hereford* 1907, *Northampton* 1904, *Redshank* 1903, *Suffolk* 1902, *Surrey* 1903, *Wiltshire* 1908.

Built by Mantle
Gipsy 1877, *Providence* 1877, *William & Eleanor* 1873.

Built by Masters
Helvellyn 1884, *J.D. Drake* 1898, *Sidwell* 1877.

Built by Shrubsall
Agreement 1878, *Aldershot* 1875, *Alice* 1875, *Anglo-Norman* 1873, *Anglo-Saxon* 1874, *Arthur* 1895, *B & S* 1883, *Bankside* 1900, *Bexhill* 1898, *Blossom* 1876, *Bluebell* 1891, *Borstal* 1874, *Bride* 1885, *Britannia* 1883, *Century* 1901, *Charles & Esther* 1884, *Charles & Isabella* 1884, *Charlotte Austin* 1895, *Chronicle* 1894, *Clyde* 1868, *Company* 1897, *Constance* 1879, *Curlew* 1881, *Early Bird* 1879, *Edith & Hilda* 1892, *Emily* 1883, *Fanny* 1879, *Florence* 1869, *Friar Bacon* 1887, *Gazelle* 1886, *Gertrude* 1874, *Godwit* 1882, *Good Templar* 1877, *Guy Fawkes* 1876, *Harriett* 1871, *Harriett Howard* 1876, *Hearts of Oak* 1879, *Heron* 1884, *Honduras* 1896, *Hope* 1885, *James Bills* 1872, *Laura* 1874, *Magnet* 1899, *Marie Stuart* 1873, *Mary Jane* 1877, *Maud* 1875, *Mayflower* 1882, *Mersey* 1869, *Mistletoe* 1876, *Myrtle* 1880, *Mystery* 1875, *New Ada* 1877, *New World* 1877, *Pall Mall* 1875, *Pastime* 1890, *Premier* 1900, *R.G.H.* 1891, *Rachel & Julia* 1873, *Rathmona* 1897, *Red Lancer* 1880, *Reliance* 1876, *Richard* 1869, *S.J.B.* 1888, *Shamrock** 1899, *Shamrock** 1899, *Sunshine* 1876, *Susie* 1874, *Swiftsure* 1875, *Tay* 1898, *Tees* 1878, *Terror* 1901, *United* 1881, *Whimbrel* 1882.

Built by Spencelaugh
Band of Hope 1878, *Thomas & Frances* 1878.

Built by Smeed Dean
Ada Mary 1887, *Alan Dean* 1908, *Annie* 1892, *Bessie* 1888, *Burton* 1880, *Cobden* 1878, *Derby* 1878, *Donald* 1898, *Elsie* 1896, *Esther* 1900, *Fred* 1881, *Garfield* 1882, *George* 1879, *George Smeed* 1882, *Georgiana* 1881, *Gladstone* 1877, *Gordon* 1884, *Gore Court* 1882, *Grace* 1890, *Graham* 1897, *Harold* 1905, *Jane Mead* 1886, *Jessie* 1888, *Joe* 1898, *Leslie* 1894, *Levitt* 1891, *Livingstone* 1880, *Lizzie* 1892, *Lowe* 1878, *Maria* 1891, *Martin Luther* 1884, *Mercy* 1896, *Persevere* 1889, *Plimsoll* 1878, *Russell* 1879, *Ruth* 1879, *S.D.* 1902, *Sam* 1895, *Spurgeon* 1883, *Vincent* 1879, *Whitehall* 1881, *Winnie* 1880, *Young Jack* 1880.

Built by Stephen and/or John Taylor
Ann 1868, *Bessie Taylor* 1865, *Cader Idris* 1884, *East Kent* 1862, *February†* 1869, *January†* 1868, *John & Edward* 1865, *June†* 1869, *S. Taylor* 1865.

Built by White

Alarm 1898, *Beatrice Maud* 1910, *Cecilia* 1903, *Clara* 1896, *Cutty Sark* 1904, *Dee* 1898, *Dreadnought* 1907, *Edith* 1904, *Edward VII* 1901, *Edwin* 1900, *Gertrude May* 1893, *G.W.* 1895, *H.M.W.* 1908, *Harry* 1898, *Her Majesty* 1897, *Invicta* 1896, *John & Mary* 1897, *Juliet* 1896, *Maria* 1898, *Mary Ann* 1900, *Mite* 1894, *Monarch* 1900, *Monarch* 1905, *Nelson* 1905, *Phillippa* 1903, *Pickwick* 1903, *Queen* 1906, *Romeo* 1896, *Sam Weller* 1903, *Shannon* 1898, *Silica* 1899, *Solent* 1904, *T.T.H.* 1897, *Tam O'Shanter* 1904, *Thetis* 1897, *Vampire* 1898, *Vectis* 1895, *Vera* 1897, *Victoria* 1897, *Viper* 1898, *Windward* 1897.

Built by Wills & Packham

Aberdeen 1892, *C.I.V.* 1901, *Ebenezer* 1891, *Edinburgh* 1891, *Five Sisters* 1891, *Glasgow* 1896, *H.T. Wills* 1889, *Henry & Jabez* 1890, *Ivy* 1894, *Llandudno* 1892, *M.M. Packham* 1890, *McKinley* 1901, *Rand* 1898, *Samuel* 1892, *Scotsman* 1899, *Shamrock* 1893, *Unique* 1903, *W. & P.* 1889.

Built at Milton by unidentified builders

Alberta 1867, *Emma* 1899, *George & Ann* 1862, *Gladiator* 1865, *Humber* 1897, *Leslie* 1902, *William & Richard* 1862.

Built at Murston by unidentified builders

Florence 1858, *Frank* 1870, *Meteor* 1869, *Surrey* 1868.

Built at Sittingbourne by unidentified builders

(The builders Stephen and John Taylor, Mantle, Masters and Spencelaugh were undoubtedly responsible for most of these barges.)

Active 1864, *Ada* 1867, *Agincourt* 1866, *Agnus* 1878, *Albion* 1864, *Alexandra* 1867, *Alfreda* 1870, *Alice Laws* 1878, *Annie Bryan* 1876, *Argosy* 1878, *Arthur* 1864, *Arthur* 1869, *Bessie Hart* 1866, *Bexon* 1869, *Brightside* 1879, *Burnham* 1864, *Butcher* 1866, *Canvey* 1876, *Cecilia* 1876, *Ceres* 1862, *Challenge* 1874, *Charles* 1861, *Clara* 1873, *Columbus* 1868, *Connaught* 1879, *Conyer* 1866, *Cryalls* 1870, *Dawn* 1890, *Deerhound* 1864, *Defence* 1869, *Diligent* 1880, *Dover Castle* 1872, *E.P.B.* 1882, *East Hall* 1893, *Ebenezer* 1879, *Echo* 1870, *Edith* 1882, *Edith Mary* 1880, *Edward* 1881, *Eliza* 1857, *Elizabeth & Mary* 1870, *Ellen* 1874, *Emily Jane* 1867, *Emma** 1868, *Emma** 1868, *Emma Seager* 1891, *Emma & Sarah* 1873, *Empress* 1877, *Ernest* 1867, *Ernest William* 1866, *Esther* 1863, *Eva Annie* 1878, *Excelsior* 1869, *Excelsior* 1879, *Fanny* 1872, *Fanny Maria* 1864, *Faversham* 1882, *Favorite* 1803, *Flora* 1873, *Four Sisters* 1877, *Foxgrove* 1866, *Frank* 1874, *Frank* 1875, *Frank* 1882, *Frank Filmer* 1866, *Frank Lloyd* 1872, *George & Alfred* 1862, *George & William* 1879, *Gleaner* 1885, *The Golden Hope* 1869, *Gondola* 1878, *Governor* 1863, *Gratitude* 1880, *Hadleigh Castle* 1880, *Harriet* 1881, *Henry* 1863, *Henry Wood* 1877, *Henry & Eliza* 1865, *Herbert Gordon* 1889, *Industry* 1863, *J.S.H.* 1877, *J.B. Gough* 1879, *James* 1868, *Jane* 1893, *John Bright* 1877, *John Huggens* 1866, *John & Sarah* 1865, *Kathleen* 1876, *Keeble* 1876, *Lady Flora* 1866, *Lizzie* 1867, *M.E.I.W.* 1880, *Maria* 1864, *Marion* 1868, *Mary Sophia* 1886, *Midget* 1894, *Milton* 1862, *Milton* 1874, *Minnie* 1876, *Moretta* 1881, *Morley* 1883, *Mundon* 1868, *Muriel* 1896, *Murston* 1885, *Murston* 1867, *Murton* 1866, *Nellie Austen* 1887, *Nil Desperandum* 1871, *Ocean Queen* 1862, *Onward* 1867, *Orient* 1879, *Oscar* 1876, *Osprey* 1866, *Percy* 1888, *Phoebe* 1878, *Pimlico* 1876, *Pioneer* 1862, *Pomona* 1878, *Preston* 1884, *Queen of the Thames* 1864, *R.O.W.* 1865, *Rawreth* 1866, *Renown* 1868, *Rettendon* 1868, *Roache* 1867, *Robert Stone* 1864, *Robert & Elizabeth* 1870, *Roberta* 1870, *Rochester Castle* 1889, *Rover* 1871, *Samuel Bowly* 1878, *Sarah Ann* 1854, *Sarah & Eliza* 1880, *Satis* 1899, *Secret* 1867, *Shah* 1874, *Shannon* 1872, *Sibyl* 1872, *Sir Wilfred Lawson* 1878, *Sophy* 1861, *Strathmore* 1899, *Surprise* 1862, *Surprise* 1864, *Teetotaler* 1877, *Thomas & Caroline* 1864, *Tom Tuff* 1878, *Triton* 1866, *Two Friends* 1865, *United* 1864, *Unity* 1871, *Valders* 1890, *Venus* 1867, *W.H. Randall* 1876, *Warden Court* 1870, *Wasp* 1866, *Wave* 1844, *Welsh Girl* 1878, *William* 1872, *William Stone* 1864, *William Wood* 1864, *William & Arthur* 1869.

Note

Absolute accuracy in the above list cannot be guaranteed, because it is very difficult to determine exactly what was happening 100 years ago, and Mercantile Registers are not always correct.

The Smeed Dean built 'stumpy' barge *Vincent*, seen here about 1935, after she had passed
to A.P.C.M.   (Photo by R. Stimson Jnr.)

Undoubtedly some Milton Creek built barges are missing from the list because their
working careers had finished by 1912.

Five barges were built at Milton Creek after 1912:

By Smeed Dean
Youngarth 1913.

By Wills & Packham
Olive Mary 1921, *Olive May* 1920, *Raybel* 1920, *Phoenician* 1922.

* Different barges — same name and year
† Built in conjunction with the Burham Brick, Cement and Lime Co.

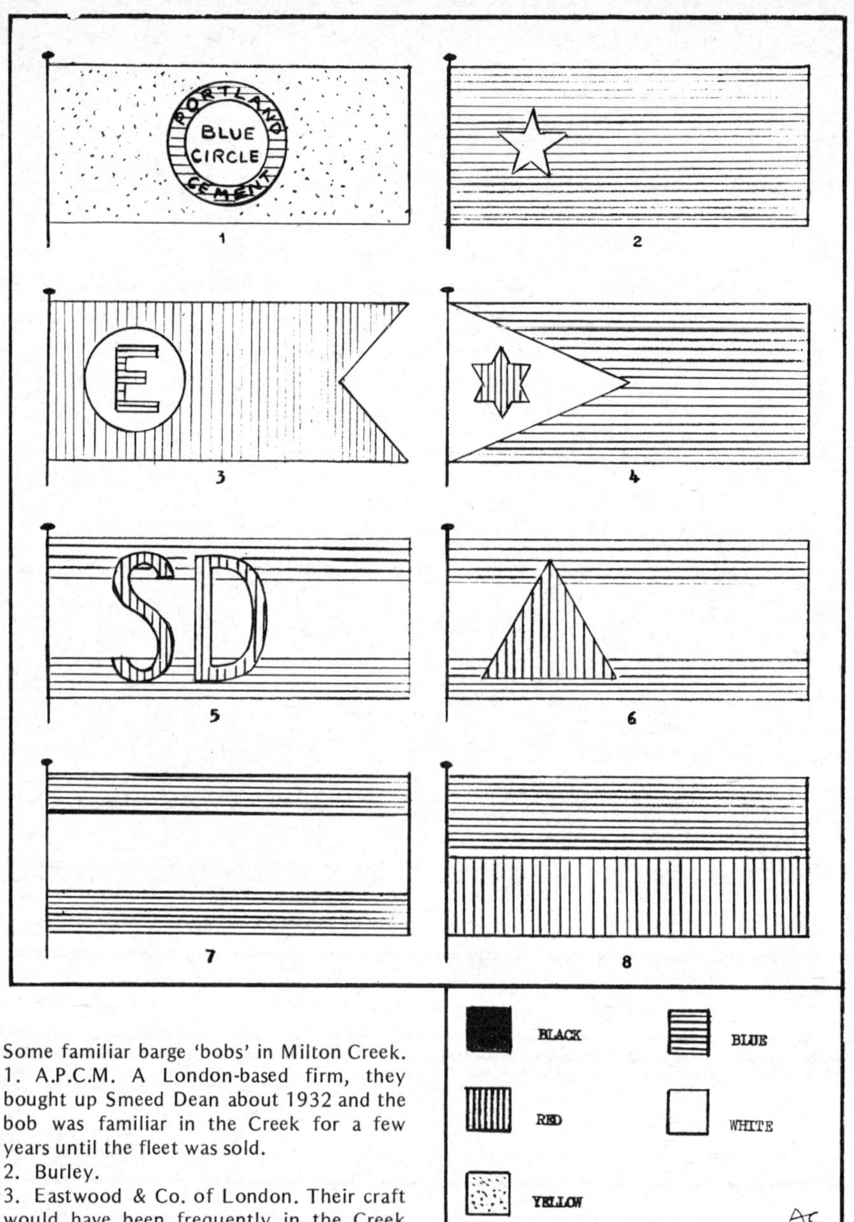

Some familiar barge 'bobs' in Milton Creek.
1. A.P.C.M. A London-based firm, they bought up Smeed Dean about 1932 and the bob was familiar in the Creek for a few years until the fleet was sold.
2. Burley.
3. Eastwood & Co. of London. Their craft would have been frequently in the Creek during the period 1890-1907 when Eastwood's Milton brickfield was operating. In later years (1930s onwards) the E became black and the bob shape was sometimes rectangular.
4. Ellis and Andrews.
5. Smeed Dean.
6. Smeed Dean during the period when they were amalgamated with the Dunstable Cement Company, ie in the Red Triangle Group, c.1927-32.
7. Bob worn by private barges working with Smeed Dean's fleet. Andrews owned or had shares in most of these craft.
8. Wills and Packham; Gransden barges also flew the same bob.

APPENDIX 2
SPRITSAIL BARGES OWNED AT MILTON CREEK

(Extracted from the 1912 Mercantile Register)

Owned by the Andrews family
Fanny, Frank, Maria, Monarch

Owned by Burchett
Phoebe

Owned by Burley
Annie Bryan, Baltic, C. & B., Cecilia, Charles, Charles Burley, Clara, Content, Dorothy, Edith, F.B., Fairy, Fanny Maria, Foxgrove, Gordon, Isle of Grain, Laurence, May, Owner's Delight, Redwing, Stanley, Sydney, Thomas & Edward, Vectis, W.B., Water Lily.

Owned by Cashman
J.S.H.

Owned by Dean
Hambrook

Owned by Drake
Sidwell

Owned by Epps
Harriett

Owned by Fenteman
Yieldsted

Owned by Filmer
Windward

Owned by Gransden
Bexhill, Premier

Owned by Goodenough
Gladstone

Owned by Greensted
Mars, Richard

Owned by Johncock
Wye

Owned by Lavers
Connaught, Gipsy, Gondola, Kathleen, Moretta, Valders, Welsh Girl

Owned by Lloyd
Pioneer, Protector

Owned by Prentis
Pomona

Owned by Smeed Dean
Ada Mary, Alan Dean, Argosy, Bessie, Burton, Cobden, Curlew, Derby, Donald, East Hall, Edith, Eliza, Elsie, Ernest, Esther, Favorite, Florence, Fred, Garfield, George, George Smeed, Georgiana, Gertrude May, Gladstone, Gordon, Gore Court, Grace, Graham, Harold, Harriet, Harry, Histed, Jane Mead, Jessie, Joe, John Bright, Leslie, Levitt, Livingstone, Lizzie, Lowe, Maria, Martin Luther, Mary Ann, Maud, Mercy, Morley, Murston, Perseverance, Persevere, Plimsoll, R.G.H., Russell, Ruth, S.D., Sam, Spurgeon, Victoria, Vincent, Whitehall, Winnie, Young Jack.*

Owned by Watson
Constance, Hope, Orient.

Owned by White
Beatrice Maud

Owned by Wills & Packham
Aberdeen, Arthur Blake, C.I.V., Ebenezer, Edinburgh, Five Sisters, Flora, Glasgow, Good Templar, H.T. Wills, Henry & Jabez, Herbert Gordon, Ivy, J.B. Gough, Llandudno, M.M. Packham, Rand, Red Lancer, Rover, Samuel, Samuel Bowly, Scotsman, Shamrock, Teetotaler, Unique, W. & P.

Owned by the Wood family
Columbus, Emma & Sarah, Excelsior, Harmony, M.E.I.W., Nesta, Richard, Strathmore, Vera, William Wood.

Note
The owners' fleets varied to a certain extent over the years. In particular, Burley, Smeed Dean and Wood bought barges during the period 1915/25, which enabled them to discard some of their older craft.

* Ketch in 1912, converted to spritsail rig 1913-14

APPENDIX 3
MILTON CREEK BARGES IN 1912 REGISTER
STILL AFLOAT TODAY

Out of the craft listed in Appendices 1 and 2, the following are still afloat (June 1979):

Beatrice Maud	(Barge-yacht, based Maldon)
C.I.V.	(Barge-yacht, based London)
Edith & Hilda	(Housebarge, Maldon)
Five Sisters	(Housebarge, R. Hamble)
George Smeed	(Housebarge, Maldon)
Leslie — built 1894	(Housebarge, Allington)
Mary Ann	(Housebarge, Hoo)
Olive May	(Barge-yacht, based London)
Persevere	(Housebarge, Conyer)
Phoenician	(Barge-yacht, based Ipswich)
Premier	(Housebarge, Burcot, R. Thames)
Queen	(Weekend home, Nr Dartmouth)
Raybel	(Barge-yacht, based London)
Scotsman	(Housebarge, Faversham)
Victoria	(Weekend home, Wrabness)
Viper	(Housebarge, Upnor)

APPENDIX 4
A MISCELLANY OF BARGE LORE
compiled by Marlin Spike and Alan Cordell

Evening red and morning grey
Are two good signs of a very fine day.
But evening grey and morning red
Makes an old sailor scratch his head.

When the gulls are flying high
You can let your skysail fly;
And when the gulls are flying low
Look out for a stronger blow.

I used to think I was too indecisive to become a barge skipper,
but now I'm not so sure.

Blessed is he that expecteth nothing,
For he shall not be disappointed.

Six days shalt thou labour
And do all thou art able,
On the seventh, holystone the deck,
And scrape the cable.

— (The Fourth Commandment according
   to Captain Walter King)

If you should a rope belay,
Coil it up, don't walk away.

The following verses are from 'A Handbook for Bargemen, Lightermen and Tugmen' by
Charles T. Perfect:

Whether sailing close hauled or running free —
    LOOK OUT!
Whatever the weather, wherever you be —
    LOOK OUT!
You cannot avoid a thing you don't see —
    so LOOK OUT!
When coming to anchor, or stowing up sail —
    LOOK OUT!
Or washing the decks with mop and pail —
    LOOK OUT!

Whatever you're doing never fail to —
   LOOK OUT!
It is easy to hit an object that's there —
   so LOOK OUT!
But it's just as easy to miss it with care —
   so LOOK OUT!
Vessels and lights spring from Lord knows where —
   so LOOK OUT!

Fast rise after low
Foretells stronger blow.
Long foretold, long last,
Short notice, soon past.

Don't get the 'wind-up' in a breeze,
But try your pumps and be at ease.

If your job you'd carry through
In a way that's straight and true,
Steer your barge, and all things do,
As though the craft belonged to you.

APPENDIX 5

POET'S CORNER

'GERTRUDE MAY'
By Marlin Spike

I 'ad a yen to go to sea,
When I was just a lad,
Me Muvver wouldn't let me go,
So I 'ad to ask me Dad,
'E fixed me up wiv Walter King,
A right old pirate he;
A saltier man there never was,
Nor ever went to sea.

The mate 'e was a Tilbury man,
Fred Outridge was 'is name,
Chewing baccy was 'is taste,
But sailing was 'is game;
The barge we sailed was *Gertrude May*,
Wiv neat flush deck an' sheer,
Beatin to wind'ard, running free,
'Er decks was dry, me dear.

So Walter, Fred, an' *Gertrude*
Taught me all they could,
Knot, splice, wash me neck,
An' make a suet pud;
Steer by compass, stow a jib,
Batten, serve, an' lash,
Clean the flippin' brass work,
Catch a mackerel, make a hash.

Made me mind me 'Ps' an' 'Qs',
An' treat 'em wiv respect,
An' if I gave 'em any lip,
A clout I could expect;
Those two old 'shell-backs' taught me much,
Did Walter King an' Fred,
Things that, later on in life,
'Ave stood me in good stead.

But *Gertrude* gave me somethin' more,
As wind bore us along,
'Er great tall spars stretched to the skies,
'Er timber hull was strong;
'Er foc'sle was me own domain,
Top bunk, port side, me rest,
The smell of oil an' yes'day's stew,
Hung where I washed me vest.

An' rock me off to sleep, she would,
But I 'ardly downed me 'ead,
When awful sounds would break me dream,
"Turn to, show a leg", by Fred;
So I came 'ome a better lad,
Than when I went away,
Those three did me a power o' good,
Walt, Fred, an' *Gertrude May*.

Captain Coward paced the deck,
His brow as black as thunder,
He only had 200 tons,
Who made this serious blunder?

— (Popular rhyme amongst bargemen, reflecting Arthur Coward's thirst for earning big money with the *Hydrogen*. See Chapter 2).

A MILTON CREEK SAILORMAN'S SAGA
By Marlin Spike

Had my fill of song and beer,
Now the reckoning time is here.
Sailing on the evening tide,
Freight of bricks for Barkingside.
Covered up and battened tight,
The old gal might 'suck down' tonight.
Light the fire and swinging lamp,
Fill the kettle (cabin's damp!)
Water on deck afore she rose,
Looks like rain, a cold wind blows.
Side lights up, bright green and red,
(Wish I was at home, in bed!)
Let go moorings fore and aft,
(Why am I here? I must be daft!)
Set the tops'l, fore and main,
Shove away, down comes the rain.
The 'Old Man' growls from the gloom,
"Get to loo'ard on the boom".
Clear the Creek, shoulders sore,
Nearly aground, on Turkey shore.[1]
Fores'l to wind'ard, coming round,
Stay-fall ready to lower down.
Startled gulls rise up ahead,
Go screeching, fit to wake the dead.
"That you, *Shamrock*?" through the dark,
"What's it look like, *Noah's Ark*?"
Huffler comments on the night, . . . !!! . . . !
All agree, without a fight.
Bear away, gear down flat,
Shoot Kingsferry,[2] fancy that!
Still its belting down with rain,
Heave up 'B. . . ' gear again.
Twist and turn round every bight,
Blue with cold, cor, what a night.
Queenbro' Jetty, Sheerness Pier,
(Can only feel I shouldn't be here!)
Now she lifts to the open sea,
Opens up the Estuary.
'Ships it green', stinging spray,
Cheerless comes the dawn of day.
Wet and weary, hungry too,
(now me boots let water through!)
Grain Spit buoy goes sliding past,
Bear away up Swatch, at last.
Wind abates, we lose the sea,
Stagger aft, to make some tea.

Cook the bacon, cut the bread,
(I must be off my blooming head!)
In spite of all the stress and strain,
I'll do the whole darned thing again!

1   Turkey shore — the site of the derelict Turkey Cement Works in the Swale opposite
Ridham Dock.
2   Kingsferry — Kingsferry Bridge. Before about 1938, barges had to lower their gear to
pass through, as the bridge was lifted only for vessels with fixed masts.

CHARTER BARGE SAIL
By George Tutton

The wind and the waves and the sound of the sea,
these things are music and much more to me.
The weather may change and the sun grow pale,
but nothing can alter the joys of a sail.
The squeal of blocks and the strain of the sheet,
the iron hard halyards and the ropes all neat.
The whip in the topmast and taunt stays and shrouds,
up through red sails to the 'Bob' in the clouds.
"Stand by to go about" from the helmsman we hear,
a pause — and then "Leeo" comes loud and clear.
(Foresail held backed to help him to steer). And
then it comes — "Let go bowline" and with frightening
force, the foresail swings over to strain at the horse.
One leeboard is lowered and the other is raised,
lowering's no trouble, hauling up one feels dazed.
We are on a close reach and moving fast,
she's an old lady and has memories past.
The wind blows strong and the water is rough,
but she pushes on hard, her bows are tough.
The foredeck is wet from the sea over the bows,
for we keep moving fast and how the wind howls.
The staysail is pulling well, a lovely sight,
to get it like that was a hell of a fight.
A muffled voice is heard calling a welcome sound,
"tea up" — big mugs full — and we gather round.
Drink up, it's not long before we end the tack,
about we go, fast, true and heading back.
Good timing, tide right, and without much fuss,
we couldn't have done better if we'd travelled by 'bus.
The crew has done well, we are pleased with
ourselves, but our old Skipper says "What a ******* ,
like spinsters you should all be on shelves!"

JOURNEY HOME
By Marlin Spike

After many years at last I took
Myself to Milton for a look;
At my old home down by the Creek,
To have, maybe, a nostalgic peek.

I hummed a tune as off I went,
To find my birthplace down in Kent,
Forgetting in my mood sublime,
The passing of 'Old Father Time'.

Alas, the old home was not there,
The street had gone, I knew not where,
And in its place, a gate, a fence,
A notice, saying 'Get you hence!'

The Mill Street that I used to know,
The little cobbler man named Joe,
The useful general shop next door,
Had disappeared for evermore.

I turned away and tried to find,
Another road I had in mind,
But soon it was to me quite clear,
There'd been a right old land grab here!

"Let's find the Creek I knew so well",
(I used to know it by the smell!)
But every path I wandered down,
Was blocked off by a 'shanty' town.

Then at last, a place I knew,
'Murston Gas' and 'Biddy's' too,
But I found to my dismay,
That both had passed to yesterday.

Ruins where cement works stood,
Rusting steel and rotting wood;
I looked across to 'Milton side' —
The Creek's now only half as wide!

Then magically I saw once more,
The hustle, bustle on the shore,
Barges lying there two wide,
With still two widths the other side.

The rattle, clang of wheels on plate,
As 'truckies' at terrific rate,
Ran heavy sacks of 'dusty gold',[1]
Down chutes, into a barge's hold.

[1] 'Dusty gold' — cement

Clouds of dust hung in the air,
Sprits and topmasts everywhere,
And passing every now and then,
Burley's, Packham's, Sailormen.

Bargemen hurrying to and fro,
Getting stores in time to go;
George Smeed, Dunstable and *Grace*,
Waiting there to take their place.

The slap of canvas, creaking gear —
Music to a bargeman's ear;
Rattling blocks and clanking pawl,
The lonely, plaintive, seagulls' call.

The sound of laughter brought me back,
Coming from a wooden shack;
Having tea-break, I suppose,
What they do there, goodness knows!

I sighed and sadly turned away,
'Cause I belong to yesterday;
'Twas then that I received the 'call' —
A pint, up at the 'Golden Ball'!

CROSSING THE BAR
By Tennyson

Sunset and evening star, and one clear call for me!
And may there be no moaning of the bar
When I put out to sea,
But such a tide as moving seems asleep,
Too full for sound and foam,
When that which drew from out the boundless deep
Turns again home.

Twilight and evening bell, and after that the dark!
And may there be no sadness of farewell
When I embark;
For tho' from out our bourne of Time and Place,
The flood may bear me far,
I hope to see my Pilot face to face,
When I have crost the bar.

Nightfall. (Photo by Alan Cordell)

NIGHTFALL
By Ronald Washington

A running tide sets *Shamrock* swinging
And dark against the coral sky,
She gyrates slowly on her mooring
Her gleaming mast light — riding high
And mirrored in the deepening cobalt
Of the ebb flow streaming by.

But now the rhythmic sweep of oarblades
Flinging arcs of splintered light
Against the fiery path of sunset,
Enriched by shadows of the night,
Disturbs the waders at the tideline
And puts some startled gulls to flight.

A lingering sun writhes in a death-throw
Above the threshold of the west
And trembles in a last convulsion
Before its crimson mass is pressed
Into the shroud of purple twilight
Which drapes the world in silent rest.

Up high against the coral streamers
Translucent in the afterglow,
A lonely heron seeks his night roost
With flapping wing beats, full and slow,
And from the sea sweep scolding seagulls
To skim the tiderace, wheeling low.

And when the darkness cloaks the estuary,
And distant shorelines wink with lights,
They match the spangled vault of Heaven
Where constellations, blazing bright,
Have comforted across the ages,
The lonely ones throughout the night.

BARGES GALORE!
By Heather Cordell, age 9

To every child who reads this,
The warning is quite clear,
Don't let Dad loose near barges,
Or you'll shed many a tear.

My Daddy is quite mad on them,
He thinks, drinks, sleeps and eats,
Nothing but barges, barges galore,
Performing nautical feats.

But ah, alas I put up with him,
And I can do no more,
Than try to wean my father off,
Barges, barges galore.

So take heed of my warning kids,
Don't let your Dads go near,
Barges, barges, or barging folk,
Listen! Do you hear?

THE MAPS

Notes

Map 3

1. 'The Snapper' was not a wharf but was a stretch of sea wall accessible by small boats at most states of tide. Hence crews of craft anchored in the Swale used to leave their boats there when they went ashore.
2. Churchfield Wharf No. 2 was often called 'The Flint Dock' by bargemen.

Map 4

Some of these wharves were previously worked by Smeed and by The Burham Brick Cement and Lime Co. Since c.1932 they have all been owned (but not all worked) by A.P.C.M., now called Blue Circle Group.

Map 5

Eastwoods abandoned their wharf about 1907 and it was later occasionally used by Gransden. Hence it is sometimes called Gransden's Wharf. But the position of this latter firm's main wharf is shown on Map 3.

Map 6

1. One early brickfield was sited to the south of this map in the area which is now Valenciennes Road. It was opened by Wills & Packham when they moved to the town from Rainham about 1870 and it closed about 1890.
2. Other probable earlier nineteenth century brickfields were those of Ashenden (which may be another field and spelling of Ashingdon given on this map), Boles, Huggens and Muggleton.

Map 8

1. Some builders ran more than one yard.
2. Masters also built at various spots on the sea wall, particularly just upstream of the Adelaide Dock entrance.
3. Other probable early nineteenth century builders were: Huggens, Matthews, Peake, Thompson, Smith, Swann and Webster.
4. *Denotes repair yard only. All of the others both built and repaired craft.

Map 9

1. Official numbers are given where there was more than one barge bearing that name.
2. *Denotes that barge was still afloat. *Dart* and *Bride* were later towed away. *May* and *Scud* were later taken to Churchfield No. 1 and burnt.
3. The identity of the four barges on Wood's Wharf are discussed in Chapter 22.

Map 10

1. This map shows craft which are easily identifiable as barges.
2. Many of the hulks on Map 9 were subsequently burnt or broken up; there are still traces of some of them, i.e, timbers lying in the mud.
3. *Genesta, Scud* (125589), *May* (99927) and *Ninety-Nine* were burnt at Churchfield Wharf No. 1 (where *Pomona* lies) during the period 1950-62. Some remains are still visible.

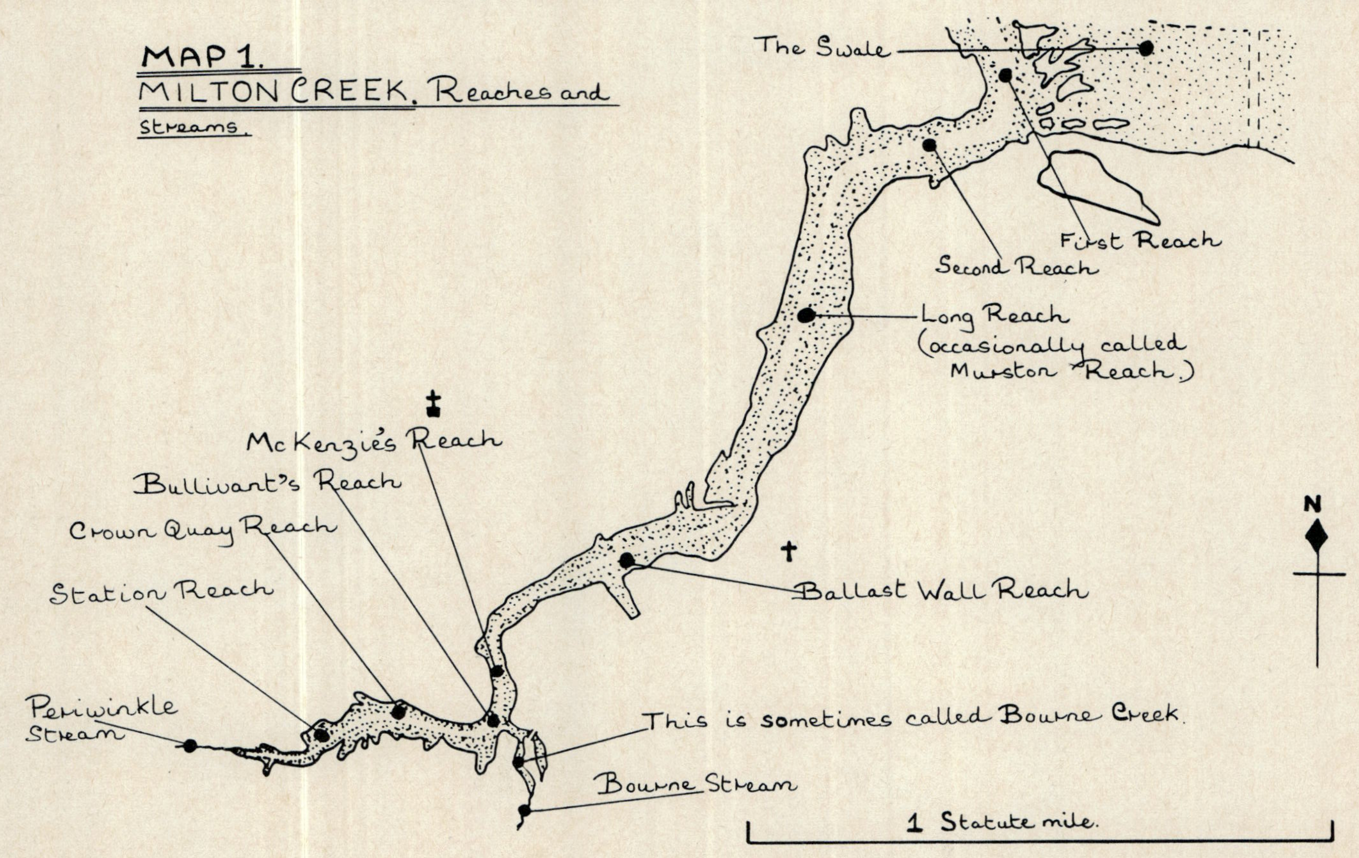

MAP 1.
MILTON CREEK, Reaches and
Streams.
The Swale
First Reach
Second Reach
Long Reach
(occasionally called
Murston Reach.)
McKenzie's Reach
Bullivant's Reach
Crown Quay Reach
Station Reach
Ballast Wall Reach
Periwinkle
Stream
This is sometimes called Bourne Creek
Bourne Stream
1 Statute mile.
N

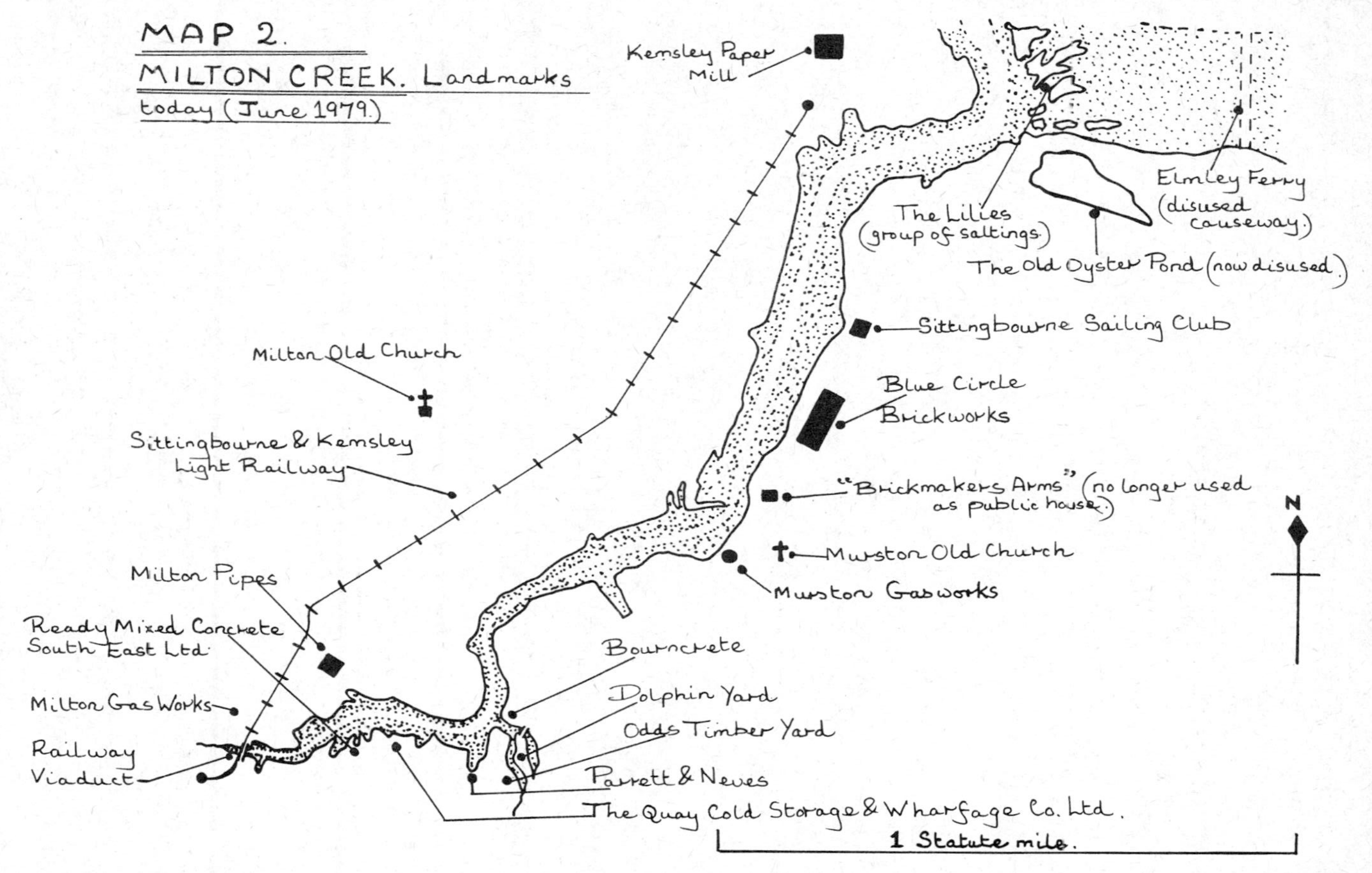

MAP 2.
MILTON CREEK. Landmarks
today (June 1979)
Kemsley Paper Mill
The Lilies (group of saltings)
Elmley Ferry (disused causeway)
The Old Oyster Pond (now disused)
Sittingbourne Sailing Club
Blue Circle Brickworks
Milton Old Church
Sittingbourne & Kemsley Light Railway
"Brickmakers Arms" (no longer used as public house)
Murston Old Church
Murston Gasworks
Milton Pipes
Bowncrete
Ready Mixed Concrete South East Ltd.
Dolphin Yard
Odds Timber Yard
Milton Gas Works
Parrett & Neves
Railway Viaduct
The Quay Cold Storage & Wharfage Co. Ltd.
1 Statute mile.
N
220

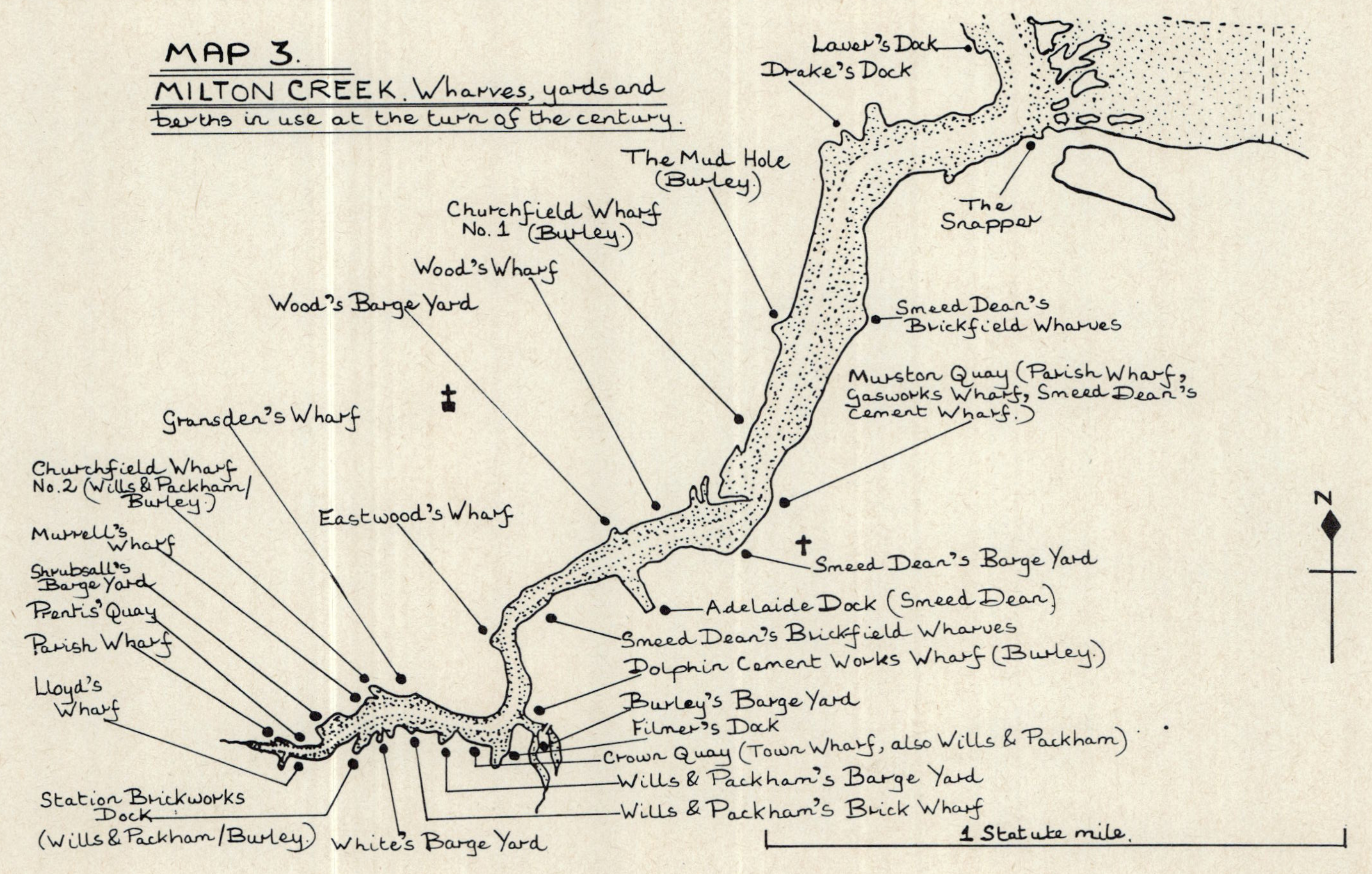

MAP 3.
MILTON CREEK. Wharves, yards and berths in use at the turn of the century.
Laver's Dock
Drake's Dock
The Mud Hole (Burley.)
The Snapper
Churchfield Wharf No. 1 (Burley.)
Wood's Wharf
Wood's Barge Yard
Smeed Dean's Brickfield Wharves
Murston Quay (Parish Wharf, Gasworks Wharf, Smeed Dean's Cement Wharf.)
Gransden's Wharf
Churchfield Wharf No. 2 (Wills & Packham/ Burley.)
Murrell's Wharf
Shrubsall's Barge Yard
Prentis' Quay
Parish Wharf
Eastwood's Wharf
Smeed Dean's Barge Yard
Adelaide Dock (Smeed Dean)
Smeed Dean's Brickfield Wharves
Dolphin Cement Works Wharf (Burley.)
Lloyd's Wharf
Burley's Barge Yard
Filmer's Dock
Crown Quay (Town Wharf, also Wills & Packham)
Wills & Packham's Barge Yard
Wills & Packham's Brick Wharf
Station Brickworks Dock
(Wills & Packham/Burley.)
White's Barge Yard
1 Statute mile.
N

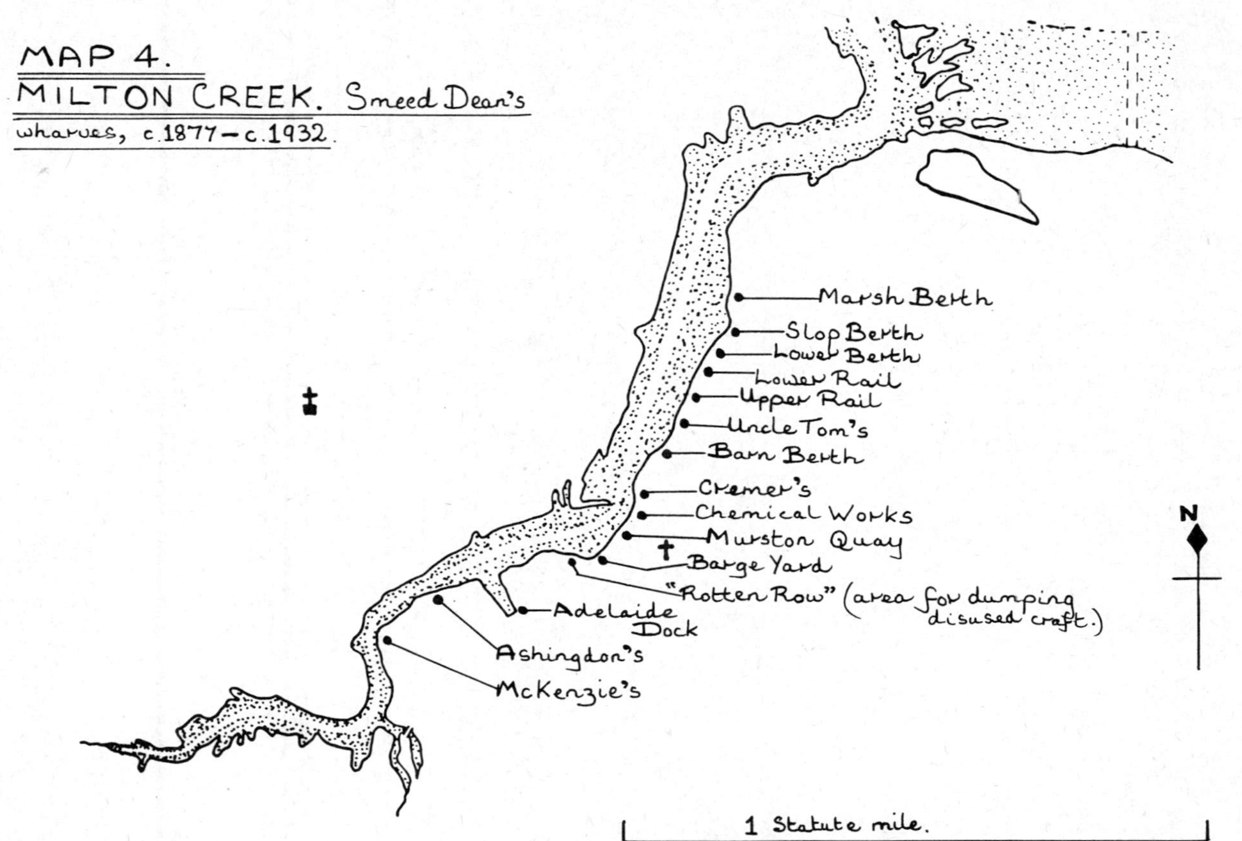

MAP 4.
MILTON CREEK. Smeed Dean's wharves, c.1877 – c.1932.

MAP 5.

MILTON CREEK. Wharves, yards and berths in use today – June 1979.

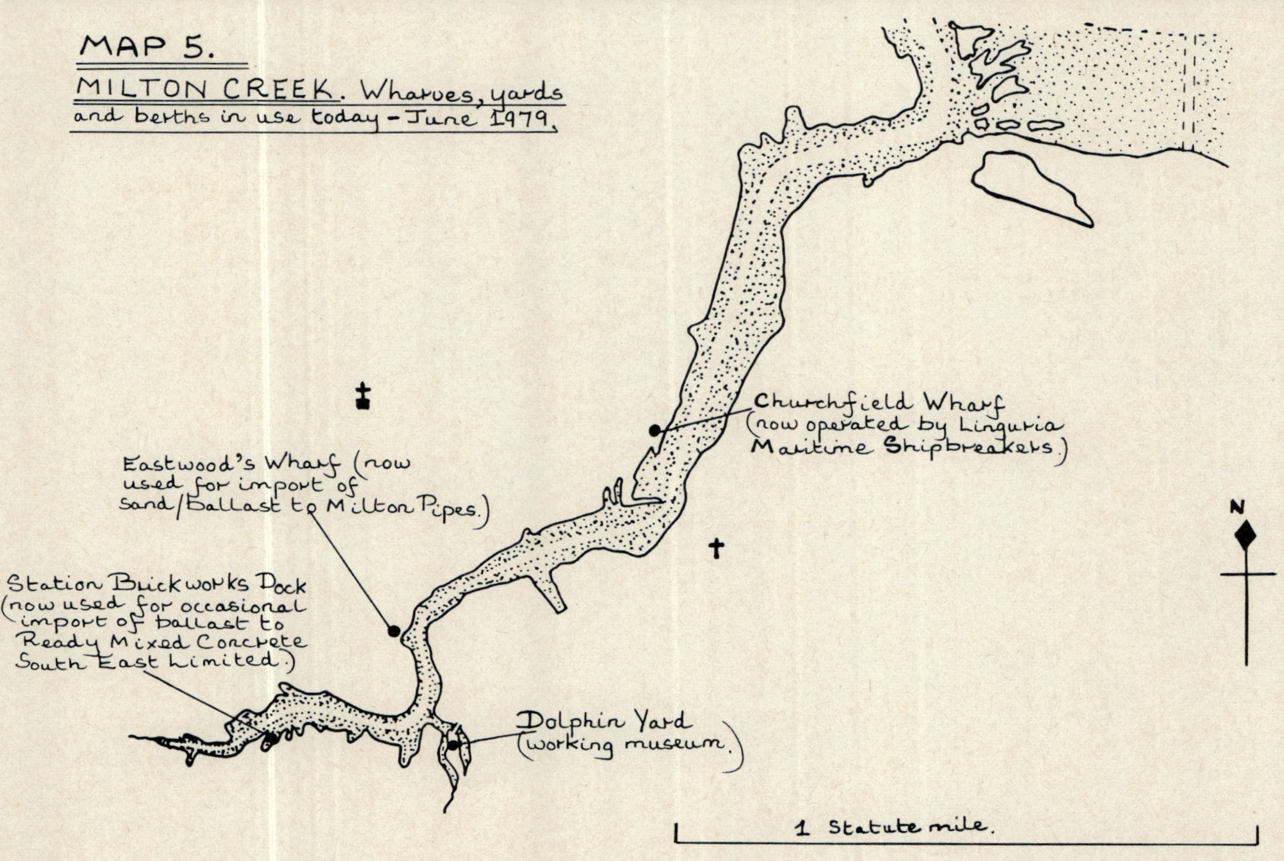

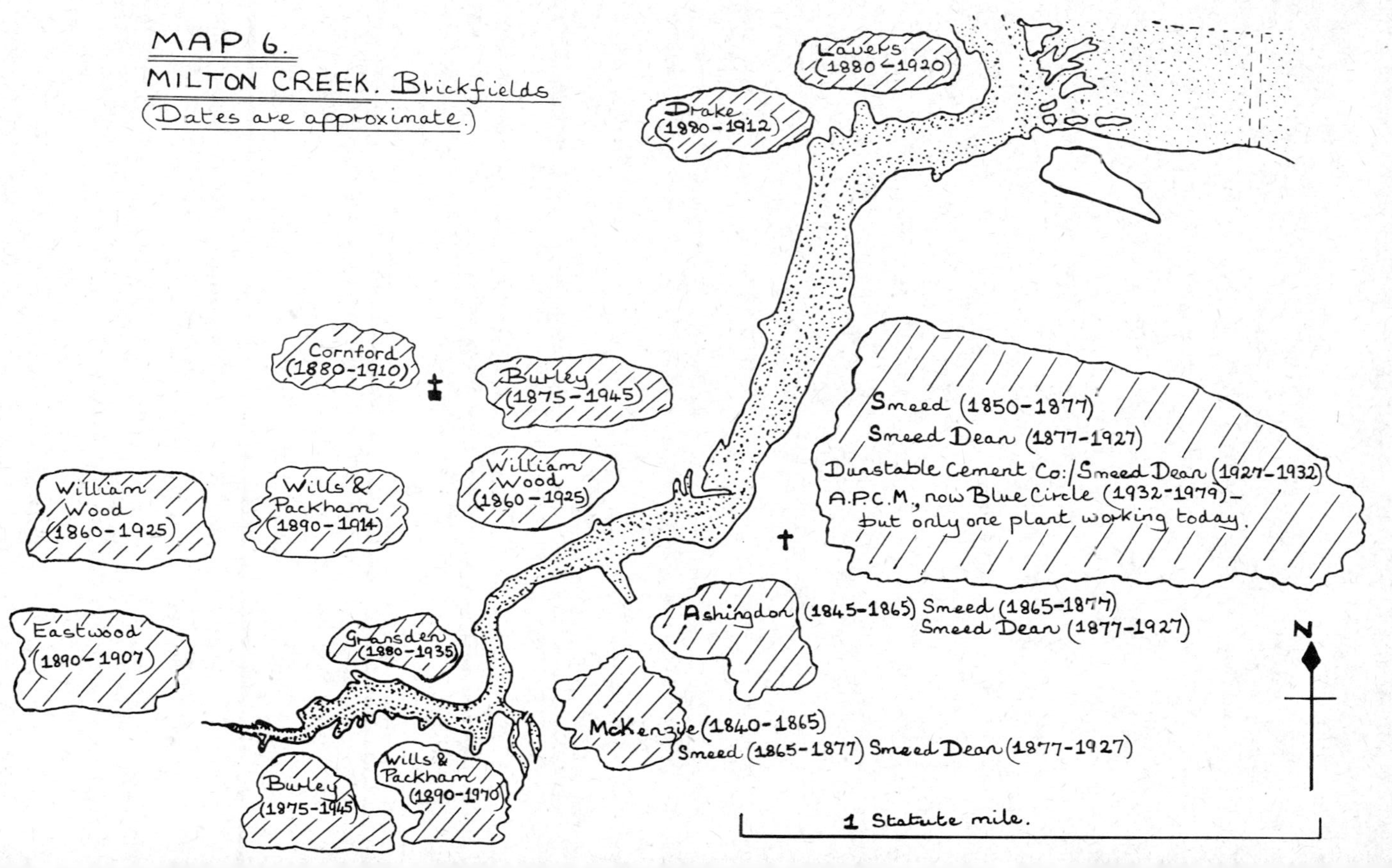

MAP 6.
MILTON CREEK. Brickfields
(Dates are approximate.)
Lavers (1880-1920)
Drake (1880-1912)
Cornford (1880-1910)
Burley (1875-1945)
William Wood (1860-1925)
Wills & Packham (1890-1914)
William Wood (1860-1925)
Eastwood (1890-1907)
Gransden (1880-1935)
Burley (1875-1945)
Wills & Packham (1890-1970)
Smeed (1850-1877)
Smeed Dean (1877-1927)
Dunstable Cement Co./Smeed Dean (1927-1932)
A.P.C.M., now Blue Circle (1932-1979) - but only one plant working today.
Ashingdon (1845-1865) Smeed (1865-1877)
Smeed Dean (1877-1927)
McKenzie (1840-1865)
Smeed (1865-1877) Smeed Dean (1877-1927)
N
1 Statute mile.

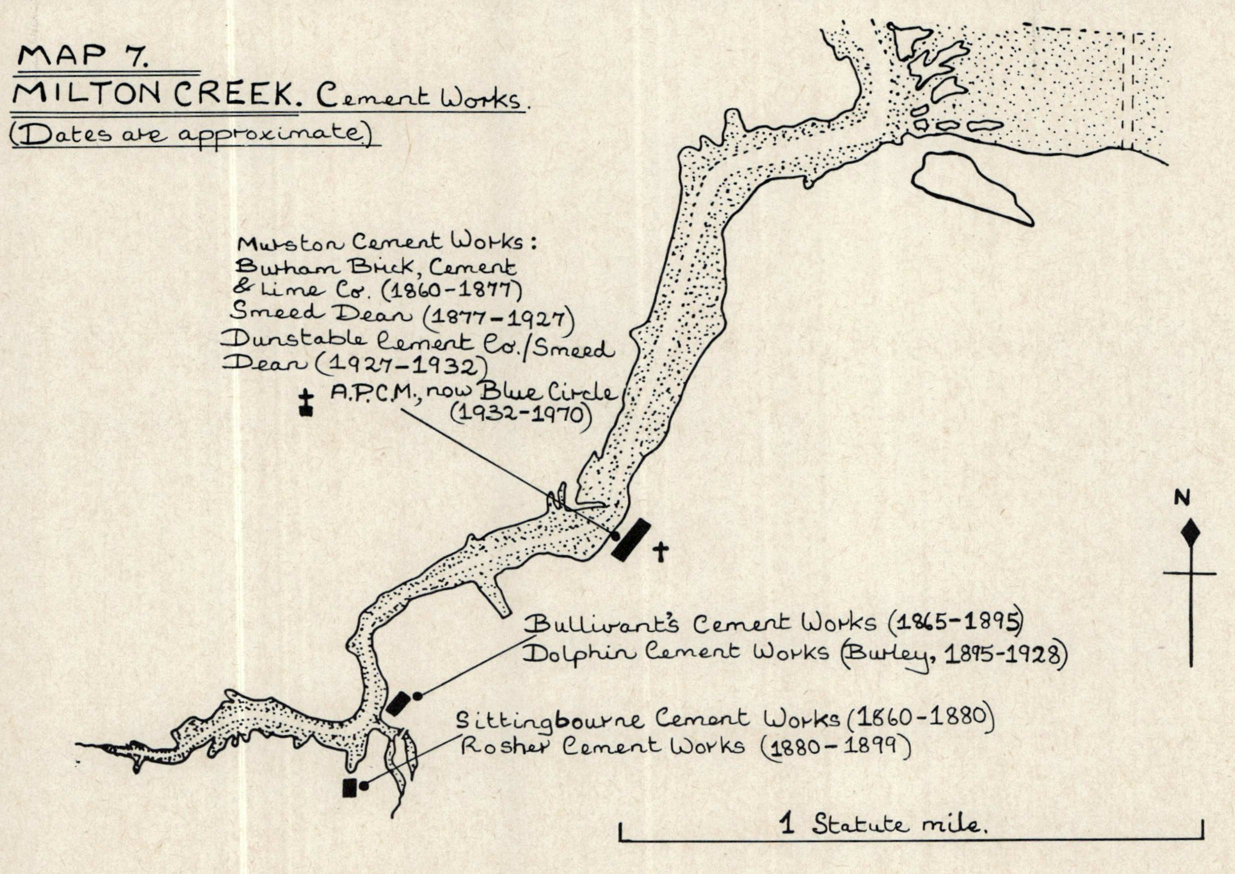

MAP 7.
MILTON CREEK. Cement Works.
(Dates are approximate)
Murston Cement Works :
Burham Brick, Cement
& Lime Co. (1860-1877)
Smeed Dean (1877-1927)
Dunstable Cement Co./Smeed
Dean (1927-1932)
A.P.C.M., now Blue Circle
(1932-1970)
Bullivant's Cement Works (1865-1895)
Dolphin Cement Works (Burley, 1895-1928)
Sittingbourne Cement Works (1860-1880)
Rosher Cement Works (1880-1899)
N
1 Statute mile.

MAP 8.
MILTON CREEK. Ship/Barge Yards
(Dates are approximate.)
George & William Mantle (1866-75)
Burley (1875-90)
White (1890-1920)
Sittingbourne Shipbuilding Co: (1920-38)
* Bowater (1938-65)
George Smeed (1845-77)
Burham Brick, Cement & Lime Co. (1860-69)
John Taylor (1869-1880)
Alf Taylor (1880-1915)
Smeed Dean (1877-1932)
* A.P.C.M. (1932-65)
* Alfred Wood (1937-47)
Shrubsall (1865-1902)
Eastwoods (1902-12)
* Lloyd (1912-35)
* Bowater (1935-38)
* William Wood (1860-1925)
Burley (1890-1965)
* Dolphin Yard (working museum, 1970-77, 1979 re-opened.)
Stephen Taylor (1820-69)
John Taylor (1840-90)
Spencelaugh (1870-80)
Wills & Packham (1890-1938)
Sittingbourne Shipbuilding Co: (1938-53)
Masters (1866-69)
N
1 Statute mile.

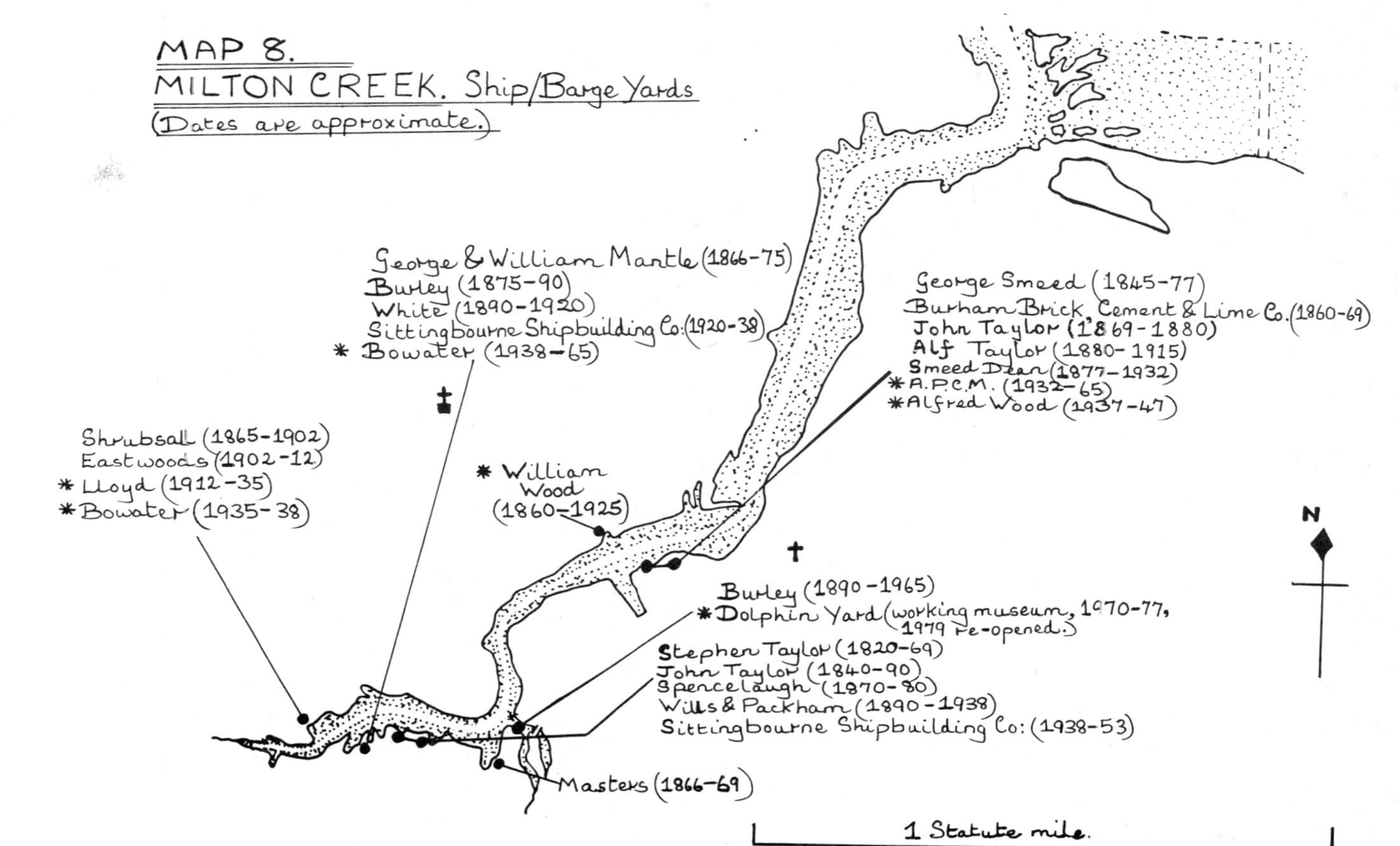

226

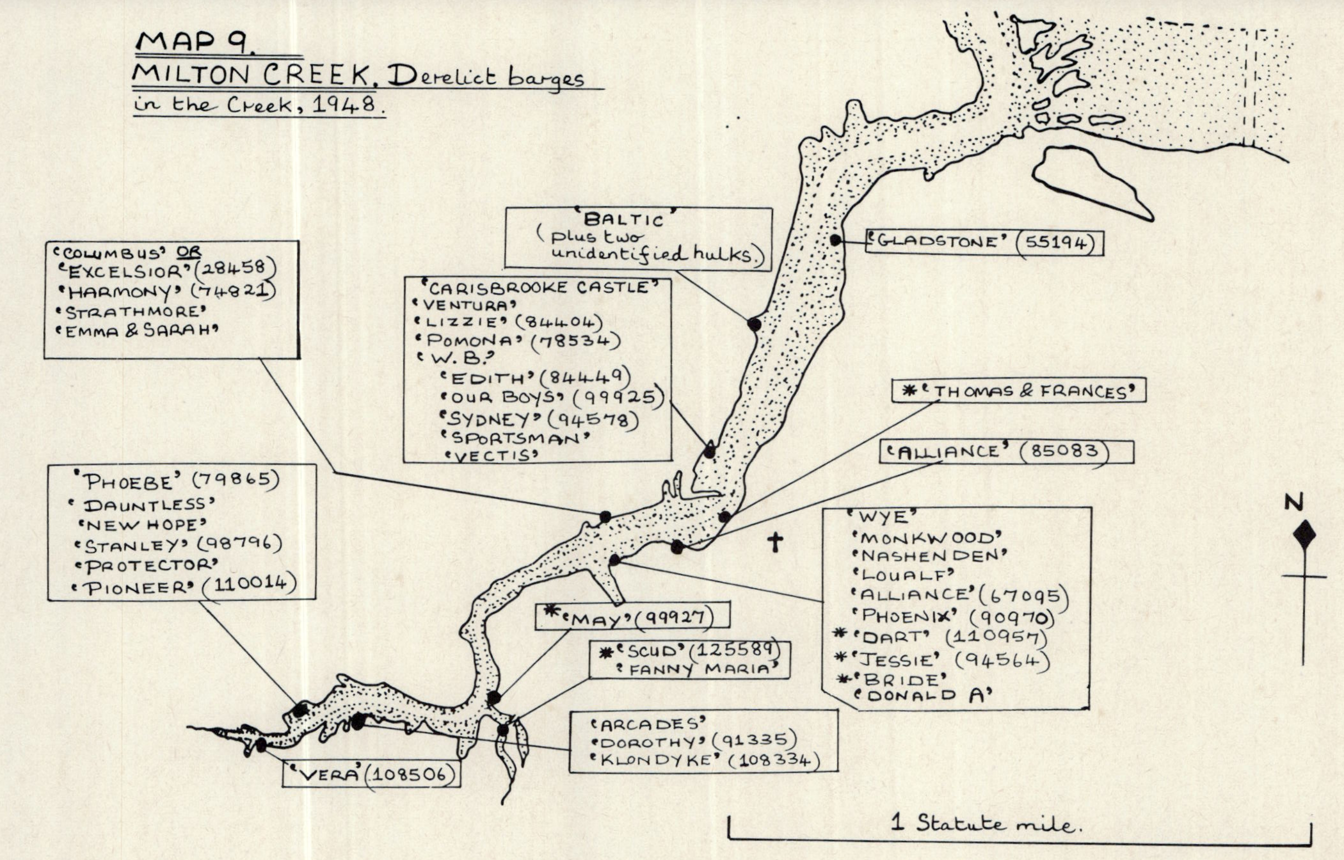

MAP 9.
MILTON CREEK, Derelict barges
in the Creek, 1948.

'BALTIC'
(plus two
unidentified hulks.)

'GLADSTONE' (55194)

'COLUMBUS' OR
'EXCELSIOR' (28458)
'HARMONY' (74821)
'STRATHMORE'
'EMMA & SARAH'

'CARISBROOKE CASTLE'
'VENTURA'
'LIZZIE' (84404)
'POMONA' (78534)
'W.B.'
'EDITH' (84449)
'OUR BOYS' (99925)
'SYDNEY' (94578)
'SPORTSMAN'
'VECTIS'

* 'THOMAS & FRANCES'

'ALLIANCE' (85083)

'PHOEBE' (79865)
'DAUNTLESS'
'NEW HOPE'
'STANLEY' (98796)
'PROTECTOR'
'PIONEER' (110014)

'WYE'
'MONKWOOD'
'NASHENDEN'
'LOUALF'
'ALLIANCE' (67095)
'PHOENIX' (90970)
* 'DART' (110957)
* 'JESSIE' (94564)
* 'BRIDE'
'DONALD A'

* 'MAY' (99927)

* 'SCUD' (125589)
'FANNY MARIA'

'ARCADES'
'DOROTHY' (91335)
'KLONDYKE' (108334)

'VERA' (108506)

N

1 Statute mile.

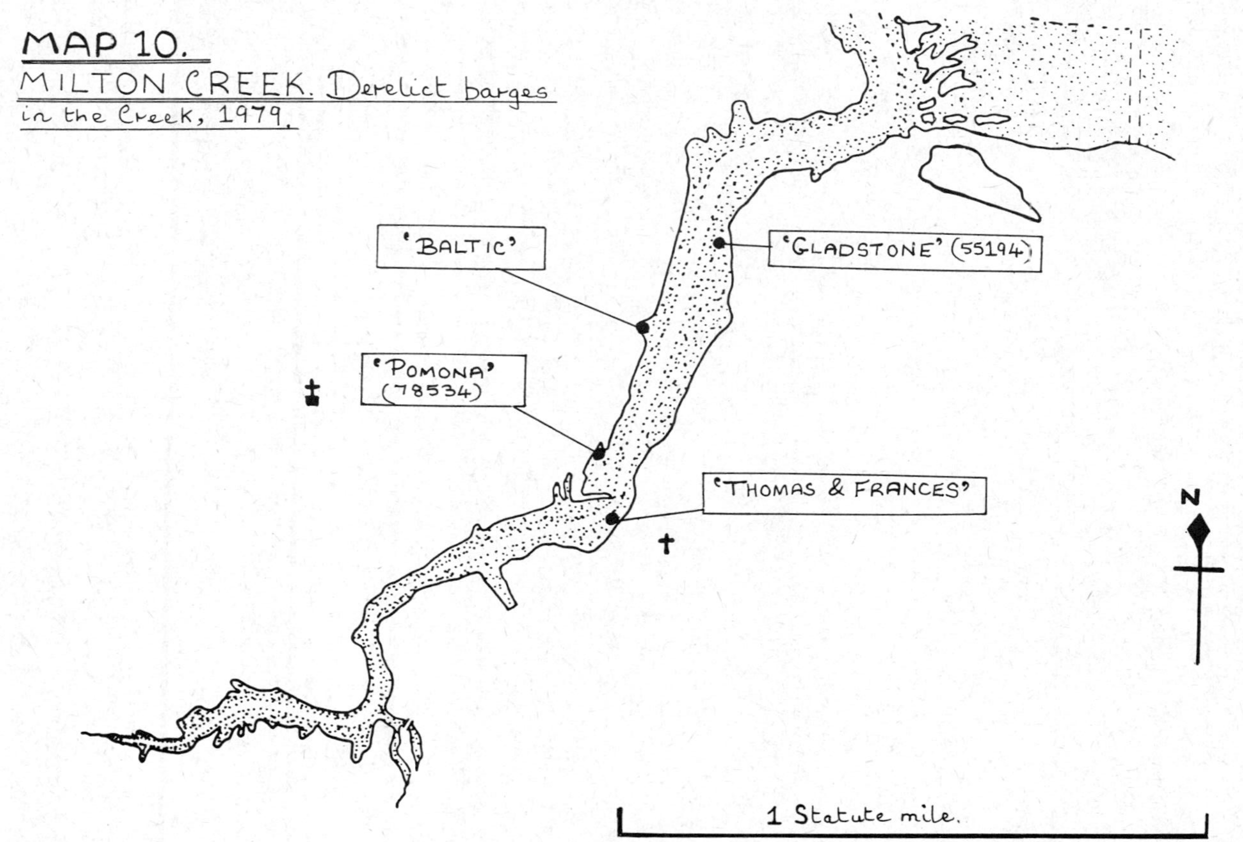

MAP 10.
MILTON CREEK. Derelict barges
in the Creek, 1979.
'BALTIC'
'GLADSTONE' (55194)
'POMONA' (78534)
'THOMAS & FRANCES'
N
1 Statute mile.

A PHOTOGRAPHIC MISCELLANY

The *Five Sisters* as a sailing-barge-yacht.
(Photo by J.S. Hines)

Dreadnought racing in the 1961 Thames Match. (Photo by Alan Cordell)

Scud laid-up at Burley's Yard, 1948.
(Photo by A.S. Bennett)

This pot lid, dating from the last century, shows that one of the Cries of London was 'Buy My Fine Milton Oysters'. It demonstrates how active the local oyster fleet was.

(Courtesy of Mr & Mrs Lee)

A history-laden scene in Sittingbourne Cemetery. The small stone in the foreground marks the resting place of well-known local barge skipper Bill Kennett. In the background is the old chapel and mortuary. Buried around the walls are some of the area's leading barge-owners and industrialists: John Andrews (an early brickfield manager and director of Smeed Dean); Daniel Wills (co-founder of Wills & Packham); John Horsford and William Cremer (both of whom had brickfields at Faversham); and finally, the two Robert Gardiners (father and son) who ran the East Kent Ironworks in Frederick Street. Robert Jnr was so keen on his barge ironwork that he studied barge sailing and served on the committee of the Medway Barge Match before his death in 1907. (Photo by Alan Cordell)

Maid of Connaught racing on the Medway, 1959. She was owned by Smeed Dean in the 1920s — they had changed her name from *The Monarch*.   (Photo by J.S. Hines)

One of Milton Creek's two 'film-star' barges, the *Surrey*, at Weybridge in 1925.
(Courtesy of A. Harknett and F.G. Willmott)

George 'Doggy' Fletcher, master of several local barges including the *Baltic*.
(Courtesy of Mrs Ada Fletcher)

Ada Fletcher in 1970 at the age of 91. She had sailed as mate with her husband in the *Baltic*. She lived on to reach her 100 years.
(Photo by Alan Cordell)

'Doggy' Fletcher towards the end of his career afloat when he was a huffler at Kingsferry Bridge. This picture was taken aboard the *Sidwell* — she had a very obvious 'joyrider' aboard! (Courtesy of Bill Kennett)

Local man Charlie Parr in 1970. He had been skipper of the *Derby* in the 1930s. (Photo by Alan Cordell)

Harold Farrington-House at the wheel of the *Pudge* (owned by Thames Barge Sailing Club), 1975. (Photo by Alan Cordell)

The *Derby*. Bill Kennett started his barging career as mate of this barge in 1895; Charlie Parr was the skipper in the 1930s.

36 Eastbourne Street, residence of Harold Farrington-House, at the time when he was resisting demolition! (Photo by Alan Cordell)

Harold's barge weather-vane remains defiant! (Photo by Alan Cordell)

Mastcase manufactured by R. Gardiner at the East Kent Ironworks.   (Photo by Ferris)

A winch of the type made by R. Gardiner.   (Photo by Ferris)

Edinburgh frozen in the ice, Swaie, 1895.   (Courtesy of Mrs Wright)

Restored souvenirs of barges, two of which came from Milton Creek craft. The *Meridian* was owned by Gransden in the 1920s and early '30s; the *Baltic* (bowbadge shown) by Burley.
(Photo by Alan Cordell)

Ernie Britton, champion racing skipper of the *Dunstable*.   (Courtesy of Mrs Hewitt)

Trophy won by Ernie Britton and the *Dunstable* — Thames Match (Staysail Class) 1937.   (Photo by Alan Cordell)

The Shrubsall-built *Mary Jane*, about 1930.   (Photo by R. Stimson Jnr).

Jim Fenteman, about 1909.   (Courtesy of Mrs Saunders)

George Faint when he was master of the yacht *Thalassa*.   (Courtesy of George Faint)

Sidwell, about 1936.   (Photo by R. Stimson Jnr.)

The crack Sittingbourne-built racing champion *Phoenician*, photographed in the early 1930s.

Mary Ann as a housebarge at Hoo St Werburgh, Kent, about 1976   (Photo by Alan Cordell)

Dunstable in the 1937 Medway Barge Match.   (Photo by H. Oliver Hill)

Harold as a sailing-barge-yacht, 1959.
(Photo by J.S. Hines)

Northdown at Burley's Yard, 1929; she had just won the Coasting Class in the Medway Match. (Courtesy of Mrs Wright)

The stern of *Lady of the Lea*, Milton Creek, 1949. The cabin top extends right out to the quarterboards — a feature seen only in very small barges. (Photo by Alan Cordell)

C.I.V. (nearest) as a sailing-barge-yacht, Hoo St Werburgh, 1970.   (Photo by Alan Cordell)

Whitstable, about 1925. The nearest barge is the *Bessier*, owned by Andrews in the 1920s and early '30s.
(Courtesy of George Faint)

A photograph taken just after the start of the 1928 Medway Match. In the foreground, with the triangle in her mainsail, is the *Favorite*.   (Courtesy of G. Wansbrough-White)

Nicholas racing under Smeed Dean (Red Triangle) ownership, 1929.

(Courtesy of Tom Redshaw)

The untidy and neglected appearance of Milton Creek today. This view was taken just below Murston Quay, looking towards the Creek mouth. (Photo by Alan Cordell)

Lord Nelson bound across the English Channel, about 1920. Owned by Arthur Wenban at that time, she was his favourite barge. In fact, he died whilst rigging her in Milton Creek, 1932. (Courtesy of George Aspin)

A scene in King George's Playing Field, which was formerly the grounds of Gore Court House, home of George Smeed (who died in 1881). In the background is the pavilion, which was originally the stables. In the foreground on the far right are the bases of the pillars of Gore Court House itself. These were all that was left when the house was demolished in 1926. This park was the original home ground of Gore Court Cricket Club, which was founded by George Smeed. (Photo by Alan Cordell)

INDEX OF BARGE CAPTAINS

Meresborough Books

7 STATION ROAD, RAINHAM, GILLINGHAM, KENT. ME8 7RS
Telephone Medway (0634) 388812

We are a specialist publisher of books about Kent. Our books are available in most bookshops in the country, including our own at this address. Alternatively you may order direct, adding 10% for post (minimum 20p, orders over £20.00 post free). ISBN prefix 0 905270 for 3 figure numbers, 094819 for 4 figure numbers. Titles in print December 1985.

BYGONE KENT. A monthly journal on all aspects of Kent history founded October 1979. £1.20 per month. Annual Subscription £13.00. All back numbers available.

HARDBACKS

LIFE AND TIMES OF THE EAST KENT CRITIC: A Kentish Chronicle compiled by Derrick Molock. Large format. ISBN 3077. £9.95.

THE PAST GLORY OF MILTON CREEK: Tales of Slipways, Sails and Setting Booms compiled by Alan Cordell and Leslie Williams. ISBN 3042. £9.95.

TALES OF VICTORIAN HEADCORN or The Oddities of Heddington by Penelope Rivers (Ellen M. Poole). ISBN 3050. £8.95. (Also available in paperback ISBN 3069. £3.95.)

ROCHESTER FROM OLD PHOTOGRAPHS compiled by the City of Rochester Society. Large format. ISBN 975. £7.95. (Also available in paperback ISBN 983. £4.95.)

THE LONDON, CHATHAM & DOVER RAILWAY by Adrian Gray. A major study of the development of railways in Kent. ISBN 886. £7.95.

THE NATURAL HISTORY OF ROMNEY MARSH by Dr F.M. Firth, M.A., Ph.D. ISBN 789. £6.95.

O FAMOUS KENT by Eric Swain. The county of Kent in old prints. ISBN 738. £9.95. **BARGAIN OFFER £4.95.**

KENT'S OWN by Robin J. Brooks. The history of 500 (County of Kent) Squadron of the R.A.A.F. ISBN 541. £5.95.

TWO HALVES OF A LIFE by Doctor Kary Pole. The autobiography of a Viennese doctor who escaped from the Nazis and established a new career in Kent. ISBN 509. £5.95.

SOUTH EAST BRITAIN: ETERNAL BATTLEGROUND by Gregory Blaxland. A military history. ISBN 444. £5.95.

KENT AIRFIELDS IN THE BATTLE OF BRITAIN by The Kent Aviation Historical Research Society. A study of nine airfields. Over 100 photographs. ISBN 363. £5.95.

HAWKINGE 1912-1961 by Roy Humphreys. A study of the former RAF Station, 100 photographs. ISBN 355. £5.95.

A NEW DICTIONARY OF KENT DIALECT by Alan Major. The first major work on the subject this century. ISBN 274. £7.50.

KENT CASTLES by John Guy. The first comprehensive guide to all the castles and castle sites in Kent. ISBN 150. £7.50.

US BARGEMEN by A.S. Bennett. A new book of sailing barge life around Kent and Essex from the author of 'June of Rochester' and 'Tide Time'. ISBN 207. £6.95.

THE GILLS by Tony Conway. A history of Gillingham Football Club. 96 large format pages packed with old photographs. ISBN 266. £5.95. **BARGAIN OFFER £1.95.**

A VIEW OF CHRIST'S COLLEGE, BLACKHEATH by A.E.O. Crombie, B.A. ISBN 223. £6.95.

JUST OFF THE SWALE by Don Sattin. The story of the barge-building village of Conyer. ISBN 045. £5.95.

TEYNHAM MANOR AND HUNDRED (798-1935) by Elizabeth Selby, MBE. ISBN 630. £5.95.

THE PLACE NAMES OF KENT by Judith Glover. A comprehensive reference work. ISBN 614. £7.50 (also available in paperback. ISBN 622. £3.95)

LARGE FORMAT PICTORIAL PAPERBACKS

GOUDHURST: A Pictorial History by John T. Wilson, M.A. ISBN 3026. £2.95.

A PICTORIAL STUDY OF ALKHAM PARISH by Susan Lees and Roy Humphreys. ISBN 3034. £2.95.

THE MOTOR BUS SERVICES OF KENT AND EAST SUSSEX — A brief history by Eric Baldock. An illustrated history from 1899 to 1984 containing 146 photographs. ISBN 959. £4.95.

ROCHESTER FROM OLD PHOTOGRAPHS — see under hardbacks.

PEMBURY IN THE PAST by Mary Standen. ISBN 916. £2.95.

OLD MARGATE by Michael David Mirams. ISBN 908. £2.95.

OLD RAMSGATE by Michael David Mirams. ISBN 797. £2.95.

EXPLORING OLD ROCHESTER by John Bryant. A guide to buildings of historic interest. ISBN 827. £2.95.

THOMAS SIDNEY COOPER OF CANTERBURY by Brian Stewart. The life and work of Britain's best cattle painter, with 10 illustrations in colour. ISBN 762. £2.95.

A FIRST PICTUREBOOK OF OLD CHATHAM by Philip MacDougall. ISBN 754. £2.95.

A SECOND PICTUREBOOK OF OLD CHATHAM by Philip MacDougall. ISBN 924. £2.95.

CRANBROOK by Jenni Rodger. A pictorial history. ISBN 746. £2.95.

KENT TOWN CRAFTS by Richard Filmer. A pictorial record of sixteen different crafts. ISBN 584. £2.95.

KENTISH RURAL CRAFTS AND INDUSTRIES by Richard Filmer.   wide variety of rural crafts. ISBN 428. £2.50.

SMARDEN: A PICTORIAL HISTORY by Jenni Rodger. ISBN 592. £2.95.

A PICTUREBOOK OF OLD SHEPPEY by Michael Thomas. 130 Old photographs, mostly from glass negatives. ISBN 657. £2.95.

FIVE MEDWAY VILLAGES by Wyn Bergess and Stephen Sage. A pictorial history of Aylesford, Burham, Wouldham, Eccles and Borstal. ISBN 649. £2.95.

OLD SANDWICH by Julian Arnold and Andrew Aubertin. 146 old photographs. ISBN 673. £2.95.

AVIATION IN KENT by Robin Brooks. A pictorial history from 19th century ballooning to 1939. ISBN 681. £2.95.

A PICTURE BOOK OF OLD RAINHAM by Barbara Mackay Miller. ISBN 606. £2.95.

THE LIFE AND ART OF ONE MAN by Dudley Pout. A Kentish farmer's son who became successful as a commercial artist and as a children's illustrator. ISBN 525. £2.95.

OLD MAIDSTONE'S PUBLIC HOUSES by Irene Hales. 123 photographs. ISBN 533. £2.95.

OLD MAIDSTONE Vol. 1 by Irene Hales and Kay Baldock. ISBN 096. £2.50.

OLD MAIDSTONE Vol. 2 by Irene Hales. ISBN 38X. £2.50.

OLD ASHFORD by Richard Filmer. A photographic study of life in Ashford over 150 years. ISBN 72X. £2.95.

OLD TONBRIDGE by Don Skinner. ISBN 398. £2.50.

KENT TRANSPORT IN OLD POSTCARDS by Eric Baldock. 146 photographs. ISBN 320. £2.95.

GEORGE BARGEBRICK Esq. by Richard-Hugh Perks. The story of Smeed Dean Ltd in Sittingbourne. 80 illustrations. ISBN 479. £2.95.